BIG IDEAS
MATH.
Integrated Mathematics II

Student Journal

- Maintaining Mathematical Proficiency

- Exploration Journal

- Notetaking with Vocabulary

- Extra Practice

BIG IDEAS LEARNING.

Erie, Pennsylvania

Photo Credits

Cover Image Mix3r/Shutterstock.com

156 *top right* Sascha Burkard/Shutterstock.com;
center left Ruslan Gi/Shutterstock.com;
157 cobalt88/Shutterstock.com, Sanchai Khudpin/Shutterstock.com;
181 Laurin Rinder/Shutterstock.com;
348 Mauro Rodrigues/Shutterstock.com;
353 *left* Elena Elisseeva/Shutterstock.com;
right © Sam Beebe / CC-BY-2.0;
378 Mark Herreid/Shutterstock.com

Printed in the United States

ISBN 13: 978-1-68033-071-7
ISBN 10: 1-68033-071-3

10 11 12 13 14-QSX-23 22 21 20 19

Contents

Contents

Contents

Contents

Contents

Contents

Contents

About the Student Journal

Maintaining Mathematical Proficiency

The Maintaining Mathematical Proficiency corresponds to the Pupil Edition Chapter Opener. Here you have the opportunity to practice prior skills necessary to move forward.

Exploration Journal

The Exploration pages correspond to the Explorations and accompanying exercises in the Pupil Edition. Here you have room to show your work and record your answers.

Notetaking with Vocabulary

This student-friendly notetaking component is designed to be a reference for key vocabulary, properties, and core concepts from the lesson. There is room to add definitions in your words and take notes about the core concepts.

Extra Practice

Each section of the Pupil Edition has an additional Practice with room for you to show your work and record your answers.

Name_____ Date_____

Chapter 1

Maintaining Mathematical Proficiency

Let $f(x) = 2x$. Graph f and g. Describe the transformation from the graph of f to the graph of g.

1. $g(x) = f(x) - 4$

2. $g(x) = f(x + 2)$

3. $g(x) = f\left(\frac{1}{2}x\right)$

4. $g(x) = 3f(x)$

5. Describe the transformation from the graph of $f(x) = x$ to the graph of $h(x) = -\frac{1}{3}x + 2$.

Graph the figure and its image after a reflection in the line $y = x$.

6. $\overline{LM}$ with endpoints $L(2, -4)$ and $M(2, 0)$

7. $\overline{ST}$ with endpoints $S(-2, 5)$ and $T(-4, -1)$

8. $\triangle ABC$ with vertices $A(6, 4)$, $B(6, -1)$, and $C(-2, 0)$

9. $\square EFGH$ with vertices $E(-2, -4)$, $F(4, -4)$, $G(4, 3)$, and $H(-2, 3)$

10. After a reflection in the line $y = -x$, a point originally in Quadrant I will be in which Quadrant?

1.1 Absolute Value Functions
For use with Exploration 1.1

Essential Question How do the values of *a*, *h*, and *k* affect the graph of the absolute value function $g(x) = a|x - h| + k$?

---

1 | **EXPLORATION:** Identifying Graphs of Absolute Value Functions

Work with a partner. Match each absolute value function with its graph. Then use a graphing calculator to verify your answers.

a. $g(x) = -|x - 2|$ **b.** $g(x) = |x - 2| + 2$ **c.** $g(x) = -|x + 2| - 2$

d. $g(x) = |x - 2| - 2$ **e.** $g(x) = 2|x - 2|$ **f.** $g(x) = -|x + 2| + 2$

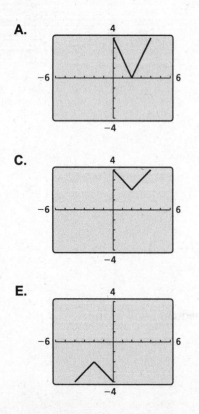

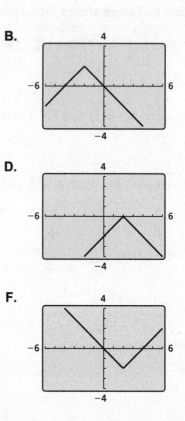

Name_____ Date_____

Communicate Your Answer

2. How do the values of a, h, and k affect the graph of the absolute value function $g(x) = a|x - h| + k$?

3. Write the equation of the absolute value function whose graph is shown. Use a graphing calculator to verify your equation.

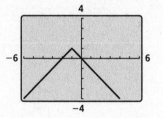

Name _____ Date _____

Notetaking with Vocabulary
For use after Lesson 1.1

In your own words, write the meaning of each vocabulary term.

absolute value function

vertex

vertex form

Notes:

Name_____ Date_____

Core Concepts

Absolute Value Function

An **absolute value function** is a function that contains an absolute value expression. The parent absolute value function is $f(x) = |x|$. The graph of $f(x) = |x|$ is V-shaped and symmetric about the y-axis. The **vertex** is the point where the graph changes direction. The vertex of the graph of $f(x) = |x|$ is $(0, 0)$.

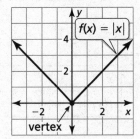

The domain of $f(x) = |x|$ is all real numbers.

The range is $y \geq 0$.

Notes:

Vertex Form of an Absolute Value Function

An absolute value function written in the form $g(x) = a|x - h| + k$, where $a \neq 0$, is in **vertex form**. The vertex of the graph of g is (h, k).

Any absolute value function can be written in vertex form, and its graph is symmetric about the line $x = h$.

Notes:

Name _____ Date _____

Extra Practice

In Exercises 1–4, graph the function. Compare the graph to the graph of
$f(x) = |x|$. Describe the domain and range.

1. $t(x) = \frac{1}{2}|x|$

x	−4	−2	0	2	4
t(x)					

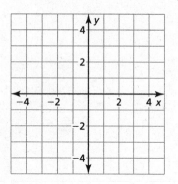

2. $u(x) = -|x|$

x	−2	−1	0	1	2
u(x)					

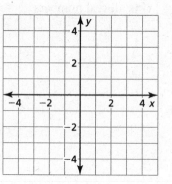

3. $p(x) = |x| - 3$

x	−2	−1	0	1	2
p(x)					

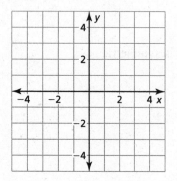

4. $r(x) = |x + 2|$

x	−4	−3	−2	−1	0
r(x)					

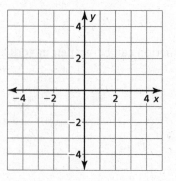

Name_____ Date_____

1.2 Piecewise Functions
For use with Exploration 1.2

Essential Question How can you describe a function that is represented by more than one equation?

1 EXPLORATION: Writing Equations for a Function

Work with a partner.

a. Does the graph represent y as a function of x? Justify your conclusion.

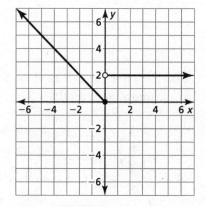

b. What is the value of the function when $x = 0$? How can you tell?

c. Write an equation that represents the values of the function when $x \leq 0$.

$f(x) = $ _____ , if $x \leq 0$

d. Write an equation that represents the values of the function when $x > 0$.

$f(x) = $ _____ , if $x > 0$

e. Combine the results of parts (c) and (d) to write a single description of the function.

$$f(x) = \begin{cases} \underline{\quad\quad}, \text{if } x \leq 0 \\ \underline{\quad\quad}, \text{if } x > 0 \end{cases}$$

1.2 **Piecewise Functions** (continued)

2 **EXPLORATION:** Writing Equations for a Function

Work with a partner.

a. Does the graph represent y as a function of x? Justify your conclusion.

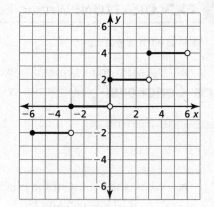

b. Describe the values of the function for the following intervals.

$$f(x) = \begin{cases} \underline{}, & \text{if } -6 \le x < -3 \\ \underline{}, & \text{if } -3 \le x < 0 \\ \underline{}, & \text{if } 0 \le x < 3 \\ \underline{}, & \text{if } 3 \le x < 6 \end{cases}$$

Communicate Your Answer

3. How can you describe a function that is represented by more than one equation?

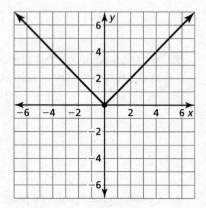

4. Use two equations to describe the function represented by the graph.

1.2 Notetaking with Vocabulary
For use after Lesson 1.2

In your own words, write the meaning of each vocabulary term.

piecewise function

step function

Core Concepts

Piecewise Function

A **piecewise function** is a function defined by two or more equations. Each "piece" of the function applies to a different part of its domain. An example is shown below.

$$f(x) = \begin{cases} x - 2, & \text{if } x \leq 0 \\ 2x + 1, & \text{if } x > 0 \end{cases}$$

- The expression $x - 2$ represents the value of f when x is less than or equal to 0.

- The expression $2x + 1$ represents the value of f when x is greater than 0.

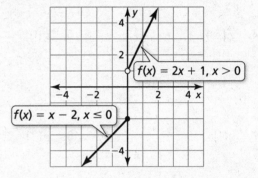

$f(x) = 2x + 1, x > 0$

$f(x) = x - 2, x \leq 0$

Notes:

1.2 **Notetaking with Vocabulary** (continued)

Extra Practice

In Exercise 1–9, evaluate the function.

$$f(x) = \begin{cases} 3x - 1, & \text{if } x \leq 1 \\ 1 - 2x, & \text{if } x > 1 \end{cases}$$

$$g(x) = \begin{cases} 3x - 1, & \text{if } x \leq -3 \\ 2, & \text{if } -3 < x < 1 \\ -3x, & \text{if } x \geq 1 \end{cases}$$

1. $f(0)$ **2.** $f(1)$ **3.** $f(5)$

4. $f(-4)$ **5.** $g(0)$ **6.** $g(-3)$

7. $g(1)$ **8.** $g(3)$ **9.** $g(-5)$

In Exercise 10–13, graph the function. Describe the domain and range.

10. $y = \begin{cases} -4x, & \text{if } x \leq 0 \\ 4, & \text{if } x > 0 \end{cases}$

11. $y = \begin{cases} 4 - x, & \text{if } x < 2 \\ x + 3, & \text{if } x \geq 2 \end{cases}$

1.2 **Notetaking with Vocabulary** (continued)

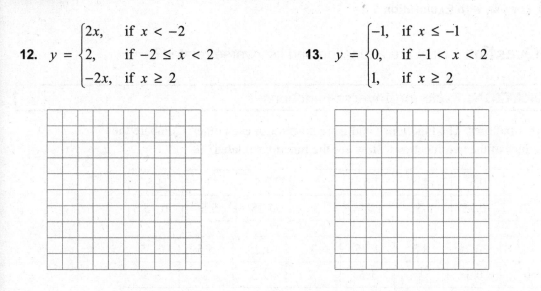

12. $y = \begin{cases} 2x, & \text{if } x < -2 \\ 2, & \text{if } -2 \le x < 2 \\ -2x, & \text{if } x \ge 2 \end{cases}$

13. $y = \begin{cases} -1, & \text{if } x \le -1 \\ 0, & \text{if } -1 < x < 2 \\ 1, & \text{if } x \ge 2 \end{cases}$

In Exercise 14 and 15, write a piecewise function for the graph.

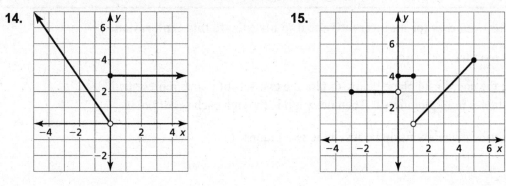

14.

15.

16. A postal service charges $4 for shipping any package weighing up to but not including 1 pound and $1 for each additional pound or portion of a pound up to but not including 5 pounds. Packages 5 pounds or over have different rates. Write and graph a step function that shows the relationship between the number x of pounds a package weighs and the total cost y for postage.

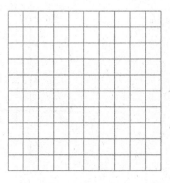

1.3 Inverse of a Function
For use with Exploration 1.3

Essential Question   How are a function and its inverse related?

1 EXPLORATION: Exploring Inverse Functions

Work with a partner. The functions *f* and *g* are *inverses* of each other. Compare the tables of values of the two functions. How are the functions related?

x	0	0.5	1	1.5	2	2.5	3	3.5
f(x)	−2	−0.75	0.5	1.75	3	4.25	5.5	6.75

x	−2	−0.75	0.5	1.75	3	4.25	5.5	6.75
g(x)	0	0.5	1	1.5	2	2.5	3	3.5

2 EXPLORATION: Exploring Inverse Functions

Go to *BigIdeasMath.com* for an interactive tool to investigate this exploration.

Work with a partner.

  a. Use the coordinate plane below to plot the two sets of points represented by the tables in Exploration 1. Then draw a line through each set of points.

  b. Describe the relationship between the two graphs.

  c. Write an equation for each function.

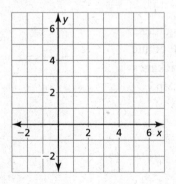

Name_____ Date_____

Communicate Your Answer

3. How are a function and its inverse related?

4. A table of values for a function f is given. Create a table of values for a function g, the inverse of f.

x	0	1	2	3	4	5	6	7
f(x)	1	2	3	4	5	6	7	8

x								
g(x)								

5. Sketch the graphs of $f(x) = x + 4$ and its inverse in the same coordinate plane. Then write an equation of the inverse of f. Explain your reasoning.

1.3 Notetaking with Vocabulary
For use after Lesson 1.3

In your own words, write the meaning of each vocabulary term.

inverse relation

inverse function

Core Concepts

Inverse Relation

When a relation contains (a, b), the inverse relation contains (b, a).

Notes:

Finding Inverses of Functions Algebraically

Step 1 Set y equal to $f(x)$.

Step 2 Switch x and y in the equation.

Step 3 Solve the equation for y.

Notes:

1.3 **Notetaking with Vocabulary** (continued)

Extra Practice

In Exercises 1–3, find the inverse of the relation.

1. $(1, -1), (2, 5), (4, -2), (6, 8), (8, 9)$

2.

Input	−3	−1	0	1	3
Output	4	2	2	5	3

Input					
Output					

3.

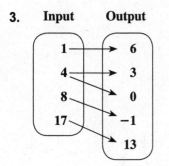

Input   Output

In Exercises 4–6, solve $y = f(x)$ for x. Then find the input when the output is 3.

4. $f(x) = x + 3$

5. $f(x) = 3x - 2$

6. $f(x) = \frac{3}{4}x + 6$

Name_____ Date _____

In Exercises 7–12, find the inverse of the function. Then graph the function and its inverse.

  7. $f(x) = 4x$ **8.** $f(x) = 3x - 1$ **9.** $f(x) = -3x + 2$

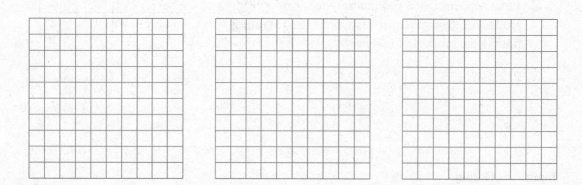

  10. $f(x) = -2x + 3$ **11.** $f(x) = \frac{1}{2}x + 2$ **12.** $f(x) = \frac{1}{3}x - \frac{2}{3}$

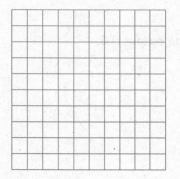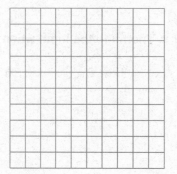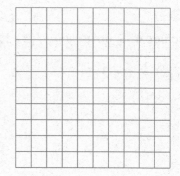

Name_____ Date_____

Essential Question How can you write general rules involving properties of exponents?

1 **EXPLORATION:** Writing Rules for Properties of Exponents

Work with a partner.

a. What happens when you multiply two powers with the same base? Write the product of the two powers as a single power. Then write a *general rule* for finding the product of two powers with the same base.

   i. $\left(2^2\right)\left(2^3\right) =$ _____   **ii.** $\left(4^1\right)\left(4^5\right) =$ _____

   iii. $\left(5^3\right)\left(5^5\right) =$ _____   **iv.** $\left(x^2\right)\left(x^6\right) =$ _____

b. What happens when you divide two powers with the same base? Write the quotient of the two powers as a single power. Then write a *general rule* for finding the quotient of two powers with the same base.

   i. $\dfrac{4^3}{4^2} =$ _____   **ii.** $\dfrac{2^5}{2^2} =$ _____

   iii. $\dfrac{x^6}{x^3} =$ _____   **iv.** $\dfrac{3^4}{3^4} =$ _____

c. What happens when you find a power of a power? Write the expression as a single power. Then write a *general rule* for finding a power of a power.

   i. $\left(2^2\right)^4 =$ _____   **ii.** $\left(7^3\right)^2 =$ _____

   iii. $\left(y^3\right)^3 =$ _____   **iv.** $\left(x^4\right)^2 =$ _____

1.4 **Properties of Exponents** (continued)

1 **EXPLORATION:** Writing Rules for Properties of Exponents (continued)

    d. What happens when you find a power of a product? Write the expression as the product of two powers. Then write a *general rule* for finding a power of a product.

        i. $(2 \bullet 5)^2 =$ _____   **ii.** $(5 \bullet 4)^3 =$ _____

        iii. $(6a)^2 =$ _____   **iv.** $(3x)^2 =$ _____

    e. What happens when you find a power of a quotient? Write the expression as the quotient of two powers. Then write a *general rule* for finding a power of a quotient.

        i. $\left(\dfrac{2}{3}\right)^2 =$ _____   **ii.** $\left(\dfrac{4}{3}\right)^3 =$ _____

       iii. $\left(\dfrac{x}{2}\right)^3 =$ _____   **iv.** $\left(\dfrac{a}{b}\right)^4 =$ _____

Communicate Your Answer

    2. How can you write general rules involving properties of exponents?

    3. There are 3^3 small cubes in the cube below. Write an expression for the number of small cubes in the large cube at the right.

Name_____ Date_____

 1.4 **Notetaking with Vocabulary**
For use after Lesson 1.4

In your own words, write the meaning of each vocabulary term.

power

exponent

base

scientific notation

Core Concepts

Zero Exponent

Words For any nonzero number a, $a^0 = 1$. The power 0^0 is undefined.

Numbers $4^0 = 1$ **Algebra** $a^0 = 1$, where $a \neq 0$

Negative Exponents

Words For any integer n and any nonzero number a, a^{-n} is the reciprocal of a^n.

Numbers $4^{-2} = \dfrac{1}{4^2}$ **Algebra** $a^{-n} = \dfrac{1}{a^n}$, where $a \neq 0$

Notes:

1.4 Notetaking with Vocabulary (continued)

Product of Powers Property

Let a be a real number, and let m and n be integers.

Words To multiply powers with the same base, add their exponents.

Numbers $4^6 \cdot 4^3 = 4^{6+3} = 4^9$ **Algebra** $a^m \cdot a^n = a^{m+n}$

Quotient of Powers Property

Let a be a nonzero real number, and let m and n be integers.

Words To divide powers with the same base, subtract their exponents.

Numbers $\dfrac{4^6}{4^3} = 4^{6-3} = 4^3$ **Algebra** $\dfrac{a^m}{a^n} = a^{m-n}$, where $a \neq 0$

Power of a Power Property

Let a be a real number, and let m and n be integers.

Words To find a power of a power, multiply the exponents.

Numbers $\left(4^6\right)^3 = 4^{6 \cdot 3} = 4^{18}$ **Algebra** $\left(a^m\right)^n = a^{mn}$

Notes:

Power of a Product Property

Let a and b be real numbers, and let m be an integer.

Words To find a power of a product, find the power of each factor and multiply.

Numbers $\left(3 \cdot 2\right)^5 = 3^5 \cdot 2^5$ **Algebra** $\left(ab\right)^m = a^m b^m$

Power of a Quotient Property

Let a and b be real numbers with $b \neq 0$, and let m be an integer.

Words To find the power of a quotient, find the power of the numerator and the power of the denominator and divide.

Numbers $\left(\dfrac{3}{2}\right)^5 = \dfrac{3^5}{2^5}$ **Algebra** $\left(\dfrac{a}{b}\right)^m = \dfrac{a^m}{b^m}$, where $b \neq 0$

Notes:

1.4 Notetaking with Vocabulary (continued)

Extra Practice

In Exercises 1–8, evaluate the expression.

1. 3^0

2. $(-2)^0$

3. 3^{-4}

4. $(-4)^{-3}$

5. $\dfrac{2^{-3}}{5^0}$

6. $\dfrac{-3^{-2}}{2^{-3}}$

7. $\dfrac{4^{-1}}{-7^0}$

8. $\dfrac{3^{-1}}{(-5)^0}$

In Exercises 9–23, simplify the expression. Write your answer using only positive exponents.

9. z^0

10. a^{-8}

11. $6a^0b^{-2}$

12. $14m^{-4}n^0$

13. $\dfrac{3^{-2}r^{-3}}{s^0}$

14. $\dfrac{2^3 a^{-3}}{8^{-1}b^{-5}c^0}$

15. $\dfrac{3^5}{3^3}$

16. $\dfrac{(-2)^7}{(-2)^5}$

17. $(-5)^3 \bullet (-5)^3$

18. $\left(q^5\right)^3$

19. $\left(a^{-4}\right)^2$

20. $\dfrac{c^4 \bullet c^3}{c^6}$

21. $(-4d)^4$

22. $(-3f)^{-3}$

23. $\left(\dfrac{4}{x}\right)^{-3}$

24. A rectangular prism has length x, width $\dfrac{x}{2}$, and height $\dfrac{x}{3}$. Which of the expressions represent the volume of the prism? Select all that apply.

A. $6^{-1}x^3$

B. $6^{-1}x^{-3}$

C. $\left(6x^{-3}\right)^{-1}$

D. $2^{-1} \bullet 3^{-1} \bullet x^3$

1.5   Radicals and Rational Exponents
For use with Exploration 1.5

Essential Question   How can you write and evaluate an *n*th root of a number?

Recall that you cube a number as follows.

3rd power

$2^3 = 2 \cdot 2 \cdot 2 = 8$ 2 cubed is 8.

To "undo" cubing a number, take the cube root of the number.

Symbol for cube root is $\sqrt[3]{}$.

$\sqrt[3]{8} = \sqrt[3]{2^3} = 2$ The cube root of 8 is 2.

---

1   EXPLORATION: Finding Cube Roots

Work with a partner. Use a cube root symbol to write the side length of each cube. Then find the cube root. Check your answers by multiplying. Which cube is the largest? Which two cubes are the same size? Explain your reasoning.

a.   Volume = 27 ft^3 b.   Volume = 125 cm^3 c.   Volume = 3375 in.^3

d.   Volume = 3.375 m^3 e.   Volume = 1 yd^3 f.   Volume = $\dfrac{125}{8} \text{ mm}^3$

Name_____ Date_____

2 EXPLORATION: Estimating *n*th Roots

Work with a partner. Estimate each positive *n*th root. Then match each *n*th root with the point on the number line. Justify your answers.

a. $\sqrt[4]{25}$

b. $\sqrt{0.5}$

c. $\sqrt[5]{2.5}$

d. $\sqrt[3]{65}$

e. $\sqrt[3]{55}$

f. $\sqrt[6]{20,000}$

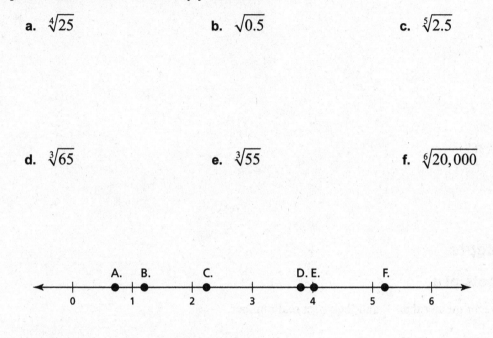

Communicate Your Answer

3. How can you write and evaluate an *n*th root of a number?

4. The body mass *m* (in kilograms) of a dinosaur that walked on two feet can be modeled by

$$m = (0.00016)C^{2.73}$$

where *C* is the circumference (in millimeters) of the dinosaur's femur. The mass of a *Tyrannosaurus rex* was 4000 kilograms. Use a calculator to approximate the circumference of its femur.

1.5 Notetaking with Vocabulary
For use after Lesson 1.5

In your own words, write the meaning of each vocabulary term.

nth root of a

radical

index of a radical

Core Concepts

Real nth Roots of a

Let n be an integer greater than 1, and let a be a real number.

- If n is odd, then a has one real nth root: $\sqrt[n]{a} = a^{1/n}$

- If n is even and $a > 0$, then a has two real nth roots: $\pm \sqrt[n]{a} = \pm a^{1/n}$

- If n is even and $a = 0$, then a has one real nth root: $\sqrt[n]{0} = 0$

- If n is even and $a < 0$, then a has no real nth roots.

Notes:

Name_____ Date _____

Rational Exponents

Let $a^{1/n}$ be an nth root of a, and let m be a positive integer.

Algebra $a^{m/n} = \left(a^{1/n}\right)^m = \left(\sqrt[n]{a}\right)^m$

Numbers $27^{2/3} = \left(27^{1/3}\right)^2 = \left(\sqrt[3]{27}\right)^2$

Notes:

Extra Practice

In Exercises 1–6, find the indicated real nth root(s) of a.

1. $n = 2, a = 64$

2. $n = 3, a = 27$

3. $n = 4, a = 256$

4. $n = 5, a = 243$

5. $n = 8, a = 256$

6. $n = 4, a = 10{,}000$

In Exercises 7–12, evaluate the expression.

7. $\sqrt[4]{625}$

8. $\sqrt[3]{-512}$

9. $\sqrt[3]{-216}$

10. $\sqrt[5]{-243}$

11. $729^{1/6}$

12. $(-81)^{1/2}$

1.5 Notetaking with Vocabulary (continued)

In Exercises 13–15, rewrite the expression in rational exponent form.

13. $\left(\sqrt[5]{4}\right)^3$

14. $\left(\sqrt[3]{-8}\right)^2$

15. $\left(\sqrt[4]{15}\right)^7$

In Exercises 16–18, rewrite the expression in radical form.

16. $(-3)^{2/5}$

17. $6^{3/2}$

18. $12^{3/4}$

In Exercises 19–24, evaluate the expression.

19. $32^{2/5}$

20. $(-64)^{3/2}$

21. $343^{2/3}$

22. $256^{7/8}$

23. $-729^{5/6}$

24. $(-625)^{3/4}$

25. The radius r of a sphere is given by the equation

$$r = \left(\frac{A}{4\pi}\right)^{1/2}$$

where A is the surface area of the sphere. The surface area of a sphere is 1493 square meters. Find the radius of the sphere to the nearest tenth of a meter. Use 3.14 for π.

Name_____ Date_____

1.6 Exponential Functions
For use with Exploration 1.6

Essential Question What are some of the characteristics of the graph of an exponential function?

1 EXPLORATION: Identifying Graphs of Exponential Functions

Work with a partner. Match each exponential function with its graph. Use a table of values to sketch the graph of the function, if necessary.

  a. $f(x) = 2^x$ b. $f(x) = 3^x$ c. $f(x) = 4^x$

  d. $f(x) = \left(\dfrac{1}{2}\right)^x$ e. $f(x) = \left(\dfrac{1}{3}\right)^x$ f. $f(x) = \left(\dfrac{1}{4}\right)^x$

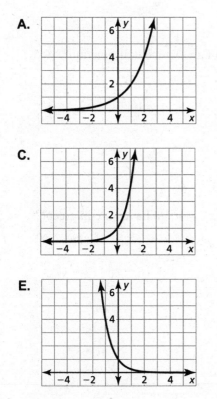

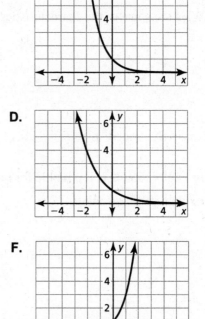

1.6   **Exponential Functions** (continued)

2   **EXPLORATION:** Characteristics of Graphs of Exponential Functions

Work with a partner. Use the graphs in Exploration 1 to determine the domain, range, and y-intercept of the graph of $f(x) = b^x$, where b is a positive real number other than 1. Explain your reasoning.

Communicate Your Answer

3. What are some of the characteristics of the graph of an exponential function?

4. In Exploration 2, is it possible for the graph of $f(x) = b^x$ to have an x-intercept? Explain your reasoning.

Name_____ Date_____

In your own words, write the meaning of each vocabulary term.

exponential function

exponential growth function

growth factor

asymptote

exponential decay function

decay factor

recursive rule

Core Concepts

Parent Function for Exponential Growth Functions

The function $f(x) = b^x$, where $b > 1$, is the parent function for the family of exponential growth functions with base b. The graph shows the general shape of an exponential growth function.

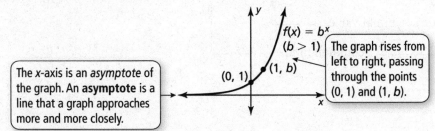

The x-axis is an *asymptote* of the graph. An **asymptote** is a line that a graph approaches more and more closely.

$f(x) = b^x$
$(b > 1)$

$(0, 1)$ $(1, b)$

The graph rises from left to right, passing through the points $(0, 1)$ and $(1, b)$.

The domain of $f(x) = b^x$ is all real numbers. The range is $y > 0$.

Notes:

1.6 **Notetaking with Vocabulary (continued)**

Parent Function for Exponential Decay Functions

The function $f(x) = b^x$, where $0 < b < 1$, is the parent function for the family of exponential decay functions with base b. The graph shows the general shape of an exponential decay function.

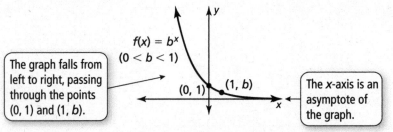

The graph falls from left to right, passing through the points $(0, 1)$ and $(1, b)$.

$f(x) = b^x$
$(0 < b < 1)$

$(0, 1)$ $(1, b)$

The x-axis is an asymptote of the graph.

The domain of $f(x) = b^x$ is all real numbers. The range is $y > 0$.

Notes:

Writing Recursive Rules for Exponential Functions

An exponential function of the form $f(x) = ab^x$ is written using a recursive rule as follows.

Recursive Rule $f(0) = a, f(n) = r \bullet f(n - 1)$, where $a \neq 0$, r is the common ratio, and n is a natural number.

Example $y = 6(3)^x$ can be written as $f(0) = 6, f(n) = 3 \bullet f(n - 1)$

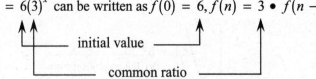

initial value

common ratio

Notes:

Name_____ Date _____

Extra Practice

In Exercises 1–4, determine whether the function represents *exponential growth* or *exponential decay*. Then graph the function.

1. $y = \left(\dfrac{1}{12}\right)^x$ **2.** $y = (1.5)^x$ **3.** $y = \left(\dfrac{7}{2}\right)^x$ **4.** $y = (0.8)^x$

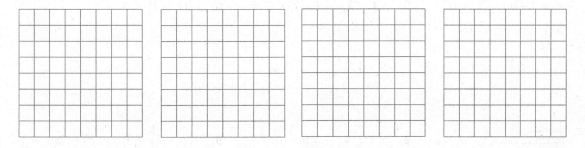

5. The number of bacteria y (in thousands) in a culture can be approximated by the model $y = 100(1.99)^t$, where t is the number of hours the culture is incubated.

   a. Tell whether the model represents exponential growth or exponential decay.

   b. Identify the hourly percent increase or decrease in the number of bacteria.

   c. Estimate when the number of bacteria will be 1,000,000.

In Exercises 6 and 7, write a recursive rule for the exponential function.

   6. $y = 2(6)^x$ **7.** $f(t) = 11(0.3)^t$

In Exercises 8 and 9, rewrite the function to determine whether it represents *exponential growth* or *exponential decay*. Then identify the percent rate of change.

   8. $y = 3(1.25)^{t+4}$ **9.** $f(t) = (0.44)^{7t}$

Chapter 2 Maintaining Mathematical Proficiency

Simplify the expression.

1. $5x - 6 + 3x$

2. $3t + 7 - 3t - 4$

3. $8s - 4 + 4s - 6 - 5s$

4. $9m + 3 + m - 3 + 5m$

5. $-4 - 3p - 7 - 3p - 4$

6. $12(z - 1) + 4$

7. $-6(x + 2) - 4$

8. $3(h + 4) - 3(h - 4)$

9. $7(z + 4) - 3(z + 2) - 2(z - 3)$

Find the greatest common factor.

10. $24, 32$

11. $30, 55$

12. $48, 84$

13. $28, 72$

14. $42, 60$

15. $35, 99$

16. Explain how to find the greatest common factor of 42, 70, and 84.

Name_____ Date_____

2.1 Adding and Subtracting Polynomials
For use with Exploration 2.1

Essential Question How can you add and subtract polynomials?

1 EXPLORATION: Adding Polynomials

Go to *BigIdeasMath.com* for an interactive tool to investigate this exploration.

Work with a partner. Write the expression modeled by the algebra tiles in each step.

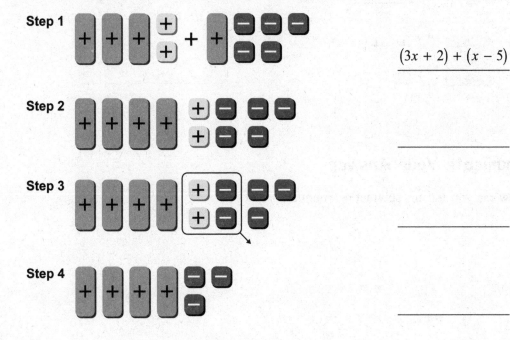

Step 1

$(3x + 2) + (x - 5)$

Step 2

_____

Step 3

_____

Step 4

_____

2 EXPLORATION: Subtracting Polynomials

Go to *BigIdeasMath.com* for an interactive tool to investigate this exploration.

Work with a partner. Write the expression modeled by the algebra tiles in each step.

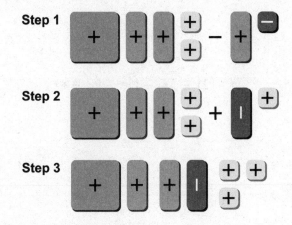

Step 1

$(x^2 + 2x + 2) - (x - 1)$

Step 2

_____

Step 3

_____

2.1 **Adding and Subtracting Polynomials** (continued)

2 **EXPLORATION:** Subtracting Polynomials (continued)

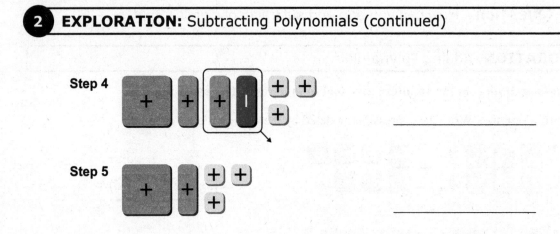

Step 4 _____

Step 5 _____

Communicate Your Answer

3. How can you add and subtract polynomials?

4. Use your methods in Question 3 to find each sum or difference.

   a. $\left(x^2 + 2x - 1\right) + \left(2x^2 - 2x + 1\right)$ **b.** $\left(4x + 3\right) + \left(x - 2\right)$

   c. $\left(x^2 + 2\right) - \left(3x^2 + 2x + 5\right)$ **d.** $\left(2x - 3x\right) - \left(x^2 - 2x + 4\right)$

Name_____ Date_____

2.1 Notetaking with Vocabulary
For use after Lesson 2.1

In your own words, write the meaning of each vocabulary term.

monomial

degree of a monomial

polynomial

binomial

trinomial

degree of a polynomial

standard form

leading coefficient

closed

Notes:

2.1 **Notetaking with Vocabulary** (continued)

Core Concepts

Polynomials

A **polynomial** is a monomial or a sum of monomials. Each monomial is called a *term* of the polynomial. A polynomial with two terms is a **binomial**. A polynomial with three terms is a **trinomial**.

Binomial	Trinomial
$5x + 2$	$x^2 + 5x + 2$

The **degree of a polynomial** is the greatest degree of its terms. A polynomial in one variable is in **standard form** when the exponents of the terms decrease from left to right. When you write a polynomial in standard form, the coefficient of the first term is the **leading coefficient**.

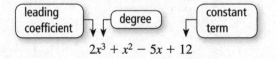

Notes:

Extra Practice

In Exercises 1–8, find the degree of the monomial.

1. $-6s$

2. w

3. 8

4. $-2abc$

5. $7x^2y$

6. $4r^2s^3t$

7. $10mn^3$

8. $\dfrac{2}{3}$

Name_____ Date _____

In Exercises 9–12, write the polynomial in standard form. Identify the degree and leading coefficient of the polynomial. Then classify the polynomial by the number of terms.

9. $x + 3x^2 + 5$

10. $\sqrt{5}\, y$

11. $3x^5 + 6x^8$

12. $f^2 - 2f + f^4$

In Exercises 13–16, find the sum.

13. $(-4x + 9) + (6x - 14)$

14. $(-3a - 2) + (7a + 5)$

15. $(x^2 + 3x + 5) + (-x^2 + 6x - 4)$

16. $(t^2 + 3t^3 - 3) + (2t^2 + 7t - 2t^3)$

In Exercises 17–20, find the difference.

17. $(g - 4) - (3g - 6)$

18. $(-5h - 2) - (7h + 6)$

19. $(-x^2 - 5) - (-3x^2 - x - 8)$

20. $(k^2 + 6k^3 - 4) - (5k^3 + 7k - 3k^2)$

2.2 Multiplying Polynomials
For use with Exploration 2.2

Essential Question How can you multiply two polynomials?

1 EXPLORATION: Multiplying Monomials Using Algebra Tiles

Work with a partner. Write each product. Explain your reasoning.

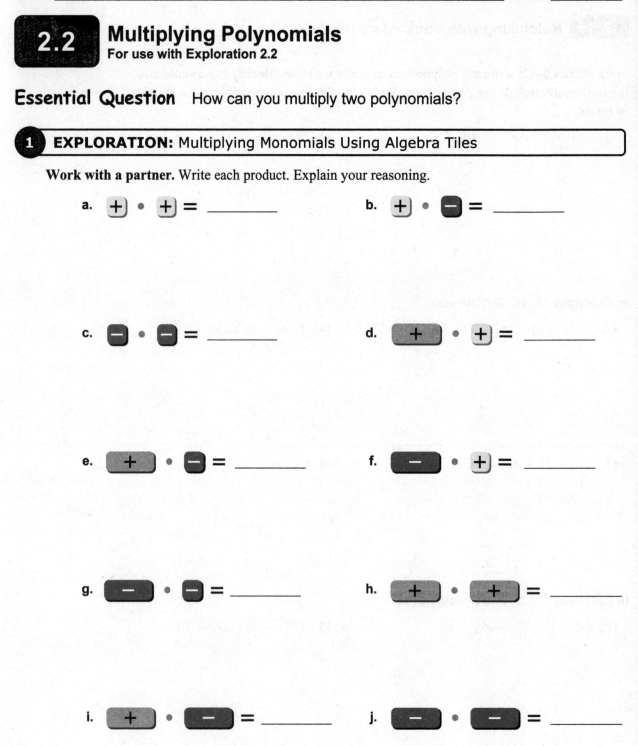

a. $\boxed{+} \cdot \boxed{+} = $ _____

b. $\boxed{+} \cdot \boxed{-} = $ _____

c. $\boxed{-} \cdot \boxed{-} = $ _____

d. $\boxed{+} \cdot \boxed{+} = $ _____

e. $\boxed{+} \cdot \boxed{-} = $ _____

f. $\boxed{-} \cdot \boxed{+} = $ _____

g. $\boxed{-} \cdot \boxed{-} = $ _____

h. $\boxed{+} \cdot \boxed{+} = $ _____

i. $\boxed{+} \cdot \boxed{-} = $ _____

j. $\boxed{-} \cdot \boxed{-} = $ _____

2.2 **Multiplying Polynomials** (continued)

2 **EXPLORATION:** Multiplying Binomials Using Algebra Tiles

Go to *BigIdeasMath.com* for an interactive tool to investigate this exploration.

Work with a partner. Write the product of two binomials modeled by each rectangular array of algebra tiles. In parts (c) and (d), first draw the rectangular array of algebra tiles that models each product.

a. $(x + 3)(x - 2) =$ _____

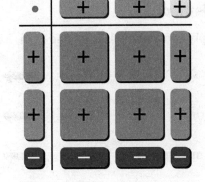

b. $(2x - 1)(2x + 1) =$ _____

c. $(x + 2)(2x - 1) =$ _____

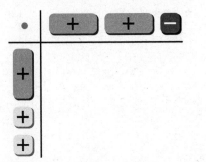

d. $(-x - 2)(x - 3) =$ _____

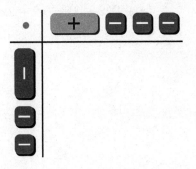

Communicate Your Answer

3. How can you multiply two polynomials?

4. Give another example of multiplying two binomials using algebra tiles that is similar to those in Exploration 2.

2.2 Notetaking with Vocabulary
For use after Lesson 2.2

In your own words, write the meaning of each vocabulary term.

FOIL Method

Core Concepts

FOIL Method

To multiply two binomials using the FOIL Method, find the sum of the products of the

First terms, $(x + 1)(x + 2)$ ➡ $x(x) = x^2$

Outer terms, $(x + 1)(x + 2)$ ➡ $x(2) = 2x$

Inner terms, and $(x + 1)(x + 2)$ ➡ $1(x) = x$

Last terms. $(x + 1)(x + 2)$ ➡ $1(2) = 2$

$$(x + 1)(x + 2) = x^2 + 2x + x + 2 = x^2 + 3x + 2$$

Notes:

Name_____ Date_____

Extra Practice

In Exercises 1–6, use the Distributive Property to find the product.

1. $(x-2)(x-1)$

2. $(b-3)(b+2)$

3. $(g+2)(g+4)$

4. $(a-1)(2a+5)$

5. $(3n-4)(n+1)$

6. $(r+3)(3r+2)$

In Exercises 7–12, use a table to find the product.

7. $(x-3)(x-2)$

8. $(y+1)(y-6)$

9. $(q+3)(q+7)$

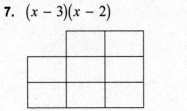

10. $(2w-5)(w-3)$

11. $(6h-2)(-3-2h)$

12. $(-3+4j)(3j+4)$

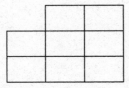

Name _____ Date _____

2.2 **Notetaking with Vocabulary** (continued)

In Exercises 13–18, use the FOIL Method to find the product.

13. $(x + 2)(x - 3)$ **14.** $(z + 3)(z + 2)$ **15.** $(h - 2)(h + 4)$

16. $(2m - 1)(m + 2)$ **17.** $(4n - 1)(3n + 4)$ **18.** $(-q - 1)(q + 1)$

In Exercises 19–24, find the product.

19. $(x - 2)(x^2 + x - 1)$ **20.** $(2 - a)(3a^2 + 3a - 5)$ **21.** $(h + 1)(h^2 - h - 1)$

22. $(d + 3)(d^2 - 4d + 1)$ **23.** $(3n^2 + 2n - 5)(2n + 1)$ **24.** $(2p^2 + p - 3)(3p - 1)$

42 **Integrated Mathematics II**
Student Journal

Copyright © Big Ideas Learning, LLC
All rights reserved.

2.3 Special Products of Polynomials
For use with Exploration 2.3

Essential Question What are the patterns in the special products $(a + b)(a - b)$, $(a + b)^2$, and $(a - b)^2$?

1 EXPLORATION: Finding a Sum and Difference Pattern

Work with a partner. Write the product of two binomials modeled by each rectangular array of algebra tiles.

a. $(x + 2)(x - 2) =$ _____

b. $(2x - 1)(2x + 1) =$ _____

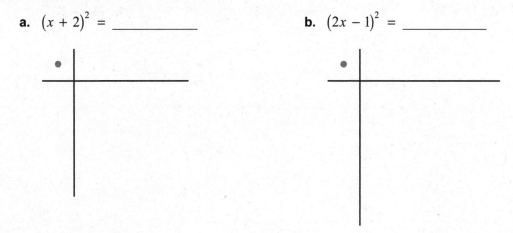

2 EXPLORATION: Finding the Square of a Binomial Pattern

Go to *BigIdeasMath.com* for an interactive tool to investigate this exploration.

Work with a partner. Draw the rectangular array of algebra tiles that models each product of two binomials. Write the product.

a. $(x + 2)^2 =$ _____

b. $(2x - 1)^2 =$ _____

2.3   **Special Products of Polynomials** (continued)

Communicate Your Answer

3. What are the patterns in the special products $(a + b)(a - b), (a + b)^2$, and $(a - b)^2$?

4. Use the appropriate special product pattern to find each product. Check your answers using algebra tiles.

    a. $(x + 3)(x - 3)$ **b.** $(x - 4)(x + 4)$ **c.** $(3x + 1)(3x - 1)$

    d. $(x + 3)^2$ **e.** $(x - 2)^2$ **f.** $(3x + 1)^2$

2.3 Notetaking with Vocabulary
For use after Lesson 2.3

In your own words, write the meaning of each vocabulary term.

binomial

Core Concepts

Square of a Binomial Pattern

Algebra

$$(a + b)^2 = a^2 + 2ab + b^2$$

$$(a - b)^2 = a^2 - 2ab + b^2$$

Example

$$(x + 5)^2 = (x)^2 + 2(x)(5) + (5)^2$$
$$= x^2 + 10x + 25$$

$$(2x - 3)^2 = (2x)^2 - 2(2x)(3) + (3)^2$$
$$= 4x^2 - 12x + 9$$

Notes:

Sum and Difference Pattern

Algebra

$$(a + b)(a - b) = a^2 - b^2$$

Example

$$(x + 3)(x - 3) = x^2 - 9$$

Notes:

2.3 Notetaking with Vocabulary (continued)

Extra Practice

In Exercises 1–18, find the product.

1. $(a + 3)^2$

2. $(b - 2)^2$

3. $(c + 4)^2$

4. $(-2x + 1)^2$

5. $(3x - 2)^2$

6. $(-4p - 3)^2$

7. $(3x + 2y)^2$

8. $(2a - 3b)^2$

9. $(-4c + 5d)^2$

10. $(x - 3)(x + 3)$

11. $(q + 5)(q - 5)$

12. $(t - 11)(t + 11)$

2.3 **Notetaking with Vocabulary** (continued)

13. $(5a - 1)(5a + 1)$

14. $\left(\dfrac{1}{4}b + 1\right)\left(\dfrac{1}{4}b - 1\right)$

15. $\left(\dfrac{1}{2}c + \dfrac{1}{3}\right)\left(\dfrac{1}{2}c - \dfrac{1}{3}\right)$

16. $(-m + 2n)(-m - 2n)$

17. $(-3j - 2k)(-3j + 2k)$

18. $\left(6a + \dfrac{1}{2}b\right)\left(-6a + \dfrac{1}{2}b\right)$

In Exercises 19–24, use special product patterns to find the product.

19. $18 \cdot 22$

20. $49 \cdot 51$

21. $19\dfrac{3}{5} \cdot 20\dfrac{2}{5}$

22. $(31)^2$

23. $(20.7)^2$

24. $(109)^2$

25. Find k so that $kx^2 - 12x + 9$ is the square of a binomial.

Name _____ Date _____

Solving Polynomial Equations in Factored Form
For use with Exploration 2.4

Essential Question How can you solve a polynomial equation?

1 EXPLORATION: Matching Equivalent Forms of an Equation

Work with a partner. An equation is considered to be in *factored form* when the product of the factors is equal to 0. Match each factored form of the equation with its equivalent standard form and nonstandard form.

Factored Form	Standard Form	Nonstandard Form
a. $(x-1)(x-3)=0$	A. $x^2-x-2=0$	1. $x^2-5x=-6$
b. $(x-2)(x-3)=0$	B. $x^2+x-2=0$	2. $(x-1)^2=4$
c. $(x+1)(x-2)=0$	C. $x^2-4x+3=0$	3. $x^2-x=2$
d. $(x-1)(x+2)=0$	D. $x^2-5x+6=0$	4. $x(x+1)=2$
e. $(x+1)(x-3)=0$	E. $x^2-2x-3=0$	5. $x^2-4x=-3$

2 EXPLORATION: Writing a Conjecture

Go to *BigIdeasMath.com* for an interactive tool to investigate this exploration.

Work with a partner. Substitute 1, 2, 3, 4, 5, and 6 for x in each equation and determine whether the equation is true. Organize your results in the table. Write a conjecture describing what you discovered.

	Equation	$x=1$	$x=2$	$x=3$	$x=4$	$x=5$	$x=6$
a.	$(x-1)(x-2)=0$						
b.	$(x-2)(x-3)=0$						
c.	$(x-3)(x-4)=0$						
d.	$(x-4)(x-5)=0$						
e.	$(x-5)(x-6)=0$						
f.	$(x-6)(x-1)=0$						

Name_____ Date_____

2.4 **Solving Polynomial Equations in Factored Form** (continued)

3 **EXPLORATION:** Special Properties of 0 and 1

Work with a partner. The numbers 0 and 1 have special properties that are shared by no other numbers. For each of the following, decide whether the property is true for 0, 1, both, or neither. Explain your reasoning.

   a. When you add _____ to a number n, you get n.

   b. If the product of two numbers is _____, then at least one of the numbers is 0.

   c. The square of _____ is equal to itself.

   d. When you multiply a number n by _____, you get n.

   e. When you multiply a number n by _____, you get 0.

   f. The opposite of _____ is equal to itself.

Communicate Your Answer

4. How can you solve a polynomial equation?

5. One of the properties in Exploration 3 is called the Zero-Product Property. It is one of the most important properties in all of algebra. Which property is it? Why do you think it is called the Zero-Product Property? Explain how it is used in algebra and why it is so important.

Name _____ Date _____

In your own words, write the meaning of each vocabulary term.

factored form

Zero-Product Property

roots

repeated roots

Core Concepts

Zero-Product Property

Words   If the product of two real numbers is 0, then at least one of the numbers
             is 0.

Algebra   If a and b are real numbers and $ab = 0$, then $a = 0$ or $b = 0$.

Notes:

Name_____ Date_____

Extra Practice

In Exercises 1–12, solve the equation.

1. $x(x + 5) = 0$

2. $a(a - 12) = 0$

3. $5p(p - 2) = 0$

4. $(c - 2)(c + 1) = 0$

5. $(2b - 6)(3b + 18) = 0$

6. $(3 - 5s)(-3 + 5s) = 0$

7. $(x - 3)^2 = 0$

8. $(3d + 7)(5d - 6) = 0$

9. $(2t + 8)(2t - 8) = 0$

10. $(w + 4)^2(w + 1) = 0$

11. $g(6 - 3g)(6 + 3g) = 0$

12. $(4 - m)\left(8 + \frac{2}{3}m\right)(-2 - 3m) = 0$

2.4 **Notetaking with Vocabulary** (continued)

In Exercises 13–18, factor the polynomial.

13. $6x^2 + 3x$

14. $4y^4 - 20y^3$

15. $18u^4 - 6u$

16. $7z^7 + 2z^6$

17. $24h^3 + 8h$

18. $15f^4 - 45f$

In Exercises 19–24, solve the equation.

19. $6k^2 + k = 0$

20. $35n - 49n^2 = 0$

21. $4z^2 + 52z = 0$

22. $6x^2 = -72x$

23. $22s = 11s^2$

24. $7p^2 = 21p$

25. A boy kicks a ball in the air. The height y (in feet) above the ground of the ball is modeled by the equation $y = -16x^2 + 80x$, where x is the time (in seconds) since the ball was kicked. Find the roots of the equation when $y = 0$. Explain what the roots mean in this situation.

Name_____ Date_____

2.5 Factoring $x^2 + bx + c$
For use with Exploration 2.5

Essential Question How can you use algebra tiles to factor the trinomial $x^2 + bx + c$ into the product of two binomials?

1 EXPLORATION: Finding Binomial Factors

Go to *BigIdeasMath.com* for an interactive tool to investigate this exploration.

Work with a partner. Use algebra tiles to write each polynomial as the product of two binomials. Check your answer by multiplying.

Sample $x^2 + 5x + 6$

Step 1 Arrange algebra tiles that model $x^2 + 5x + 6$ into a rectangular array.

Step 2 Use additional algebra tiles to model the dimensions of the rectangle.

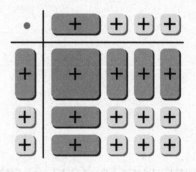

Step 3 Write the polynomial in factored form using the dimensions of the rectangle.

width   length

Area $= x^2 + 5x + 6 = (x + 2)(x + 3)$

a. $x^2 - 3x + 2 =$ _____

b. $x^2 + 5x + 4 =$ _____

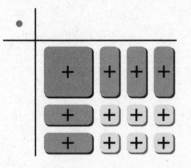

2.5 **Factoring $x^2 + bx + c$** (continued)

1 **EXPLORATION: Finding Binomial Factors (continued)**

c. $x^2 - 7x + 12 =$ _____

d. $x^2 + 7x + 12 =$ _____

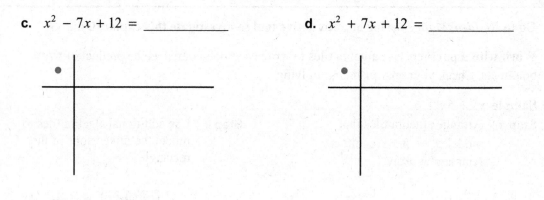

Communicate Your Answer

2. How can you use algebra tiles to factor the trinomial $x^2 + bx + c$ into the product of two binomials?

3. Describe a strategy for factoring the trinomial $x^2 + bx + c$ that does not use algebra tiles.

2.5 Notetaking with Vocabulary
For use after Lesson 2.5

In your own words, write the meaning of each vocabulary term.

polynomial

FOIL Method

Zero-Product Property

Core Concepts

Factoring $x^2 + bx + c$ When c Is Positive

Algebra $x^2 + bx + c = (x + p)(x + q)$ when $p + q = b$ and $pq = c$.

When c is positive, p and q have the same sign as b.

Examples $x^2 + 6x + 5 = (x + 1)(x + 5)$

$x^2 - 6x + 5 = (x - 1)(x - 5)$

Notes:

Factoring $x^2 + bx + c$ When c Is Negative

Algebra $x^2 + bx + c = (x + p)(x + q)$ when $p + q = b$ and $pq = c$.

When c is negative, p and q have different signs.

Example $x^2 - 4x - 5 = (x + 1)(x - 5)$

Notes:

2.5 Notetaking with Vocabulary (continued)

Extra Practice

In Exercises 1–12, factor the polynomial.

1. $c^2 + 8c + 7$ **2.** $a^2 + 16a + 64$ **3.** $x^2 + 11x + 18$

4. $d^2 + 6d + 8$ **5.** $s^2 + 11s + 10$ **6.** $u^2 + 10u + 9$

7. $b^2 + 3b - 54$ **8.** $y^2 - y - 2$ **9.** $u^2 + 3u - 18$

10. $z^2 - z - 56$ **11.** $h^2 + 2h - 24$ **12.** $f^2 - 3f - 40$

2.5 **Notetaking with Vocabulary** (continued)

In Exercises 13–18, solve the equation.

13. $g^2 - 13g + 40 = 0$ 14. $k^2 - 5k + 6 = 0$ 15. $w^2 - 7w + 10 = 0$

16. $x^2 - x = 30$ 17. $r^2 - 3r = -2$ 18. $t^2 - 7t = 8$

19. The area of a right triangle is 16 square miles. One leg of the triangle is 4 miles longer than the other leg. Find the length of each leg.

20. You have two circular flower beds, as shown. The sum of the areas of the two flower beds is 136π square feet. Find the radius of each bed.

(r – 4) ft

r ft

2.6 Factoring $ax^2 + bx + c$
For use with Exploration 2.6

Essential Question How can you use algebra tiles to factor the trinomial $ax^2 + bx + c$ into the product of two binomials?

1 EXPLORATION: Finding Binomial Factors

Go to BigIdeasMath.com for an interactive tool to investigate this exploration.

Work with a partner. Use algebra tiles to write each polynomial as the product of two binomials. Check your answer by multiplying.

Sample $2x^2 + 5x + 2$

Step 1 Arrange algebra tiles that model $2x^2 + 5x + 2$ into a rectangular array.

Step 2 Use additional algebra tiles to model the dimensions of the rectangle.

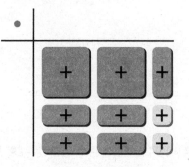
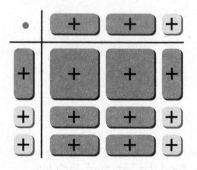

Step 3 Write the polynomial in factored form using the dimensions of the rectangle.

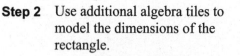

$$\text{Area} = 2x^2 + 5x + 2 = (x + 2)(2x + 1)$$

with width ⟶, length ⟶

a. $3x^2 + 5x + 2 =$ _____

2.6 **Factoring $ax^2 + bx + c$ (continued)**

1 **EXPLORATION:** Finding Binomial Factors (continued)

b. $4x^2 + 4x - 3 = $ _____   **c.** $2x^2 - 11x + 5 = $ _____

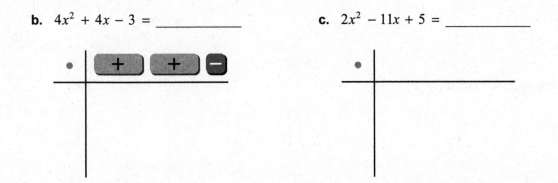

Communicate Your Answer

2. How can you use algebra tiles to factor the trinomial $ax^2 + bx + c$ into the product of two binomials?

3. Is it possible to factor the trinomial $2x^2 + 2x + 1$? Explain your reasoning.

Name _____ Date _____

2.6 Notetaking with Vocabulary
For use after Lesson 2.6

In your own words, write the meaning of each vocabulary term.

polynomial

greatest common factor (GCF)

Zero-Product Property

Notes:

2.6 Notetaking with Vocabulary (continued)

Extra Practice

In Exercises 1–18, factor the polynomial.

1. $2c^2 - 14c - 36$

2. $4a^2 + 8a - 140$

3. $3x^2 - 6x - 24$

4. $2d^2 - 2d - 60$

5. $5s^2 + 55s + 50$

6. $3q^2 + 30q + 27$

7. $12g^2 - 37g + 28$

8. $6k^2 - 11k + 4$

9. $9w^2 + 9w + 2$

10. $12a^2 + 5a - 2$

11. $15b^2 + 14b - 8$

12. $5t^2 + 12t - 9$

2.6 **Notetaking with Vocabulary (continued)**

13. $-12b^2 + 5b + 2$ **14.** $-6x^2 + x + 15$ **15.** $-60g^2 - 11g + 1$

16. $-2d^2 - d + 6$ **17.** $-3r^2 - 4r - 1$ **18.** $-8x^2 + 14x - 5$

19. The length of a rectangular shaped park is $(3x + 5)$ miles. The width is $(2x + 8)$ miles. The area of the park is 360 square miles. What are the dimensions of the park?

20. The sum of two numbers is 8. The sum of the squares of the two numbers is 34. What are the two numbers?

2.7 Factoring Special Products
For use with Exploration 2.7

Essential Question How can you recognize and factor special products?

---

1 EXPLORATION: Factoring Special Products

Go to *BigIdeasMath.com* for an interactive tool to investigate this exploration.

Work with a partner. Use algebra tiles to write each polynomial as the product of two binomials. Check your answer by multiplying. State whether the product is a "special product" that you studied in Section 2.3.

a. $4x^2 - 1 = $ _____

b. $4x^2 - 4x + 1 = $ _____

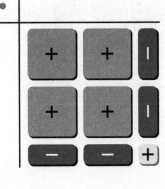

c. $4x^2 + 4x + 1 = $ _____

d. $4x^2 - 6x + 2 = $ _____

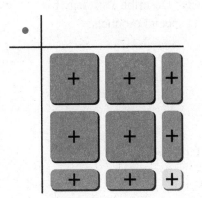

2.7 **Factoring Special Products** (continued)

2 **EXPLORATION:** Factoring Special Products

Go to *BigIdeasMath.com* for an interactive tool to investigate this exploration.

Work with a partner. Use algebra tiles to complete the rectangular arrays in three different ways, so that each way represents a different special product. Write each special product in standard form and in factored form.

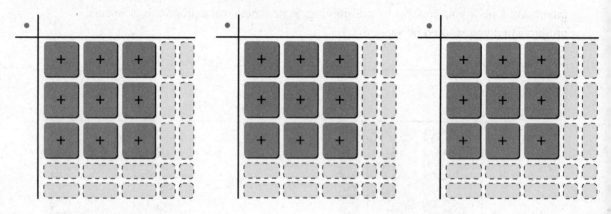

Communicate Your Answer

3. How can you recognize and factor special products? Describe a strategy for recognizing which polynomials can be factored as special products.

4. Use the strategy you described in Question 3 to factor each polynomial.

   a. $25x^2 + 10x + 1$ **b.** $25x^2 - 10x + 1$ **c.** $25x^2 - 1$

2.7 Notetaking with Vocabulary
For use after Lesson 2.7

In your own words, write the meaning of each vocabulary term.

polynomial

trinomial

Core Concepts

Difference of Two Squares Pattern

Algebra

$$a^2 - b^2 = (a + b)(a - b)$$

Example

$$x^2 - 9 = x^2 - 3^2 = (x + 3)(x - 3)$$

Notes:

Perfect Square Trinomial Pattern

Algebra

$$a^2 + 2ab + b^2 = (a + b)^2$$

$$a^2 - 2ab + b^2 = (a - b)^2$$

Example

$$x^2 + 6x + 9 = x^2 + 2(x)(3) + 3^2$$
$$= (x + 3)^2$$

$$x^2 - 6x + 9 = x^2 - 2(x)(3) + 3^2$$
$$= (x - 3)^2$$

Notes:

Name_____ Date _____

Extra Practice

In Exercises 1–6, factor the polynomial.

1. $s^2 - 49$

2. $t^2 - 81$

3. $16 - x^2$

4. $4g^2 - 25$

5. $36h^2 - 121$

6. $81 - 49k^2$

In Exercises 7–12, use a special product pattern to evaluate the expression.

7. $57^2 - 53^2$

8. $38^2 - 32^2$

9. $68^2 - 64^2$

10. $45^2 - 40^2$

11. $79^2 - 71^2$

12. $86^2 - 84^2$

Name_____ Date_____

In Exercises 13–18, factor the polynomial.

13. $x^2 + 16x + 64$ **14.** $p^2 + 28p + 196$ **15.** $r^2 - 26r + 169$

16. $a^2 - 18a + 81$ **17.** $36c^2 + 84c + 49$ **18.** $100x^2 - 20x + 1$

In Exercises 19–24, solve the equation.

19. $x^2 - 144 = 0$ **20.** $9y^2 = 49$ **21.** $c^2 + 14c + 49 = 0$

22. $d^2 - 4d + 4 = 0$ **23.** $n^2 + \frac{2}{3}n = -\frac{1}{9}$ **24.** $-\frac{6}{5}k + \frac{9}{25} = -k^2$

25. The dimensions of a rectangular prism are $(x + 1)$ feet by $(x + 2)$ feet by 4 feet. The volume of the prism is $(24x - 1)$ cubic feet. What is the value of x?

2.8 Factoring Polynomials Completely
For use with Exploration 2.8

Essential Question   How can you factor a polynomial completely?

1   EXPLORATION: Writing a Product of Linear Factors

Work with a partner. Write the product represented by the algebra tiles. Then multiply to write the polynomial in standard form.

a. $(+ \; +)(+ \; +)(- \; -)$

b. $(+ \; + \; +)(+ \; +)(-)$

c. $(+ \; + \; + \; +)(+)(+ \; +)$

d. $(+ \; +)(+ \; -)(+)$

e. $(- \; +)(+ \; +)(-)$

f. $(- \; -)(+ \; +)(- \; -)$

2   EXPLORATION: Matching Standard and Factored Forms

Work with a partner. Match the standard form of the polynomial with the equivalent factored form on the next page. Explain your strategy.

a. $x^3 + x^2$

b. $x^3 - x$

c. $x^3 + x^2 - 2x$

d. $x^3 - 4x^2 + 4x$

e. $x^3 - 2x^2 - 3x$

f. $x^3 - 2x^2 + x$

g. $x^3 - 4x$

h. $x^3 + 2x^2$

i. $x^3 - x^2$

j. $x^3 - 3x^2 + 2x$

k. $x^3 + 2x^2 - 3x$

l. $x^3 - 4x^2 + 3x$

m. $x^3 - 2x^2$

n. $x^3 + 4x^2 + 4x$

o. $x^3 + 2x^2 + x$

2.8 **Factoring Polynomials Completely** (continued)

2 **EXPLORATION:** Matching Standard and Factored Forms (continued)

A. $x(x + 1)(x - 1)$ **B.** $x(x - 1)^2$ **C.** $x(x + 1)^2$

D. $x(x + 2)(x - 1)$ **E.** $x(x - 1)(x - 2)$ **F.** $x(x + 2)(x - 2)$

G. $x(x - 2)^2$ **H.** $x(x + 2)^2$ **I.** $x^2(x - 1)$

J. $x^2(x + 1)$ **K.** $x^2(x - 2)$ **L.** $x^2(x + 2)$

M. $x(x + 3)(x - 1)$ **N.** $x(x + 1)(x - 3)$ **O.** $x(x - 1)(x - 3)$

Communicate Your Answer

3. How can you factor a polynomial completely?

4. Use your answer to Question 3 to factor each polynomial completely.

   a. $x^3 + 4x^2 + 3x$ **b.** $x^3 - 6x^2 + 9x$ **c.** $x^3 + 6x^2 + 9x$

2.8 Notetaking with Vocabulary
For use after Lesson 2.8

In your own words, write the meaning of each vocabulary term.

factoring by grouping

factored completely

Core Concepts

Factoring by Grouping

To factor a polynomial with four terms, group the terms into pairs. Factor the GCF out of each pair of terms. Look for and factor out the common binomial factor. This process is called **factoring by grouping**.

Notes:

Guidelines for Factoring Polynomials Completely

To factor a polynomial completely, you should try each of these steps.

1. Factor out the greatest common monomial factor. $3x^2 + 6x = 3x(x + 2)$

___

2. Look for a difference of two squares or a perfect square trinomial. $x^2 + 4x + 4 = (x + 2)^2$

___

3. Factor a trinomial of the form $ax^2 + bx + c$ into a product of binomial factors. $3x^2 - 5x - 2 = (3x + 1)(x - 2)$

___

4. Factor a polynomial with four terms by grouping. $x^3 + x - 4x^2 - 4 = (x^2 + 1)(x - 4)$

___

Notes:

Name_____ Date_____

Extra Practice

In Exercises 1–8, factor the polynomial by grouping.

1. $b^3 - 4b^2 + b - 4$

2. $ac + ad + bc + bd$

3. $d^2 + 2c + cd + 2d$

4. $5t^3 + 6t^2 + 5t + 6$

5. $8s^3 + s - 64s^2 - 8$

6. $12a^3 + 2a^2 - 30a - 5$

7. $4x^3 - 12x^2 - 5x + 15$

8. $21h^3 + 18h^2 - 35h - 30$

2.8 Notetaking with Vocabulary (continued)

In Exercises 9–16, factor the polynomial completely.

9. $4c^3 - 4c$

10. $100x^4 - 25x^2$

11. $2a^2 + 3a - 2$

12. $9x^2 + 3x - 14$

13. $20p^2 + 22p - 12$

14. $12x^2 - 20x - 48$

15. $3s^3 + 2s^2 - 21s - 14$

16. $2t^4 + t^3 - 10t - 5$

In Exercises 17–22, solve the equation.

17. $3x^2 - 21x + 30 = 0$

18. $5y^2 - 5y - 30 = 0$

19. $c^4 - 81c^2 = 0$

20. $9d + 9 = d^3 + d^2$

21. $48n - 3n^2 = 0$

22. $x^3 + 3x^2 = 16x + 48$

Name_____ Date_____

Graph the linear equation.

1. $y = 4x - 5$

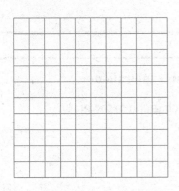

2. $y = -2x + 3$

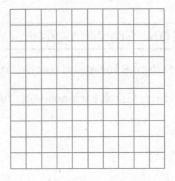

3. $y = \dfrac{1}{2}x + 3$

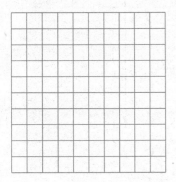

4. $y = -x + 2$

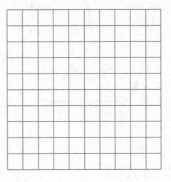

Evaluate the expression when $x = -4$.

5. $2x^2 + 8$

6. $-x^2 + 3x - 4$

7. $-3x^2 - 4$

8. $5x^2 - x + 8$

9. $4x^2 - 8x$

10. $6x^2 - 5x + 3$

11. $-2x^2 + 4x + 4$

12. $3x^2 + 2x + 2$

3.1 Graphing $f(x) = ax^2$

For use with Exploration 3.1

Essential Question What are some of the characteristics of the graph of a quadratic function of the form $f(x) = ax^2$?

1 **EXPLORATION:** Graphing Quadratic Functions

Go to *BigIdeasMath.com* for an interactive tool to investigate this exploration.

Work with a partner. Graph each quadratic function. Compare each graph to the graph of $f(x) = x^2$.

a. $g(x) = 3x^2$

b. $g(x) = -5x^2$

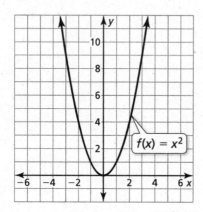

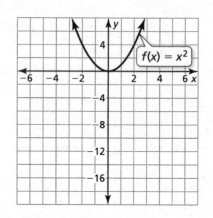

c. $g(x) = -0.2x^2$

d. $g(x) = \dfrac{1}{10}x^2$

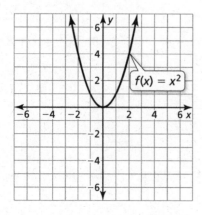

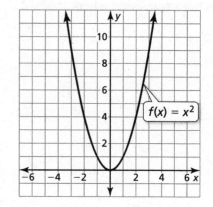

3.1 Graphing $f(x) = ax^2$ (continued)

Communicate Your Answer

2. What are some of the characteristics of the graph of a quadratic function of the form $f(x) = ax^2$?

3. How does the value of a affect the graph of $f(x) = ax^2$? Consider $0 < a < 1$, $a > 1, -1 < a < 0$, and $a < -1$. Use a graphing calculator to verify your answers.

4. The figure shows the graph of a quadratic function of the form $y = ax^2$. Which of the intervals in Question 3 describes the value of a? Explain your reasoning.

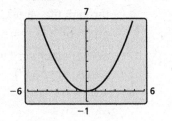

3.1 Notetaking with Vocabulary
For use after Lesson 3.1

In your own words, write the meaning of each vocabulary term.

quadratic function

parabola

vertex

axis of symmetry

Core Concepts

Characteristics of Quadratic Functions

The *parent quadratic function* is $f(x) = x^2$. The graphs of all other quadratic functions are *transformations* of the graph of the parent quadratic function.

The lowest point on a parabola that opens up or the highest point on a parabola that opens down is the **vertex.** The vertex of the graph of $f(x) = x^2$ is (0, 0).

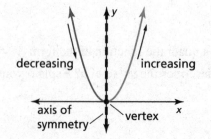

The vertical line that divides the parabola into two symmetric parts is the **axis of symmetry.** The axis of symmetry passes through the vertex. For the graph of $f(x) = x^2$, the axis of symmetry is the y-axis, or $x = 0$.

Notes:

Name_____ Date _____

Graphing $f(x) = ax^2$ When $a > 0$

- When $0 < a < 1$, the graph of $f(x) = ax^2$ is a vertical shrink of the graph of $f(x) = x^2$.

- When $a > 1$, the graph of $f(x) = ax^2$ is a vertical stretch of the graph of $f(x) = x^2$.

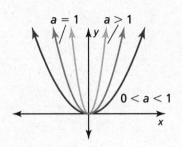

Graphing $f(x) = ax^2$ When $a < 0$

- When $-1 < a < 0$, the graph of $f(x) = ax^2$ is a vertical shrink with a reflection in the x-axis of the graph of $f(x) = x^2$.

- When $a < -1$, the graph of $f(x) = ax^2$ is a vertical stretch with a reflection in the x-axis of the graph of $f(x) = x^2$.

Notes:

Extra Practice

In Exercises 1 and 2, identify characteristics of the quadratic function and its graph.

1.

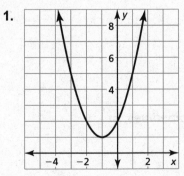

2.

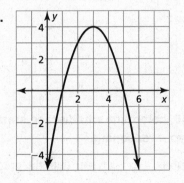

Name _____ Date _____

In Exercises 3–8, graph the function. Compare the graph to the graph of $f(x) = x^2$.

3. $g(x) = 5x^2$

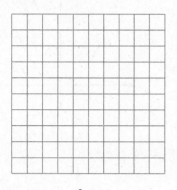

4. $m(x) = -4x^2$

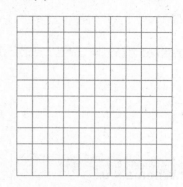

5. $k(x) = -x^2$

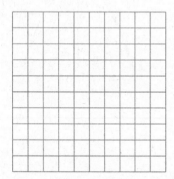

6. $l(x) = -7x^2$

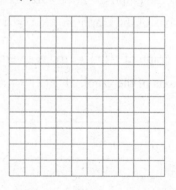

7. $n(x) = -\frac{1}{5}x^2$

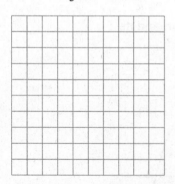

8. $p(x) = 0.6x^2$

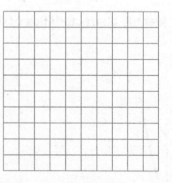

In Exercises 9 and 10, determine whether the statement is *always, sometimes,* or *never* true. Explain your reasoning.

9. The graph of $g(x) = ax^2$ is wider than the graph of $f(x) = x^2$ when $a > 0$.

10. The graph of $g(x) = ax^2$ is narrower than the graph of $f(x) = x^2$ when $|a| < 1$.

3.2 Graphing $f(x) = ax^2 + c$
For use with Exploration 3.2

Essential Question How does the value of c affect the graph of $f(x) = ax^2 + c$?

 EXPLORATION: Graphing $y = ax^2 + c$

Go to *BigIdeasMath.com* for an interactive tool to investigate this exploration.

Work with a partner. Sketch the graphs of the functions in the same coordinate plane. What do you notice?

   a. $f(x) = x^2$ and $g(x) = x^2 + 2$

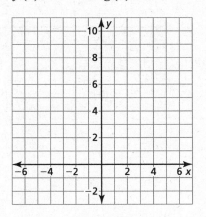

   b. $f(x) = 2x^2$ and $g(x) = 2x^2 - 2$

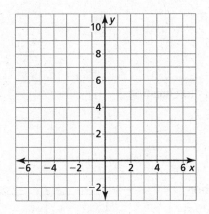

Name _____ Date _____

3.2 Graphing $f(x) = ax^2 + c$ (continued)

2 **EXPLORATION:** Finding x-Intercepts of Graphs

Go to *BigIdeasMath.com* for an interactive tool to investigate this exploration.

Work with a partner. Graph each function. Find the x-intercepts of the graph. Explain how you found the x-intercepts.

a. $y = x^2 - 7$

b. $y = -x^2 + 1$

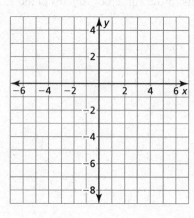

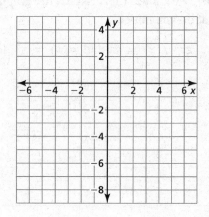

Communicate Your Answer

3. How does the value of c affect the graph of $f(x) = ax^2 + c$?

4. Use a graphing calculator to verify your answers to Question 3.

5. The figure shows the graph of a quadratic function of the form $y = ax^2 + c$. Describe possible values of a and c. Explain your reasoning.

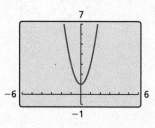

80 **Integrated Mathematics II**
Student Journal

Name_____ Date_____

In your own words, write the meaning of each vocabulary term.

zero of a function

Core Concepts

Graphing $f(x) = ax^2 + c$

- When $c > 0$, the graph of $f(x) = ax^2 + c$ is a vertical translation c units up of the graph of $f(x) = ax^2$.

- When $c < 0$, the graph of $f(x) = ax^2 + c$ is a vertical translation $|c|$ units down of the graph of $f(x) = ax^2$.

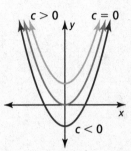

The vertex of the graph of $f(x) = ax^2 + c$ is $(0, c)$, and the axis of symmetry is $x = 0$.

Notes:

3.2 **Notetaking with Vocabulary (continued)**

Extra Practice

In Exercises 1–4, graph the function. Compare the graph to the graph of $f(x) = x^2$.

  1. $g(x) = x^2 + 5$

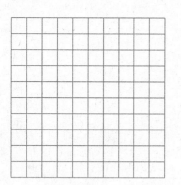

  2. $m(x) = x^2 - 3$

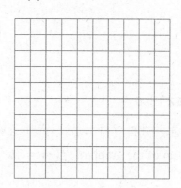

  3. $n(x) = -3x^2 - 2$

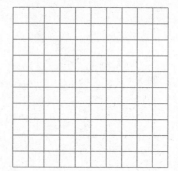

  4. $q(x) = \frac{1}{2}x^2 - 4$

3.2 Notetaking with Vocabulary (continued)

In Exercises 5–8, find the zeros of the function.

5. $y = -x^2 + 1$

6. $y = -4x^2 + 16$

7. $n(x) = -x^2 + 64$

8. $p(x) = -9x^2 + 1$

In Exercises 9 and 10, sketch a parabola with the given characteristics.

9. The parabola opens down, and the vertex is $(0, 5)$.

10. The lowest point on the parabola is $(0, 4)$.

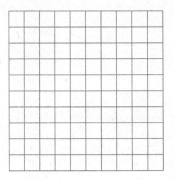

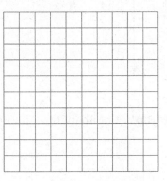

11. The function $f(t) = -16t^2 + s_0$ represents the approximate height (in feet) of a falling object t seconds after it is dropped from an initial height s_0 (in feet). A tennis ball falls from a height of 400 feet.

   a. After how many seconds does the tennis ball hit the ground?

   b. Suppose the initial height is decreased by 384 feet. After how many seconds does the ball hit the ground?

3.3 Graphing $f(x) = ax^2 + bx + c$

For use with Exploration 3.3

Essential Question How can you find the vertex of the graph of $f(x) = ax^2 + bx + c$?

1 EXPLORATION: Comparing x-Intercepts with the Vertex

Go to BigIdeasMath.com for an interactive tool to investigate this exploration.

Work with a partner.

    a. Sketch the graphs of $y = 2x^2 - 8x$ and $y = 2x^2 - 8x + 6$.

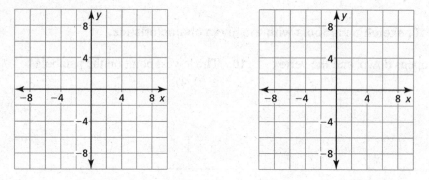

    b. What do you notice about the x-coordinate of the vertex of each graph?

    c. Use the graph of $y = 2x^2 - 8x$ to find its x-intercepts. Verify your answer by solving $0 = 2x^2 - 8x$.

    d. Compare the value of the x-coordinate of the vertex with the values of the x-intercepts.

3.3 Graphing $f(x) = ax^2 + bx + c$ (continued)

---

2 **EXPLORATION:** Finding x-Intercepts

Work with a partner.

    a. Solve $0 = ax^2 + bx$ for x by factoring.

    b. What are the x-intercepts of the graph of $y = ax^2 + bx$?

    c. Complete the table to verify your answer.

x	$y = ax^2 + bx$
0	
$-\dfrac{b}{a}$	

---

3 **EXPLORATION:** Deductive Reasoning

Work with a partner. Complete the following logical argument.

The x-intercepts of the graph of $y = ax^2 + bx$ are 0 and $-\dfrac{b}{a}$.

The vertex of the graph of $y = ax^2 + bx$ occurs when $x = $ _____.

The vertices of the graphs of $y = ax^2 + bx$ and $y = ax^2 + bx + c$ have the same x-coordinate.

The vertex of the graph of $y = ax^2 + bx + c$ occurs when $x = $ _____.

Communicate Your Answer

    4. How can you find the vertex of the graph of $f(x) = ax^2 + bx + c$?

    5. Without graphing, find the vertex of the graph of $f(x) = x^2 - 4x + 3$.
       Check your result by graphing.

3.3 Notetaking with Vocabulary
For use after Lesson 3.3

In your own words, write the meaning of each vocabulary term.

maximum value

minimum value

Core Concepts

Graphing $f(x) = ax^2 + bx + c$

- The graph opens up when $a > 0$, and the graph opens down when $a < 0$.

- The y-intercept is c.

- The x-coordinate of the vertex is $-\dfrac{b}{2a}$.

- The axis of symmetry is $x = -\dfrac{b}{2a}$.

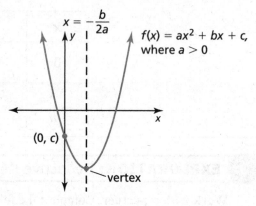

$x = -\dfrac{b}{2a}$

$f(x) = ax^2 + bx + c$, where $a > 0$

$(0, c)$

vertex

Notes:

Name_____ Date_____

Maximum and Minimum Values

The y-coordinate of the vertex of the graph of $f(x) = ax^2 + bx + c$ is the **maximum value** of the function when $a < 0$ or the **minimum value** of the function when $a > 0$.

$$f(x) = ax^2 + bx + c, a < 0 \qquad\qquad f(x) = ax^2 + bx + c, a > 0$$

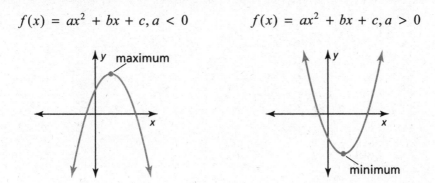

Notes:

Extra Practice

In Exercises 1–4, find (a) the axis of symmetry and (b) the vertex of the graph of the function.

1. $f(x) = x^2 - 10x + 2$

2. $y = -4x^2 + 16x$

3. $y = -2x^2 - 8x + 5$

4. $f(x) = -3x^2 + 6x + 1$

Name _____ Date _____

In Exercises 5–7, graph the function. Describe the domain and range.

5. $f(x) = 3x^2 + 6x + 2$ **6.** $y = 2x^2 - 8x - 1$ **7.** $y = -\frac{1}{5}x^2 - x + 5$

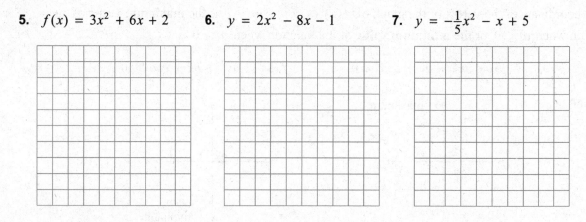

In Exercises 8–13, tell whether the function has a minimum value or a maximum value. Then find the value.

8. $y = -\frac{1}{2}x^2 - 5x + 2$ **9.** $y = 8x^2 + 16x - 2$ **10.** $y = -x^2 - 4x - 7$

11. $y = -7x^2 + 7x + 5$ **12.** $y = 9x^2 + 6x + 4$ **13.** $y = -\frac{1}{4}x^2 + x - 6$

14. The function $h = -16t^2 + 250t$ represents the height h (in feet) of a rocket t seconds after it is launched. The rocket explodes at its highest point.

a. When does the rocket explode?

b. At what height does the rocket explode?

3.4 Graphing $f(x) = a(x-h)^2 + k$
For use with Exploration 3.4

Essential Question How can you describe the graph of $f(x) = a(x-h)^2$?

---

1 EXPLORATION: Graphing $y = a(x - h)^2$ When $h > 0$

Go to *BigIdeasMath.com* for an interactive tool to investigate this exploration.

Work with a partner. Sketch the graphs of the functions in the same coordinate plane. How does the value of h affect the graph of $y = a(x - h)^2$?

   a. $f(x) = x^2$ and $g(x) = (x - 2)^2$

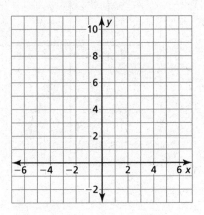

   b. $f(x) = 2x^2$ and $g(x) = 2(x - 2)^2$

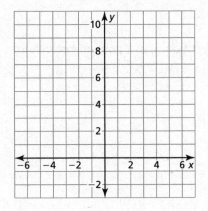

3.4 Graphing $f(x) = a(x - h)^2 + k$ (continued)

---

2 **EXPLORATION:** Graphing $y = a(x - h)^2$ When $h < 0$

Go to *BigIdeasMath.com* for an interactive tool to investigate this exploration.

Work with a partner. Sketch the graphs of the functions in the same coordinate plane. How does the value of h affect the graph of $y = a(x - h)^2$?

a. $f(x) = -x^2$ and $g(x) = -(x + 2)^2$

b. $f(x) = -2x^2$ and $g(x) = -2(x + 2)^2$

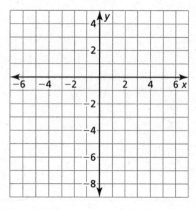
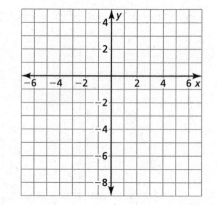

Communicate Your Answer

3. How can you describe the graph of $f(x) = a(x - h)^2$?

4. Without graphing, describe the graph of each function. Use a graphing calculator to check your answer.

a. $y = (x - 3)^2$

b. $y = (x + 3)^2$

c. $y = -(x - 3)^2$

Name_____ Date_____

3.4 Notetaking with Vocabulary
For use after Lesson 3.4

In your own words, write the meaning of each vocabulary term.

even function

odd function

vertex form (of a quadratic function)

Core Concepts

Even and Odd Functions

A function $y = f(x)$ is **even** when $f(-x) = f(x)$ for each x in the domain of f. The graph of an even function is symmetric about the y-axis.

A function $y = f(x)$ is **odd** when $f(-x) = -f(x)$ for each x in the domain of f. The graph of an odd function is symmetric about the origin. A graph is *symmetric about the origin* when it looks the same after reflections in the x-axis and then in the y-axis.

Notes:

Graphing $f(x) = a(x - h)^2$

- When $h > 0$, the graph of $f(x) = a(x - h)^2$ is a horizontal translation h units right of the graph $f(x) = ax^2$.

- When $h < 0$, the graph of $f(x) = a(x - h)^2$ is a horizontal translation $|h|$ units left of the graph of $f(x) = ax^2$.

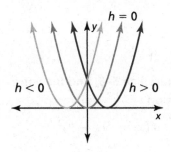

The vertex of the graph of $f(x) = a(x - h)^2$ is $(h, 0)$, and the axis of symmetry is $x = h$.

Notes:

3.4 Notetaking with Vocabulary (continued)

Graphing $f(x) = a(x-h)^2 + k$

The **vertex form** of a quadratic function is $f(x) = a(x - h)^2 + k$, where $a \neq 0$. The graph of $f(x) = a(x - h)^2 + k$ is a translation h units horizontally and k units vertically of the graph of $f(x) = ax^2$.

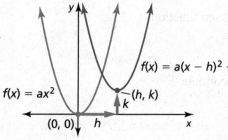

The vertex of the graph of $f(x) = a(x - h)^2 + k$ is (h, k), and the axis of symmetry is $x = h$.

Notes:

Extra Practice

In Exercises 1–4, determine whether the function is *even, odd,* or *neither.*

1. $f(x) = 5x$

2. $f(x) = -4x^2$

3. $h(x) = \dfrac{1}{2}x^2$

4. $f(x) = -3x^2 + 2x + 1$

In Exercises 5–8, find the vertex and the axis of symmetry of the graph of the function.

5. $f(x) = 5(x - 2)^2$

6. $f(x) = -4(x + 8)^2$

Name_____ Date_____

7. $p(x) = -\dfrac{1}{2}(x - 1)^2 + 4$

8. $g(x) = -(x + 1)^2 - 5$

In Exercises 9 and 10, graph the function. Compare the graph to the graph of $f(x) = x^2$.

9. $m(x) = 3(x + 2)^2$

10. $g(x) = -\dfrac{1}{4}(x - 6)^2 + 4$

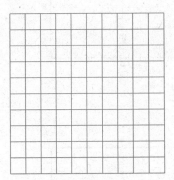
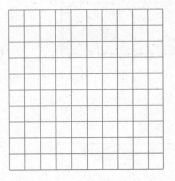

In Exercises 11 and 12, graph g.

11. $f(x) = 3(x + 1)^2 - 1;\ g(x) = f(x + 2)$

12. $f(x) = \dfrac{1}{2}(x - 3)^2 - 5;\ g(x) = -f(x)$

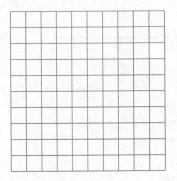

3.5 Graphing $f(x) = a(x - p)(x - q)$

For use with Exploration 3.5

Essential Question What are some of the characteristics of the graph of $f(x) = a(x - p)(x - q)$?

---

1 **EXPLORATION:** Using Zeros to Write Functions

Work with a partner. Each graph represents a function of the form $f(x) = (x - p)(x - q)$ or $f(x) = -(x - p)(x - q)$. Write the function represented by each graph. Explain your reasoning.

a.
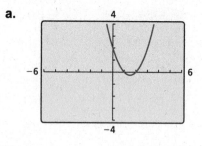

b.
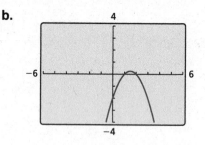

c.
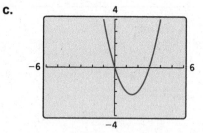

d.
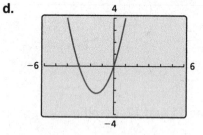

e.
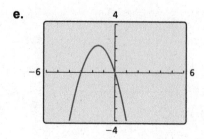

f.
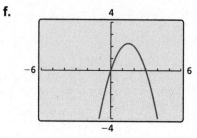

3.5 **Graphing** $f(x) = a(x - p)(x - q)$ **(continued)**

1 **EXPLORATION:** Using Zeros to Write Functions (continued)

g.

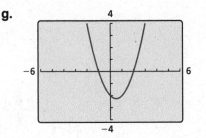

h.

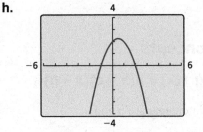

Communicate Your Answer

2. What are some of the characteristics of the graph of $f(x) = a(x - p)(x - q)$?

3. Consider the graph of $f(x) = a(x - p)(x - q)$.

   a. Does changing the sign of a change the x-intercepts? Does changing the sign of a change the y-intercept? Explain your reasoning.

   b. Does changing the value of p change the x-intercepts? Does changing the value of p change the y-intercept? Explain your reasoning.

Name _____ Date _____

3.5 Notetaking with Vocabulary
For use after Lesson 3.5

In your own words, write the meaning of each vocabulary term.

intercept form

Core Concepts

Graphing $f(x) = a(x - p)(x - q)$

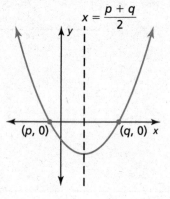

$x = \dfrac{p + q}{2}$

- The x-intercepts are p and q.

- The axis of symmetry is halfway between $(p, 0)$ and $(q, 0)$. So, the axis of symmetry is $x = \dfrac{p + q}{2}$.

- The graph opens up when $a > 0$, and the graph opens down when $a < 0$.

$(p, 0)$ $(q, 0)$ x

Notes:

Factors and Zeros

For any factor $x - n$ of a polynomial, n is a zero of the function defined by the polynomial.

Notes:

3.5 **Notetaking with Vocabulary** (continued)

Extra Practice

In Exercises 1 and 2, find the *x*-intercepts and axis of symmetry of the graph of the function.

1. $y = (x + 2)(x - 4)$

2. $y = -3(x - 2)(x - 3)$

In Exercises 3–6, graph the quadratic function. Label the vertex, axis of symmetry, and *x*-intercepts. Describe the domain and range of the function.

3. $m(x) = (x + 5)(x + 1)$

4. $y = -4(x - 3)(x - 1)$

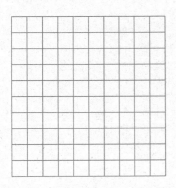

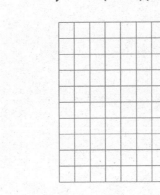

5. $y = x^2 - 4$

6. $f(x) = x^2 + 2x - 15$

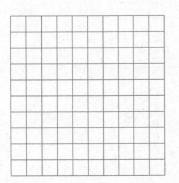

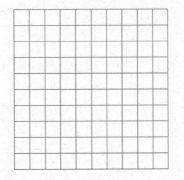

Name _____ Date _____

In Exercises 7 and 8, find the zero(s) of the function.

7. $y = 6x^2 - 6$

8. $y = x^2 + 9x + 20$

In Exercises 9–12, use zeros to graph the function.

9. $f(x) = x^2 - 3x - 10$

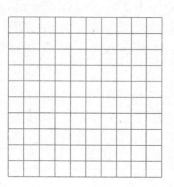

10. $f(x) = -2(x + 3)(x - 1)$

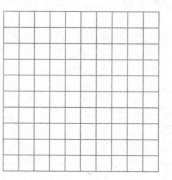

11. $f(x) = x^2 - 9$

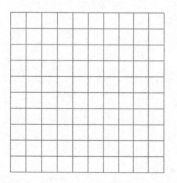

12. $f(x) = 2x^2 - 12x + 10$

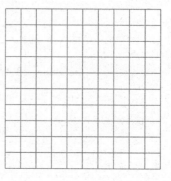

3.6 Focus of a Parabola
For use with Exploration 3.6

Essential Question What is the focus of a parabola?

---

1 **EXPLORATION: Analyzing Satellite Dishes**

Go to *BigIdeasMath.com* for an interactive tool to investigate this exploration.

Work with a partner. Vertical rays enter a satellite dish whose cross section is a parabola. When the rays hit the parabola, they reflect at the same angle at which they entered. (See Ray 1 in the figure.)

a. Draw the reflected rays so that they intersect the *y*-axis.

b. What do the reflected rays have in common?

c. The optimal location for the receiver of the satellite dish is at a point called the *focus* of the parabola. Determine the location of the focus. Explain why this makes sense in this situation.

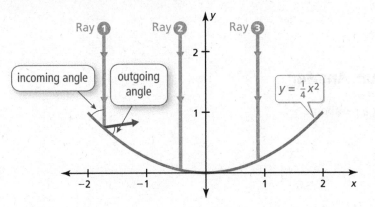

3.6 Focus of a Parabola (continued)

2 EXPLORATION: Analyzing Spotlights

Go to *BigIdeasMath.com* **for an interactive tool to investigate this exploration.**

Work with a partner. Beams of light are coming from the bulb in a spotlight, located at the focus of the parabola. When the beams hit the parabola, they reflect at the same angle at which they hit. (See Beam 1 in the figure.) Draw the reflected beams. What do they have in common? Would you consider this to be the optimal result? Explain.

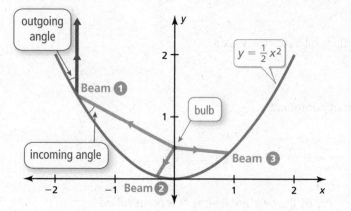

Communicate Your Answer

3. What is the focus of a parabola?

4. Describe some of the properties of the focus of a parabola.

Name_____ Date_____

Notetaking with Vocabulary
For use after Lesson 3.6

In your own words, write the meaning of each vocabulary term.

focus

directrix

Core Concepts

Standard Equations of a Parabola with Vertex at the Origin

Vertical axis of symmetry $(x = 0)$

Equation: $y = \dfrac{1}{4p}x^2$

Focus: $(0, p)$

Directrix: $y = -p$

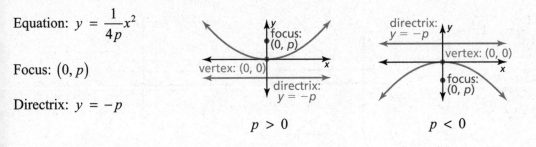

$p > 0$ $p < 0$

Horizontal axis of symmetry $(y = 0)$

Equation: $x = \dfrac{1}{4p}y^2$

Focus: $(p, 0)$

Directrix: $x = -p$

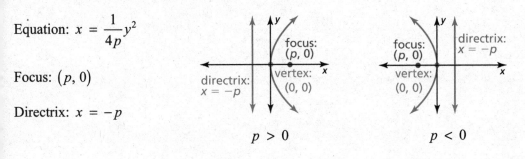

$p > 0$ $p < 0$

Notes:

Name _____ Date _____

Standard Equations of a Parabola with Vertex at (h, k)

Vertical axis of symmetry $(x = h)$

Equation: $y = \dfrac{1}{4p}(x - h)^2 + k$

Focus: $(h, k + p)$

Directrix: $y = k - p$

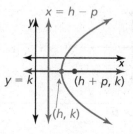

$p > 0$

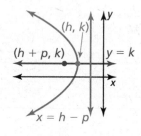

$p < 0$

Horizontal axis of symmetry $(y = k)$

Equation: $x = \dfrac{1}{4p}(y - k)^2 + h$

Focus: $(h + p, k)$

Directrix: $x = h - p$

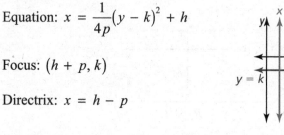

$p > 0$ $p < 0$

Notes:

Extra Practice

In Exercises 1 and 2, use the Distance Formula to write an equation of the parabola.

1. focus: $(0, -8)$

   directrix: $y = 8$

2. vertex: $(0, 0)$

   focus: $(0, 1)$

Name_____ Date_____

In Exercises 3–5, identify the focus, directrix, and axis of symmetry of the parabola. Graph the equation.

3. $x^2 = -2y$

4. $-5x + \frac{1}{3}y^2 = 0$

5. $y = -2(x + 1)^2 - 3$

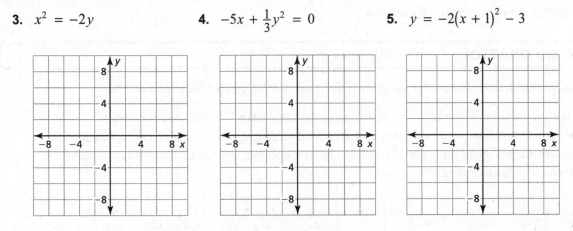

In Exercises 6–8, write an equation of the parabola shown.

6.

7.

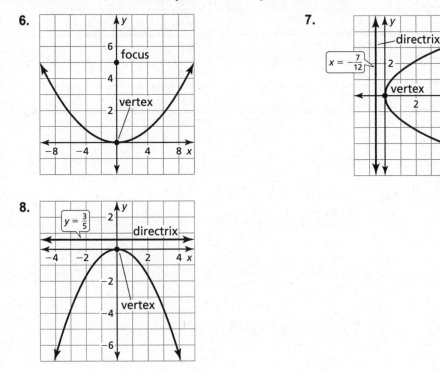

8.

9. The cross section of a parabolic sound reflector at the Olympics has a diameter of 20 inches and is 25 inches deep. Write an equation that represents the cross section of the reflector with its vertex at $(0, 0)$ and its focus to the left of the vertex.

Name _____ Date _____

3.7 Comparing Linear, Exponential, and Quadratic Functions
For use with Exploration 3.7

Essential Question How can you compare the growth rates of linear, exponential, and quadratic functions?

1 EXPLORATION: Comparing Speeds

Go to *BigIdeasMath.com* for an interactive tool to investigate this exploration.

Work with a partner. Three cars start traveling at the same time. The distance traveled in t minutes is y miles. Complete each table and sketch all three graphs in the same coordinate plane. Compare the speeds of the three cars. Which car has a constant speed? Which car is accelerating the most? Explain your reasoning.

t	$y = t$
0	
0.2	
0.4	
0.6	
0.8	
1.0	

t	$y = 2^t - 1$
0	
0.2	
0.4	
0.6	
0.8	
1.0	

t	$y = t^2$
0	
0.2	
0.4	
0.6	
0.8	
1.0	

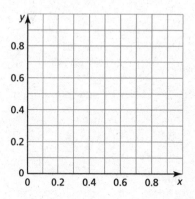

3.7 Comparing Linear, Exponential, and Quadratic Functions (continued)

2 EXPLORATION: Comparing Speeds

Work with a partner. Analyze the speeds of the three cars over the given time periods. The distance traveled in t minutes is y miles. Which car eventually overtakes the others?

t	$y = t$
1.0	
1.5	
2.0	
2.5	
3.0	
3.5	
4.0	
4.5	
5.0	

t	$y = 2^t - 1$
1.0	
1.5	
2.0	
2.5	
3.0	
3.5	
4.0	
4.5	
5.0	

t	$y = t^2$
1.0	
1.5	
2.0	
2.5	
3.0	
3.5	
4.0	
4.5	
5.0	

Communicate Your Answer

3. How can you compare the growth rates of linear, exponential, and quadratic functions?

4. Which function has a growth rate that is eventually much greater than the growth rates of the other two functions? Explain your reasoning.

Name _____ Date _____

3.7 Notetaking with Vocabulary
For use after Lesson 3.7

Core Concepts

Linear, Exponential, and Quadratic Functions

Linear Function

$$y = mx + b$$

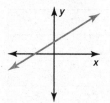

Exponential Function

$$y = ab^x$$

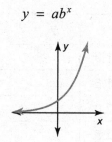

Quadratic Function

$$y = ax^2 + bx + c$$

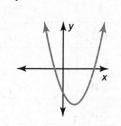

Notes:

Differences and Ratios of Functions

You can use patterns between consecutive data pairs to determine which type of function models the data. The differences of consecutive y-values are called *first differences*. The differences of consecutive first differences are called *second differences*.

- **Linear Function** The first differences are constant.

- **Exponential Function** Consecutive y-values have a common *ratio*.

- **Quadratic Function** The second differences are constant.

In all cases, the differences of consecutive x-values need to be constant.

Notes:

106 Integrated Mathematics II
Student Journal

Copyright © Big Ideas Learning, LLC
All rights reserved.

Name_____ Date _____

Comparing Functions Using Average Rates of Change

- As a and b increase, the average rate of change between $x = a$ and $x = b$ of an increasing exponential function $y = f(x)$ will eventually exceed the average rate of change between $x = a$ and $x = b$ of an increasing quadratic function $y = g(x)$ or an increasing linear function $y = h(x)$. So, as x increases, $f(x)$ will eventually exceed $g(x)$ or $h(x)$.

- As a and b increase, the average rate of change between $x = a$ and $x = b$ of an increasing quadratic function $y = g(x)$ will eventually exceed the average rate of change between $x = a$ and $x = b$ of an increasing linear function $y = h(x)$. So, as x increases, $g(x)$ will eventually exceed $h(x)$.

Notes:

Extra Practice

In Exercises 1–4, plot the points. Tell whether the points appear to represent a *linear*, an *exponential*, or a *quadratic* function.

1. $(-3, 2), (-2, 4), (-4, 4), (-1, 8), (-5, 8)$ **2.** $(-3, 1), (-2, 2), (-1, 4), (0, 8), (2, 14)$

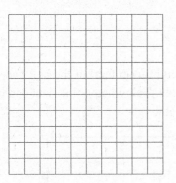

3. $(4, 0), (2, 1), (0, 3), (-1, 6), (-2, 10)$ **4.** $(2, -4), (0, -2), (-2, 0), (-4, 2), (-6, 4)$

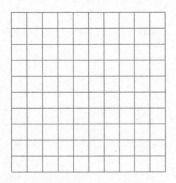
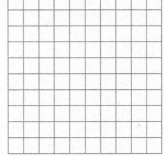

3.7   Notetaking with Vocabulary (continued)

In Exercises 5 and 6, tell whether the table of values represents a *linear*, an *exponential*, or a *quadratic* function.

5.

x	−2	−1	0	1	2
y	7	4	1	−2	−5

6.

x	−2	−1	0	1	2
y	6	2	0	2	6

In Exercises 7 and 8, tell whether the data represent a *linear*, an *exponential*, or a *quadratic* function. Then write the function.

7. $(-2, -4), (-1, -1), (0, 2), (1, 5), (2, 8)$

8. $(-2, -9), (-1, 0), (0, 3), (1, 0), (2, -9)$

9. A ball is dropped from a height of 305 feet. The table shows the height h (in feet) of the ball t seconds after being dropped. Let the time t represent the independent variable. Tell whether the data can be modeled by a *linear*, an *exponential*, or a *quadratic* function. Explain.

Time, t	0	1	2	3	4
Height, h	305	289	241	161	49

Chapter 4

Maintaining Mathematical Proficiency

Factor the trinomial.

1. $x^2 - 6x + 9$

2. $x^2 + 4x + 4$

3. $x^2 - 14x + 49$

4. $x^2 + 22x + 121$

5. $x^2 - 24x + 144$

6. $x^2 + 26x + 169$

Solve the system of linear equations by graphing.

7. $y = 2x - 1$
   $y = -3x + 9$

8. $y = -\dfrac{1}{2}x - 1$
   $y = \dfrac{1}{4}x - 4$

9. $y = 2x + 3$
   $y = -3x - 2$

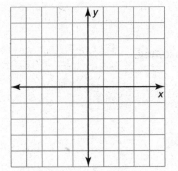
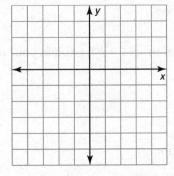
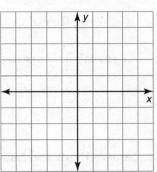

10. $y = x + 3$
    $y = -\dfrac{1}{3}x - 1$

11. $y = x + 1$
    $y = 3x - 1$

12. $y = 2x - 3$
    $y = x + 1$

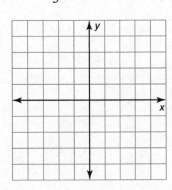
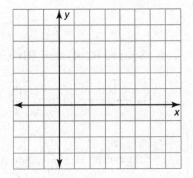

Name _____ Date _____

Essential Question How can you multiply and divide square roots?

---

1 **EXPLORATION:** Operations with Square Roots

Work with a partner. For each operation with square roots, compare the results obtained using the two indicated orders of operations. What can you conclude?

a. Square Roots and Addition

Is $\sqrt{36} + \sqrt{64}$ equal to $\sqrt{36 + 64}$?

In general, is $\sqrt{a} + \sqrt{b}$ equal to $\sqrt{a + b}$? Explain your reasoning.

b. Square Roots and Multiplication

Is $\sqrt{4} \cdot \sqrt{9}$ equal to $\sqrt{4 \cdot 9}$?

In general, is $\sqrt{a} \cdot \sqrt{b}$ equal to $\sqrt{a \cdot b}$? Explain your reasoning.

c. Square Roots and Subtraction

Is $\sqrt{64} - \sqrt{36}$ equal to $\sqrt{64 - 36}$?

In general, is $\sqrt{a} - \sqrt{b}$ equal to $\sqrt{a - b}$? Explain your reasoning.

d. Square Roots and Division

Is $\dfrac{\sqrt{100}}{\sqrt{4}}$ equal to $\sqrt{\dfrac{100}{4}}$

In general, is $\dfrac{\sqrt{a}}{\sqrt{b}}$ equal to $\sqrt{\dfrac{a}{b}}$? Explain your reasoning.

4.1 **Properties of Radicals** (continued)

2 **EXPLORATION:** Writing Counterexamples

Work with a partner. A **counterexample** is an example that proves that a general statement is *not* true. For each general statement in Exploration 1 that is not true, write a counterexample different from the example given.

Communicate Your Answer

3. How can you multiply and divide square roots?

4. Give an example of multiplying square roots and an example of dividing square roots that are different from the examples in Exploration 1.

5. Write an algebraic rule for each operation.

   a. the product of square roots

   b. the quotient of square roots

Name _____ Date _____

4.1 Notetaking with Vocabulary
For use after Lesson 4.1

In your own words, write the meaning of each vocabulary term.

counterexample

radical expression

simplest form

rationalizing the denominator

conjugates

like radicals

Core Concepts

Product Property of Square Roots

Words   The square root of a product equals the product of the square roots of the factors.

Numbers $\sqrt{9 \cdot 5} = \sqrt{9} \cdot \sqrt{5} = 3\sqrt{5}$

Algebra $\sqrt{ab} = \sqrt{a} \cdot \sqrt{b}$, where $a, b \geq 0$

Notes:

4.1 **Notetaking with Vocabulary** (continued)

Quotient Property of Square Roots

Words   The square root of a quotient equals the quotient of the square roots of the numerator and denominator.

Numbers $\sqrt{\dfrac{3}{4}} = \dfrac{\sqrt{3}}{\sqrt{4}} = \dfrac{\sqrt{3}}{2}$ **Algebra** $\sqrt{\dfrac{a}{b}} = \dfrac{\sqrt{a}}{\sqrt{b}}$, where $a \geq 0$ and $b > 0$

Notes:

Extra Practice

In Exercises 1–12, simplify the expression.

1. $\sqrt{24}$ **2.** $-\sqrt{48}$ **3.** $\sqrt{162g^6}$ **4.** $-\sqrt{512h^7}$

5. $\sqrt{\dfrac{25}{64}}$ **6.** $-\sqrt{\dfrac{6}{49}}$ **7.** $-\sqrt{\dfrac{196}{r^4}}$ **8.** $\sqrt{\dfrac{49x^3}{64y^2}}$

9. $\sqrt[3]{-135}$ **10.** $\sqrt[3]{729}$ **11.** $-\sqrt[3]{-192x^5}$ **12.** $\sqrt[3]{\dfrac{12a^6}{512b^4}}$

Name _____ Date _____

In Exercises 13–20, simplify the expression.

13. $\dfrac{\sqrt{15}}{\sqrt{500}}$

14. $\sqrt{\dfrac{8}{100}}$

15. $\dfrac{\sqrt{3x^2y^3}}{\sqrt{80xy^3}}$

16. $\dfrac{8}{\sqrt[3]{16}}$

17. $\dfrac{5}{-3 - 3\sqrt{3}}$

18. $\dfrac{3}{4 + 4\sqrt{5}}$

19. $\dfrac{4}{\sqrt{2} - 5\sqrt{3}}$

20. $\dfrac{\sqrt{5}}{\sqrt{3} + \sqrt{5}}$

21. The ratio of the length to the width of a *golden rectangle* is $\left(1 + \sqrt{5}\right) : 2$. The length of a golden rectangle is 62 meters. What is the width? Round your answer to the nearest meter.

In Exercises 22–27, simplify the expression.

22. $3\sqrt{8} + 3\sqrt{2}$

23. $2\sqrt{18} - 2\sqrt{20} - 2\sqrt{5}$

24. $3\sqrt{12} + 3\sqrt{18} + 2\sqrt{27}$

25. $2\sqrt{5}\left(\sqrt{6} + 2\right)$

26. $\left(\sqrt{7} - \sqrt{3}\right)\left(\sqrt{7} + \sqrt{3}\right)$

27. $\sqrt[3]{2}\left(\sqrt[3]{108} - \sqrt[3]{135}\right)$

4.2 Solving Quadratic Equations by Graphing
For use with Exploration 4.2

Essential Question How can you use a graph to solve a quadratic equation in one variable?

1 EXPLORATION: Solving a Quadratic Equation by Graphing

Go to *BigIdeasMath.com* for an interactive tool to investigate this exploration.

Work with a partner.

a. Sketch the graph of $y = x^2 - 2x$.

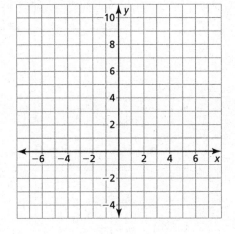

b. What is the definition of an x-intercept of a graph? How many x-intercepts does this graph have? What are they?

c. What is the definition of a solution of an equation in x? How many solutions does the equation $x^2 - 2x = 0$ have? What are they?

d. Explain how you can verify the solutions you found in part (c).

2 EXPLORATION: Solving Quadratic Equations by Graphing

Go to *BigIdeasMath.com* for an interactive tool to investigate this exploration.

Work with a partner. Solve each equation by graphing.

a. $x^2 - 4 = 0$

b. $x^2 + 3x = 0$

4.2 **Solving Quadratic Equations by Graphing** (continued)

2 **EXPLORATION:** Solving Quadratic Equations by Graphing (continued)

c. $-x^2 + 2x = 0$

d. $x^2 - 2x + 1 = 0$

e. $x^2 - 3x + 5 = 0$

f. $-x^2 + 3x - 6 = 0$

Communicate Your Answer

3. How can you use a graph to solve a quadratic equation in one variable?

4. After you find a solution graphically, how can you check your result algebraically? Check your solutions for parts (a)–(d) in Exploration 2 algebraically.

5. How can you determine graphically that a quadratic equation has no solution?

4.2 Notetaking with Vocabulary
For use after Lesson 4.2

In your own words, write the meaning of each vocabulary term.

quadratic equation

Core Concepts

Solving Quadratic Equations by Graphing

Step 1 Write the equation in standard form, $ax^2 + bx + c = 0$.

Step 2 Graph the related function $y = ax^2 + bx + c$.

Step 3 Find the x-intercepts, if any.

The solutions, or *roots*, of $ax^2 + bx + c = 0$ are the x-intercepts of the graph.

Notes:

Number of Solutions of a Quadratic Equation

A quadratic equation has:

- two real solutions when the graph of its related function has two x-intercepts.

- one real solution when the graph of its related function has one x-intercept.

- no real solutions when the graph of its related function has no x-intercepts.

Notes:

4.2 **Notetaking with Vocabulary** (continued)

Extra Practice

In Exercises 1–9, solve the equation by graphing.

1. $x^2 + 4x = 0$

2. $-x^2 = -2x + 1$

3. $x^2 + 2x + 4 = 0$

4. $x^2 - 5x + 4 = 0$

5. $x^2 + 6x + 9 = 0$

6. $x^2 = 2x - 6$

7. $x^2 - x - 12 = 0$

8. $x^2 - 10x + 25 = 0$

9. $x^2 + 4 = 0$

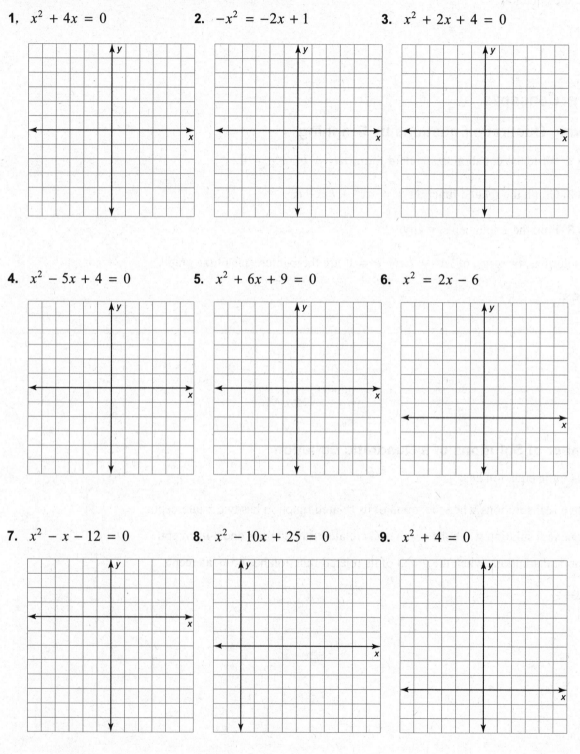

4.2 **Notetaking with Vocabulary** (continued)

In Exercises 10–15, find the zero(s) of f.

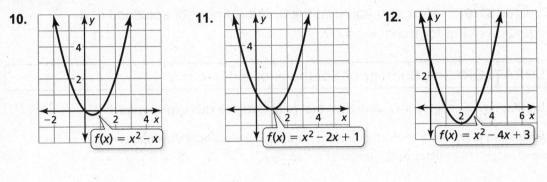

10. $f(x) = x^2 - x$

11. $f(x) = x^2 - 2x + 1$

12. $f(x) = x^2 - 4x + 3$

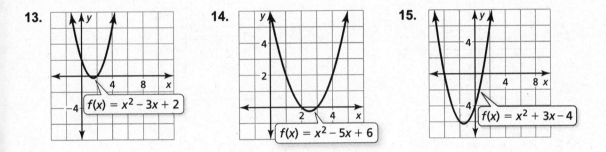

13. $f(x) = x^2 - 3x + 2$

14. $f(x) = x^2 - 5x + 6$

15. $f(x) = x^2 + 3x - 4$

In Exercises 16–18, approximate the zeros of f to the nearest tenth.

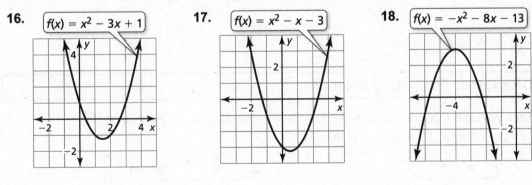

16. $f(x) = x^2 - 3x + 1$

17. $f(x) = x^2 - x - 3$

18. $f(x) = -x^2 - 8x - 13$

4.3 Solving Quadratic Equations Using Square Roots

For use with Exploration 4.3

Essential Question How can you determine the number of solutions of a quadratic equation of the form $ax^2 + c = 0$?

1 **EXPLORATION:** The Number of Solutions of $ax^2 + c = 0$

Go to *BigIdeasMath.com* for an interactive tool to investigate this exploration.

Work with a partner. Solve each equation by graphing. Explain how the number of solutions of $ax^2 + c = 0$ relates to the graph of $y = ax^2 + c$.

a. $x^2 - 4 = 0$

b. $2x^2 + 5 = 0$

c. $x^2 = 0$

d. $x^2 - 5 = 0$

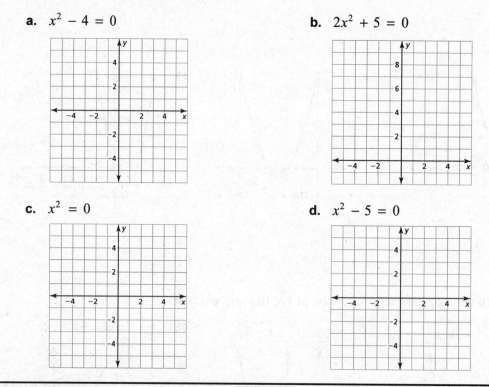

2 **EXPLORATION:** Estimating Solutions

Work with a partner. Complete each table. Use the completed tables to estimate the solutions of $x^2 - 5 = 0$. Explain your reasoning.

a.

x	$x^2 - 5$
2.21	
2.22	
2.23	
2.24	
2.25	
2.26	

b.

x	$x^2 - 5$
−2.21	
−2.22	
−2.23	
−2.24	
−2.25	
−2.26	

Name_____ Date_____

---

3 **EXPLORATION: Using Technology to Estimate Solutions**

Work with a partner. Two equations are equivalent when they have the same solutions.

a. Are the equations $x^2 - 5 = 0$ and $x^2 = 5$ equivalent? Explain your reasoning.

b. Use the square root key on a calculator to estimate the solutions of $x^2 - 5 = 0$. Describe the accuracy of your estimates in Exploration 2.

c. Write the exact solutions of $x^2 - 5 = 0$.

Communicate Your Answer

4. How can you determine the number of solutions of a quadratic equation of the form $ax^2 + c = 0$?

5. Write the exact solutions of each equation. Then use a calculator to estimate the solutions.

    a. $x^2 - 2 = 0$

    b. $3x^2 - 18 = 0$

    c. $x^2 = 8$

4.3 Notetaking with Vocabulary
For use after Lesson 4.3

In your own words, write the meaning of each vocabulary term.

square root

zero of a function

Core Concepts

Solutions of $x^2 = d$

- When $d > 0$, $x^2 = d$ has two real solutions, $x = \pm\sqrt{d}$.

- When $d = 0$, $x^2 = d$ has one real solution, $x = 0$.

- When $d < 0$, $x^2 = d$ has no real solutions.

Notes:

Name_____ Date_____

Extra Practice

In Exercises 1–18, solve the equation using square roots.

1. $x^2 + 49 = 0$

2. $x^2 - 25 = 0$

3. $x^2 + 6 = 6$

4. $2x^2 + 84 = 0$

5. $2x^2 - 72 = 0$

6. $-x^2 - 12 = -12$

7. $8x^2 - 49 = 151$

8. $-3x^2 + 16 = -11$

9. $81x^2 - 49 = -24$

10. $16x^2 - 1 = 0$

11. $25x^2 + 9 = 0$

12. $16 - 2x^2 = 16$

13. $(x - 4)^2 = 0$

14. $(x + 2)^2 = 196$

15. $(2x + 7)^2 = 49$

4.3 **Notetaking with Vocabulary** (continued)

16. $16(x - 3)^2 = 25$ **17.** $81(3x + 1)^2 = 49$ **18.** $(4x - 3)^2 = 64$

In Exercises 19–24, solve the equation using square roots. Round your solutions to the nearest hundredth.

19. $x^2 + 6 = 8$ **20.** $x^2 - 12 = 3$ **21.** $x^2 + 25 = 49$

22. $3x^2 - 4 = 14$ **23.** $6x^2 + 5 = 20$ **24.** $20 - 4x^2 = 18$

25. A ball is dropped from a window at a height of 81 feet. The function $h = -16x^2 + 81$ represents the height (in feet) of the ball after x seconds. How long does it take for the ball to hit the ground?

26. The volume of a cone with height h and radius r is given by the formula $V = \dfrac{1}{3}\pi r^2 h$. Solve the formula for r. Then find the radius of a cone with volume 27π cubic inches and height 4 inches.

4.4 Solving Quadratic Equations by Completing the Square

For use with Exploration 4.4

Essential Question How can you use "completing the square" to solve a quadratic equation?

---

1 **EXPLORATION:** Solving by Completing the Square

Go to *BigIdeasMath.com* for an interactive tool to investigate this exploration.

Work with a partner.

a. Write the equation modeled by the algebra tiles. This is the equation to be solved.

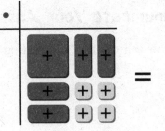

b. Four algebra tiles are added to the left side to "complete the square." Why are four algebra tiles also added to the right side?

c. Use algebra tiles to label the dimensions of the square on the left side and simplify on the right side.

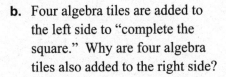

d. Write the equation modeled by the algebra tiles so that the left side is the square of a binomial. Solve the equation using square roots.

4.4 **Solving Quadratic Equations by Completing the Square** (continued)

2 **EXPLORATION:** Solving by Completing the Square

Go to *BigIdeasMath.com* for an interactive tool to investigate this exploration.

Work with a partner.

   a. Write the equation modeled
   by the algebra tiles.

   b. Use algebra tiles to "complete
   the square."

   c. Write the solutions of the equation.

   d. Check each solution in the original equation.

Communicate Your Answer

   3. How can you use "completing the square" to solve a quadratic equation?

   4. Solve each quadratic equation by completing the square.

   a. $x^2 - 2x = 1$ **b.** $x^2 - 4x = -1$ **c.** $x^2 + 4x = -3$

4.4 Notetaking with Vocabulary
For use after Lesson 4.4

In your own words, write the meaning of each vocabulary term.

completing the square

Core Concepts

Completing the Square

Words To complete the square for an expression of the form $x^2 + bx$, follow these steps.

Step 1 Find one-half of b, the coefficient of x.

Step 2 Square the result from Step 1.

Step 3 Add the result from Step 2 to $x^2 + bx$.

Factor the resulting expression as the square of a binomial.

Algebra $x^2 + bx + \left(\dfrac{b}{2}\right)^2 = \left(x + \dfrac{b}{2}\right)^2$

Notes:

4.4 Notetaking with Vocabulary (continued)

Extra Practice

In Exercises 1–6, complete the square for the expression. Then factor the trinomial.

1. $x^2 + 12x$

2. $x^2 - 14x$

3. $x^2 + 4x$

4. $x^2 + 18x$

5. $x^2 - 7x$

6. $x^2 + 11x$

In Exercises 7–18, solve the equation by completing the square. Round your solutions to the nearest hundredth, if necessary.

7. $x^2 - 8x = -15$

8. $x^2 + 2x = 3$

9. $x^2 + 7x = 30$

10. $x^2 - 26x = -9$

11. $x^2 - 12x = 10$

12. $x^2 - 15x = 18$

13. $x^2 - 12x + 9 = 0$

14. $x^2 + 14x - 10 = 0$

15. $x^2 + 2x - 99 = 0$

4.4 **Notetaking with Vocabulary** (continued)

16. $10x^2 - 13x - 9 = 0$ **17.** $3x^2 + 6x - 1 = 0$ **18.** $12x^2 - 8x - 2 = 0$

In Exercises 19–24, determine whether the quadratic function has a maximum or minimum value. Then find the value.

19. $y = -x^2 + 4x + 3$ **20.** $y = x^2 + 6x + 10$ **21.** $y = -x^2 + 8x - 2$

22. $y = x^2 - 10x + 8$ **23.** $y = 3x^2 + 3x - 1$ **24.** $y = -4x^2 + 8x + 12$

25. A diver jumps off a diving board. The function $h = -16x^2 + 6x + 5$ represents the height (in feet) of the diver after x seconds. What is the maximum height above the water of the diver? How many seconds did it take for the diver to reach the maximum height? Round your answers to the nearest hundredth.

4.5 Solving Quadratic Equations Using the Quadratic Formula

For use with Exploration 4.5

Essential Question How can you derive a formula that can be used to write the solutions of any quadratic equation in standard form?

---

1 EXPLORATION: Deriving the Quadratic Formula

Work with a partner. The following steps show a method of solving $ax^2 + bx + c = 0$. Explain what was done in each step.

$$ax^2 + bx + c = 0$$ 1. Write the equation.

$$4a^2x^2 + 4abx + 4ac = 0$$ 2. _____

$$4a^2x^2 + 4abx + 4ac + b^2 = b^2$$ 3. _____

$$4a^2x^2 + 4abx + b^2 = b^2 - 4ac$$ 4. _____

$$(2ax + b)^2 = b^2 - 4ac$$ 5. _____

$$2ax + b = \pm\sqrt{b^2 - 4ac}$$ 6. _____

$$2ax = -b \pm \sqrt{b^2 - 4ac}$$ 7. _____

Quadratic Formula: $x = \dfrac{-b \pm \sqrt{b^2 - 4ac}}{2a}$ 8. _____

Name_____ Date_____

4.5 **Solving Quadratic Equations Using the Quadratic Formula** (continued)

2 **EXPLORATION: Deriving the Quadratic Formula by Completing the Square**

Work with a partner.

a. Solve $ax^2 + bx + c = 0$ by completing the square. (*Hint:* Subtract c from each side, divide each side by a, and then proceed by completing the square.)

b. Compare this method with the method in Exploration 1. Explain why you think $4a$ and b^2 were chosen in Steps 2 and 3 of Exploration 1.

Communicate Your Answer

3. How can you derive a formula that can be used to write the solutions of any quadratic equation in standard form?

4. Use the Quadratic Formula to solve each quadratic equation.

a. $x^2 + 2x - 3 = 0$ **b.** $x^2 - 4x + 4 = 0$ **c.** $x^2 + 4x + 5 = 0$

5. Use the Internet to research *imaginary numbers*. How are they related to quadratic equations?

Copyright © Big Ideas Learning, LLC
All rights reserved.

Integrated Mathematics II **131**
Student Journal

4.5 Notetaking with Vocabulary
For use after Lesson 4.5

In your own words, write the meaning of each vocabulary term.

Quadratic Formula

discriminant

Core Concepts

Quadratic Formula

The real solutions of the quadratic equation $ax^2 + bx + c = 0$ are

$$x = \frac{-b \pm \sqrt{b^2 - 4ac}}{2a}$$ Quadratic Formula

where $a \neq 0$ and $b^2 - 4ac \geq 0$.

Notes:

Interpreting the Discriminant

$b^2 - 4ac > 0$ $b^2 - 4ac = 0$ $b^2 - 4ac < 0$

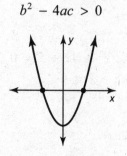
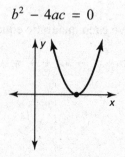
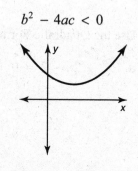

- two real solutions   • one real solution   • no real solutions

- two x-intercepts   • one x-intercept   • no x-intercepts

Notes:

Name_____ Date_____

Methods for Solving Quadratic Equations

Method	Advantages	Disadvantages
Factoring (*Lessons 2.5–2.8*)	• Straightforward when the equation can be factored easily	• Some equations are not factorable.
Graphing (*Lesson 4.2*)	• Can easily see the number of solutions • Use when approximate solutions are sufficient. • Can use a graphing calculator	• May not give exact solutions
Using Square Roots (*Lesson 4.3*)	• Used to solve equations of the form $x^2 = d$.	• Can only be used for certain equations
Completing the Square (*Lesson 4.4*)	• Best used when $a = 1$ and b is even	• May involve difficult calculations
Quadratic Formula (*Lesson 4.5*)	• Can be used for any quadratic equation • Gives exact solutions	• Takes time to do calculations

Notes:

Extra Practice

In Exercises 1–6, solve the equation using the Quadratic Formula. Round your solutions to the nearest tenth, if necessary.

1. $x^2 - 10x + 16 = 0$ **2.** $x^2 + 2x - 8 = 0$ **3.** $3x^2 - x - 2 = 0$

4. $x^2 + 6x = -13$ **5.** $-3x^2 + 5x - 1 = -7$ **6.** $-4x^2 + 8x + 12 = 6$

Name _____ Date _____

4.5 **Notetaking with Vocabulary (continued)**

7. A square pool has a side length of x feet. A uniform border around the pool is 1 foot wide. The total area of the pool and the border is 361 square feet. What is the area of the pool?

In Exercises 8–10, determine the number of real solutions of the equation.

8. $-x^2 + 6x + 3 = 0$

9. $x^2 + 6x + 9 = 0$

10. $x^2 + 3x + 8 = 0$

In Exercises 11–13 find the number of x-intercepts of the graph of the function.

11. $y = -x^2 + 4x + 3$

12. $y = x^2 + 14x + 49$

13. $y = -x^2 - 8x - 18$

In Exercises 14–16, solve the equation using any method. Explain your choice of method.

14. $x^2 - 4x + 4 = 16$

15. $x^2 - 8x + 7 = 0$

16. $3x^2 + x - 5 = 0$

Name_____ Date_____

4.6 Complex Numbers
For use with Exploration 4.6

Essential Question What are the subsets of the set of complex numbers?

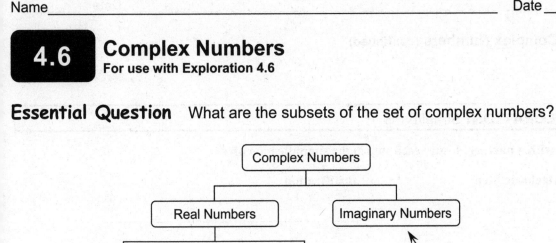

1 EXPLORATION: Classifying Numbers

Work with a partner. Determine which subsets of the set of complex numbers contain each number.

a. $\sqrt{9}$

b. $\sqrt{0}$

c. $-\sqrt{4}$

d. $\sqrt{\dfrac{4}{9}}$

e. $\sqrt{2}$

f. $\sqrt{-1}$

4.6 **Complex Numbers** (continued)

2 **EXPLORATION: Simplifying** i^2

Work with a partner. Justify each step in the simplification of i^2.

Algebraic Step   **Justification**

$i^2 = \left(\sqrt{-1}\right)^2$ _____

$ = -1$ _____

Communicate Your Answer

3. What are the subsets of the set of complex numbers? Give an example of a number in each subset.

4. Is it possible for a number to be both whole and natural? natural and rational? rational and irrational? real and imaginary? Explain your reasoning.

5. Your friend claims that the conclusion in Exploration 2 is incorrect because $i^2 = i \bullet i = \sqrt{-1} \bullet \sqrt{-1} = \sqrt{-1(-1)} = \sqrt{1} = 1$. Is your friend correct? Explain.

4.6 Notetaking with Vocabulary
For use after Lesson 4.6

In your own words, write the meaning of each vocabulary term.

imaginary unit i

complex number

imaginary number

pure imaginary number

complex conjugates

Core Concepts

The Square Root of a Negative Number

Property

1. If r is a positive real number, then $\sqrt{-r} = i\sqrt{r}$.

2. By the first property, it follows that $\left(i\sqrt{r}\right)^2 = -r$.

Example

$\sqrt{-3} = i\sqrt{3}$

$\left(i\sqrt{3}\right)^2 = i^2 \bullet 3 = -3$

Notes:

4.6 **Notetaking with Vocabulary** (continued)

Sums and Differences of Complex Numbers

To add (or subtract) two complex numbers, add (or subtract) their real parts and their imaginary parts separately.

Sum of complex numbers: $(a + bi) + (c + di) = (a + c) + (b + d)i$

Difference of complex numbers: $(a + bi) - (c + di) = (a - c) + (b - d)i$

Notes:

Extra Practice

In Exercises 1–6, find the square root of the number.

1. $\sqrt{-49}$ **2.** $\sqrt{-4}$ **3.** $\sqrt{-45}$

4. $-2\sqrt{-100}$ **5.** $6\sqrt{-121}$ **6.** $5\sqrt{-75}$

In Exercises 7 and 8, find the values of x and y that satisfy the equation.

7. $-10x + i = 30 - yi$ **8.** $44 - \frac{1}{2}yi = -\frac{1}{4}x - 7i$

Name_____ Date_____

In Exercises 9–14, simplify the expression. Then classify the result as a *real number* or *imaginary number*. If the result is an *imaginary number*, specify if it is a *pure imaginary number*.

9. $(-8 + 3i) + (-1 - 2i)$

10. $(36 - 3i) - (12 + 24i)$

11. $(16 + i) + (-16 - 8i)$

12. $(-5 - 5i) - (-6 - 6i)$

13. $(-1 + 9i)(15 - i)$

14. $(6 - 7i)(-5 + 8i)$

15. Find the impedance of the series circuit.

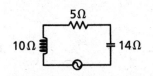

In Exercises 16–18, multiply the complex number by this complex conjugate.

16. $8 + i$

17. $3 - 2i$

18. $-7 - 5i$

Name _____ Date _____

Essential Question How can you determine whether a quadratic equation has real solutions or imaginary solutions?

---

1 **EXPLORATION:** Using Graphs to Solve Quadratic Equations

Work with a partner. Use the discriminant of $f(x) = 0$ and the sign of the leading coefficient of $f(x)$ to match each quadratic function with its graph. Explain your reasoning. Then find the real solution(s) (if any) of each quadratic equation $f(x) = 0$.

a. $f(x) = x^2 - 2x$ **b.** $f(x) = x^2 - 2x + 1$ **c.** $f(x) = x^2 - 2x + 2$

d. $f(x) = -x^2 + 2x$ **e.** $f(x) = -x^2 + 2x - 1$ **f.** $f(x) = -x^2 + 2x - 2$

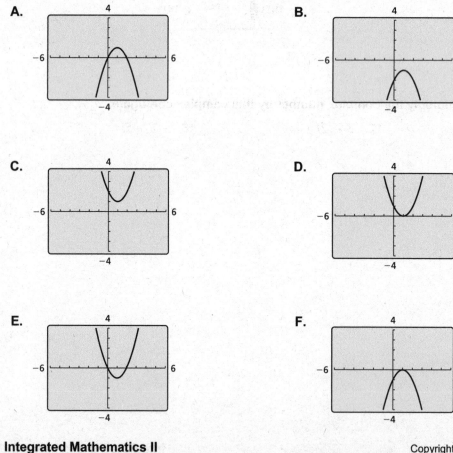

4.7 Solving Quadratic Equations with Complex Solutions (continued)

2 EXPLORATION: Finding Imaginary Solutions

Work with a partner. What do you know about the discriminants of quadratic equations that have no real solutions? Use the Quadratic Formula and what you learned about the imaginary unit i to find the *imaginary* solutions of each equation in Exploration 1 that has no real solutions. Use substitution to check your answer.

Communicate Your Answer

3. How can you determine whether a quadratic equation has real solutions or imaginary solutions?

4. Describe the number and type of solutions of $x^2 + 2x + 3 = 0$. How do you know? What are the solutions?

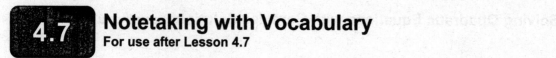

4.7

Notetaking with Vocabulary
For use after Lesson 4.7

Notes:

Name_____ Date_____

Extra Practice

In Exercises 1–3, solve the equation using the Quadratic Formula.

1. $x^2 - 7x - 18 = 0$ 2. $w^2 = 4w - 1$ 3. $-7z = -4z^2 - 3$

In Exercises 4–7, determine whether you would use factoring, square roots, or completing the square to solve the equation. Explain your reasoning. Then solve the equation.

4. $x^2 + 7x = 0$ 5. $(x - 1)^2 = 35$

6. $x^2 - 255 = 0$ 7. $4x^2 + 8x + 12 = 0$

Name _____ Date _____

8. A baseball player hits a foul ball straight up in the air from a height of 4 feet off the ground with an initial velocity of 85 feet per second.

   a. Write a quadratic function that represents the height h of the ball t seconds after it hits the bat.

   b. When is the ball 110 feet off the ground? Explain your reasoning.

   c. The catcher catches the ball 6 feet from the ground. How long is the ball in the air?

9. A golfer hits a golf ball on the fairway with an initial velocity of 80 feet per second. The height h (in feet) of the golf ball t seconds after it is hit can be modeled by the function $h(t) = -16t^2 + 80t + 0.1$.

   a. Find the maximum height of the golf ball.

   b. How long does the ball take to hit the ground?

4.8 Solving Nonlinear Systems of Equations
For use with Exploration 4.8

Essential Question How can you solve a system of two equations when one is linear and the other is quadratic?

---

1 EXPLORATION: Solving a System of Equations

Go to *BigIdeasMath.com* for an interactive tool to investigate this exploration.

Work with a partner. Solve the system of equations by graphing each equation and finding the points of intersection.

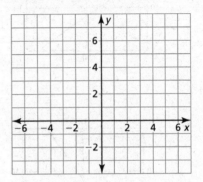

System of Equations

$y = x + 2$ Linear

$y = x^2 + 2x$ Quadratic

---

2 EXPLORATION: Analyzing Systems of Equations

Work with a partner. Match each system of equations with its graph (shown on the next page). Then solve the system of equations.

a. $y = x^2 - 4$
   $y = -x - 2$

b. $y = x^2 - 2x + 2$
   $y = 2x - 2$

c. $y = x^2 + 1$
   $y = x - 1$

d. $y = x^2 - x - 6$
   $y = 2x - 2$

4.8 **Solving Nonlinear Systems of Equations** (continued)

2 **EXPLORATION: Analyzing Systems of Equations (continued)**

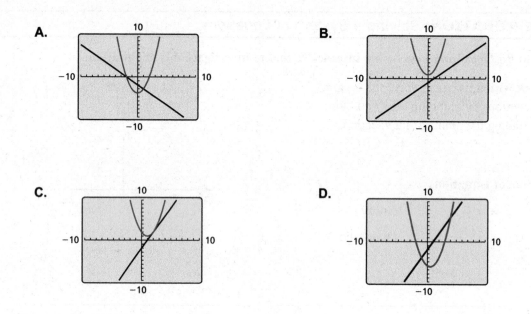

A.

B.

C.

D.

Communicate Your Answer

3. How can you solve a system of two equations when one is linear and the other is quadratic?

4. Write a system of equations (one linear and one quadratic) that has (a) no solutions, (b) one solution, and (c) two solutions. Your systems should be different from those in Explorations 1 and 2.

Name_____ Date_____

Notetaking with Vocabulary
For use after Lesson 4.8

In your own words, write the meaning of each vocabulary term.

system of nonlinear equations

Notes:

4.8   Notetaking with Vocabulary (continued)

Extra Practice

In Exercises 1–6, solve the system by graphing.

1. $y = x^2 + 5x + 6$
     $y = -x + 1$

2. $y = x^2 + x - 3$
     $y = x + 1$

3. $y = \frac{1}{2}x^2 - 2x + 1$
     $y = -x + 1$

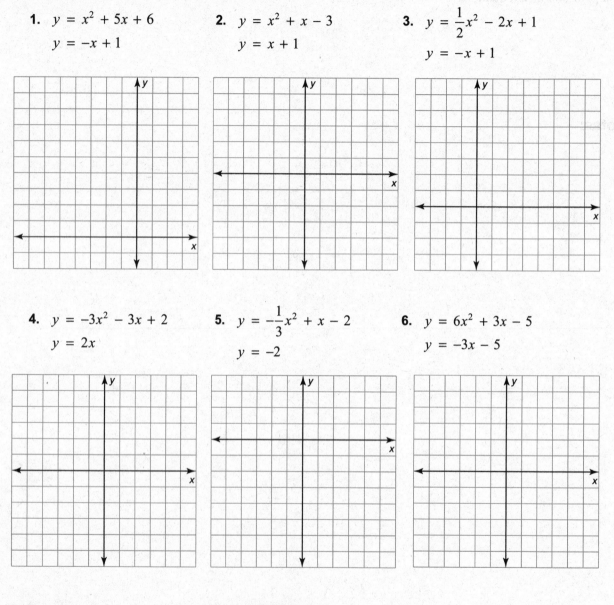

4. $y = -3x^2 - 3x + 2$
     $y = 2x$

5. $y = -\frac{1}{3}x^2 + x - 2$
     $y = -2$

6. $y = 6x^2 + 3x - 5$
     $y = -3x - 5$

In Exercises 7–9, solve the equation by substitution.

7. $y - 2 = x^2$
     $y = 6$

8. $y = -2x^2$
     $y = 3x + 2$

9. $y = x - 4$
     $y = x^2 + 3x - 4$

Name_____ Date_____

In Exercises 10–12, solve the equation by elimination.

10. $y = x^2$
    $y = x - 3$

11. $y = x^2 + 3x - 5$
    $y = 3x - 1$

12. $y = x^2 + x - 2$
    $y = x + 14$

In Exercises 13–18, solve the equation. Round your solution(s) to the nearest hundredth, if necessary.

13. $-6x + 14 = x^2 - 9x + 16$

14. $-x^2 + 4x = -2x + 8$

15. $4x^2 - 9 = 4x - 1$

16. $-\dfrac{1}{2}x + 1 = -x^2 + 4x$

17. $2x^2 - 4 = -x^2 + 6$

18. $-3\left(\dfrac{2}{3}\right)^x + 2 = x^2 - 2$

4.9 Quadratic Inequalities
For use with Exploration 4.9

Essential Question How can you solve a quadratic inequality?

---

1 EXPLORATION: Solving a Quadratic Inequality

Work with a partner. The graphing calculator screen shows the graph of

$$f(x) = x^2 + 2x - 3.$$

Explain how you can use the graph to solve the inequality

$$x^2 + 2x - 3 \le 0.$$

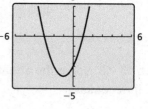

Then solve the inequality.

---

2 EXPLORATION: Solving Quadratic Inequalities

Work with a partner. Match each inequality with the graph of its related quadratic function on the next page. Then use the graph to solve the inequality.

a. $x^2 - 3x + 2 > 0$ **b.** $x^2 - 4x + 3 \le 0$ **c.** $x^2 - 2x - 3 < 0$

d. $x^2 + x - 2 \ge 0$ **e.** $x^2 - x - 2 < 0$ **f.** $x^2 - 4 > 0$

4.9 **Quadratic Inequalities** (continued)

A.

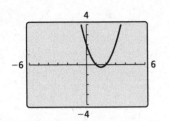

B.

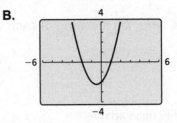

C.

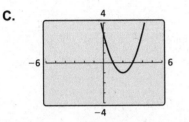

D.

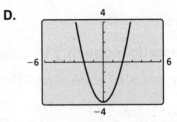

E.

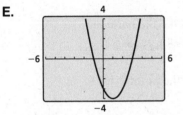

F.

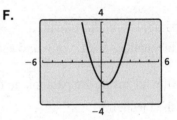

Communicate Your Answer

3. How can you solve a quadratic inequality?

4. Explain how you can use the graph in Exploration 1 to solve each inequality.
Then solve each inequality.

   a. $x^2 + 2x - 3 > 0$ **b.** $x^2 + 2x - 3 < 0$ **c.** $x^2 + 2x - 3 \geq 0$

4.9 Notetaking with Vocabulary
For use after Lesson 4.9

In your own words, write the meaning of each vocabulary term.

quadratic inequality in two variables

quadratic inequality in one variable

Core Concepts

Graphing a Quadratic Inequality in Two Variables

To graph a quadratic inequality in one of the following forms,

$$y < ax^2 + bx + c \qquad y > ax^2 + bx + c$$
$$y \le ax^2 + bx + c \qquad y \ge ax^2 + bx + c,$$

follow these steps.

Step 1 Graph the parabola with the equation $y = ax^2 + bx + c$. Make the parabola *dashed* for inequalities with $<$ or $>$ and *solid* for inequalities with $\le$ or $\ge$.

Step 2 Test a point (x, y) inside the parabola to determine whether the point is a solution of the inequality.

Step 3 Shade the region inside the parabola if the point from Step 2 is a solution. Shade the region outside the parabola if it is not a solution.

Notes:

Name_____ Date _____

Extra Practice

In Exercises 1–4, match the graph with its inequality. Explain your reasoning.

1.
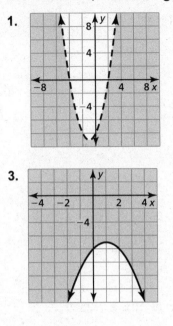

2.
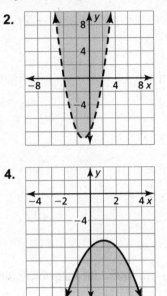

3.

4.

A. $y < x^2 + 2x - 8$

B. $y \le -x^2 + 2x - 8$

C. $y > x^2 + 2x - 8$

D. $y \ge -x^2 + 2x - 8$

In Exercises 5–8, graph the inequality.

5. $y < x^2 + 2$

6. $y \le -5x^2$

7. $y \ge -(x + 4)^2 - 1$

8. $y < 4x^2 + 4x + 1$

9. Accident investigators use the formula $d = 0.01875v^2$, where d is the braking distance of a car (in feet) and v is the speed of the car (in miles per hour) to determine how fast a car is going at the time of an accident. For what speeds v would a car leave a tire mark on the road of over 1 foot?

4.9 **Notetaking with Vocabulary** (continued)

In Exercises 10–12, graph the system of quadratic inequalities.

10. $y \leq -x^2$

$y > -3x^2 + 3$

11. $y \geq x^2 + 5x$

$y \geq (x + 2)^2 - 1$

12. $y > x^2 - 7x - 8$

$y < -x^2 + 6x + 5$

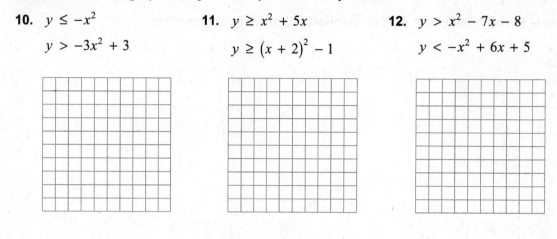

In Exercises 13–15, solve the inequality algebraically.

13. $16x^2 > 100$

14. $x^2 \leq 15x - 34$

15. $-\frac{1}{5}x^2 + 10x \geq -25$

16. The profit for a hot dog company is given by the equation $y = -0.02x^2 + 140x - 2500$, where x is the number of hot dogs produced and y is the profit (in dollars). How many hot dogs must be produced so that the company will generate a profit of at least \$150,000?

Name_____ Date_____

Chapter 5

Maintaining Mathematical Proficiency

Write and solve a proportion to answer the question.

1. What percent of 260 is 65?

2. What number is 32% of 75?

3. 15.01 is what percent of 19?

Display the data in a histogram.

4.

Number of Strike-outs in One Game		
Strike-outs	0–3	4–7	8–11
Frequency	34	20	8

5.

Number of Days of Exercise in One Week			
Days of Exercise	0–1	2–3	4–5	6–7
Frequency	4	26	22	6

5.1 Sample Spaces and Probability
For use with Exploration 5.1

Essential Question How can you list the possible outcomes in the sample space of an experiment?

The **sample space** of an experiment is the set of all possible outcomes for that experiment.

---

1 **EXPLORATION:** Finding the Sample Space of an Experiment

Work with a partner. In an experiment, three coins are flipped. List the possible outcomes in the sample space of the experiment.

---

2 **EXPLORATION:** Finding the Sample Space of an Experiment

Work with a partner. List the possible outcomes in the sample space of the experiment.

    a. One six-sided die is rolled.

                                 b. Two six-sided dice are rolled.

---

3 **EXPLORATION:** Finding the Sample Space of an Experiment

Work with a partner. In an experiment, a spinner is spun.

    a. How many ways can you spin a 1? 2? 3? 4? 5?

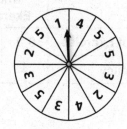

Name_____ Date _____

3 **EXPLORATION:** Finding the Sample Space of an Experiment (continued)

    b. List the sample space.

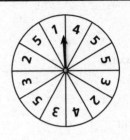

    c. What is the total number of outcomes?

4 **EXPLORATION:** Finding the Sample Space of an Experiment

Work with a partner. In an experiment, a bag contains 2 blue marbles and 5 red marbles. Two marbles are drawn from the bag.

    a. How many ways can you choose two blue? a red then blue? a blue then red? two red?

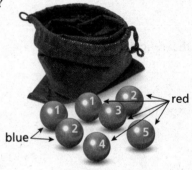

    b. List the sample space.

    c. What is the total number of outcomes?

Communicate Your Answer

  5. How can you list the possible outcomes in the sample space of an experiment?

  6. For Exploration 3, find the ratio of the number of each possible outcome to the total number of outcomes. Then find the sum of these ratios. Repeat for Exploration 4. What do you observe?

Notetaking with Vocabulary
For use after Lesson 5.1

In your own words, write the meaning of each vocabulary term.

probability experiment

outcome

event

sample space

probability of an event

theoretical probability

experimental probability

odds

Core Concepts

Probability of the Complement of an Event

The probability of the complement of event A is

$$P\left(\overline{A}\right) = 1 - P(A).$$

Notes:

5.1 Notetaking with Vocabulary (continued)

Extra Practice

**In Exercises 1 and 2, find the number of possible outcomes in the sample space.
Then list the possible outcomes.**

1. A stack of cards contains the thirteen clubs from a standard deck of cards. You pick a card from the stack and flip two coins.

2. You spin a spinner with the numbers 1–5 on it and roll a die.

3. When two tiles with numbers between 1 and 10 are chosen from two different bags, there are 100 possible outcomes. Find the probability that (a) the sum of the two numbers is not 10 and (b) the product of the numbers is greater than 10.

4. At a school dance, the parents sell pizza slices. The table shows the number of pizza slices that are available. A student chooses a slice at random. What is the probability that the student chooses a thin crust slice with pepperoni?

	Pepperoni	Plain Cheese
Thin Crust	34	36
Thick Crust	8	12

5.1   **Notetaking with Vocabulary** (continued)

5. Find the probability that the polynomial $x^2 - x - c$ can be factored if c is a randomly chosen integer from 1 to 12.

6. The sections of a spinner are numbered 1 through 12. Each section of the spinner has the same area. You spin the spinner 180 times. The table shows the results. For which number is the experimental probability of stopping on the number the same as the theoretical probability?

Spinner Results											
1	2	3	4	5	6	7	8	9	10	11	12
13	21	22	20	11	8	14	9	15	12	18	17

7. Use the spinner in Exercise 6 to find the given odds.

   a. in favor of stopping on a number greater than 8

   b. against stopping on a number that is a multiple of 3

Name_____ Date_____

Essential Question   How can you determine whether two events are independent or dependent?

Two events are **independent events** when the occurrence of one event does not affect the occurrence of the other event. Two events are **dependent events** when the occurrence of one event *does* affect the occurrence of the other event.

---

1   EXPLORATION: Identifying Independent and Dependent Events

Work with a partner. Determine whether the events are independent or dependent. Explain your reasoning.

   a.   Two six-sided dice are rolled.

   b.   Six pieces of paper, numbered 1 through 6, are in a bag. Two pieces of paper are selected one at a time without replacement.

---

2   EXPLORATION: Finding Experimental Probabilities

Go to *BigIdeasMath.com* for an interactive tool to investigate this exploration.

Work with a partner.

   a.   In Exploration 1(a), experimentally estimate the probability that the sum of the two numbers rolled is 7. Describe your experiment.

   b.   In Exploration 1(b), experimentally estimate the probability that the sum of the two numbers selected is 7. Describe your experiment.

Name_____ Date _____

5.2 **Independent and Dependent Events** (continued)

3 **EXPLORATION:** Finding Theoretical Probabilities

Work with a partner.

   a. In Exploration 1(a), find the theoretical probability that the sum of the two numbers rolled is 7. Then compare your answer with the experimental probability you found in Exploration 2(a).

   b. In Exploration 1(b), find the theoretical probability that the sum of the two numbers selected is 7. Then compare your answer with the experimental probability you found in Exploration 2(b).

   c. Compare the probabilities you obtained in parts (a) and (b).

Communicate Your Answer

  4. How can you determine whether two events are independent or dependent?

  5. Determine whether the events are independent or dependent. Explain your reasoning.

   a. You roll a 4 on a six-sided die and spin red on a spinner.

   b. Your teacher chooses a student to lead a group, chooses another student to lead a second group, and chooses a third student to lead a third group.

Name_____ Date_____

5.2 Notetaking with Vocabulary
For use after Lesson 5.2

In your own words, write the meaning of each vocabulary term.

independent events

dependent events

conditional probability

Core Concepts

Probability of Independent Events

Words Two events A and B are independent events if and only if the probability that both events occur is the product of the probabilities of the events.

Symbols $P(A \text{ and } B) = P(A) \bullet P(B)$

Notes:

5.2 Notetaking with Vocabulary (continued)

Probability of Dependent Events

Words If two events A and B are dependent events, then the probability that both events occur is the product of the probability of the first event and the conditional probability of the second event given the first event.

Symbols $P(A \text{ and } B) = P(A) \bullet P(B|A)$

Example Using the information in Example 2:

$P(\text{girl first and girl second}) = P(\text{girl first}) \bullet P(\text{girl second}|\text{girl first})$

$$= \frac{9}{12} \bullet \frac{6}{9} = \frac{1}{2}$$

Notes:

Extra Practice

In Exercises 1 and 2, determine whether the events are independent. Explain your reasoning.

1. You have three white golf balls and two yellow golf balls in a bag. You randomly select one golf ball to hit now and another golf ball to place in your pocket. Use a sample space to determine whether randomly selecting a white golf ball first and then a white golf ball second are independent events.

2. Your friend writes a phone number down on a piece of paper but the last three numbers get smudged after being in your pocket all day long. You decide to randomly choose numbers for each of the three digits. Use a sample space to determine whether guessing the first digit correctly and the second digit correctly are independent events.

5.2   **Notetaking with Vocabulary** (continued)

3. You are trying to guess a three-letter password that uses only the letters A, E, I, O, U, and Y. Letters can be used more than once. Find the probability that you pick the correct password "YOU."

4. You are trying to guess a three-letter password that uses only the letters A, E, I, O, U, and Y. Letters *cannot* be used more than once. Find the probability that you pick the correct password "AIE."

5. The table shows the number of male and female college students who played collegiate basketball and collegiate soccer in the United States in a recent year.

	Collegiate Soccer	Collegiate Basketball
Male	37,240	31,863
Female	36,523	28,002

   a. Find the probability that a randomly selected collegiate soccer player is female.

   b. Find the probability that a randomly selected male student is a collegiate basketball player.

Name _____ Date _____

 Two-Way Tables and Probability
For use with Exploration 5.3

Essential Question   How can you construct and interpret a two-way table?

---

1   EXPLORATION: Completing and Using a Two-Way Table

Work with a partner. A *two-way table* displays the same information as a Venn diagram. In a two-way table, one category is represented by the rows and the other category is represented by the columns.

The Venn diagram shows the results of a survey in which 80 students were asked whether they play a musical instrument and whether they speak a foreign language. Use the Venn diagram to complete the two-way table. Then use the two-way table to answer each question.

Survey of 80 Students

Play an instrument: 25 | 16 | Speak a foreign language: 30

9

	Play an Instrument	Do Not Play an Instrument	Total
Speak a Foreign Language			
Do Not Speak a Foreign Language			
Total			

a. How many students play an instrument?

b. How many students speak a foreign language?

c. How many students play an instrument and speak a foreign language?

d. How many students do not play an instrument and do not speak a foreign language?

e. How many students play an instrument and do not speak a foreign language?

---

2   EXPLORATION: Two-Way Tables and Probability

Work with a partner. In Exploration 1, one student is selected at random from the 80 students who took the survey. Find the probability that the student

a. plays an instrument.

5.3 **Two-Way Tables and Probability** (continued)

---

2 EXPLORATION: Two-Way Tables and Probability (continued)

    b. speaks a foreign language.

    c. plays an instrument and speaks a foreign language.

    d. does not play an instrument and does not speak a foreign language.

    e. plays an instrument and does not speak a foreign language.

---

3 EXPLORATION: Conducting a Survey

Go to *BigIdeasMath.com* for an interactive tool to investigate this exploration.

Work with your class. Conduct a survey of students in your class. Choose two categories that are different from those given in Explorations 1 and 2. Then summarize the results in both a Venn diagram and a two-way table. Discuss the results.

Communicate Your Answer

    4. How can you construct and interpret a two-way table?

    5. How can you use a two-way table to determine probabilities?

Name _____ Date _____

5.3 Notetaking with Vocabulary
For use after Lesson 5.3

In your own words, write the meaning of each vocabulary term.

two-way table

joint frequency

marginal frequency

joint relative frequency

marginal relative frequency

conditional relative frequency

Core Concepts

Relative and Conditional Relative Frequencies

A **joint relative frequency** is the ratio of a frequency that is not in the total row or the total column to the total number of values or observations.

A **marginal relative frequency** is the sum of the joint relative frequencies in a row or a column.

A **conditional relative frequency** is the ratio of a joint relative frequency to the marginal relative frequency. You can find a conditional relative frequency using a row total or a column total of a two-way table.

Notes:

5.3 **Notetaking with Vocabulary** (continued)

Extra Practice

In Exercises 1 and 2, complete the two-way table.

1.

		Arrival		
		Tardy	On Time	Total
Method	Walk	22		
	City Bus			60
	Total		58	130

2.

		Response		
		Yes	No	Total
Age	Under 21		24	25
	Over 21	29		
	Total	30		75

3. A survey was taken of 100 families with one child and 86 families with two or more children to determine whether they were saving for college. Of those, 94 of the families with one child and 60 of the families with two or more children were saving for college. Organize these results in a two-way table. Then find and interpret the marginal frequencies.

5.3 Notetaking with Vocabulary (continued)

4. In a survey, 214 ninth graders played video games every day of the week and 22 ninth graders did not play video games every day of the week. Of those that played every day of the week, 36 had trouble sleeping at night. Of those that did not play every day of the week, 7 had trouble sleeping at night. Make a two-way table that shows the joint and marginal relative frequencies.

5. For financial reasons, a school district is debating about eliminating a Computer Programming class at the high school. The district surveyed parents, students, and teachers. The results, given as joint relative frequencies, are shown in the two-way table.

<table>
<tr><th></th><th></th><th colspan="3">Population</th></tr>
<tr><th></th><th></th><th>Parents</th><th>Students</th><th>Teachers</th></tr>
<tr><th rowspan="2">Response</th><th>Yes</th><td>0.58</td><td>0.08</td><td>0.10</td></tr>
<tr><th>No</th><td>0.06</td><td>0.15</td><td>0.03</td></tr>
</table>

a. What is the probability that a randomly selected parent voted to eliminate the class?

b. What is the probability that a randomly selected student did not want to eliminate the class?

c. Determine whether voting to eliminate the class and being a teacher are independent events.

5.4 Probability of Disjoint and Overlapping Events
For use with Exploration 5.4

Essential Question How can you find probabilities of disjoint and overlapping events?

Two events are **disjoint**, or **mutually exclusive**, when they have no outcomes in common. Two events are **overlapping** when they have one or more outcomes in common.

 1 EXPLORATION: Disjoint Events and Overlapping Events

Go to *BigIdeasMath.com* for an interactive tool to investigate this exploration.

Work with a partner. A six-sided die is rolled. Draw a Venn diagram that relates the two events. Then decide whether the events are disjoint or overlapping.

a. Event *A*: The result is an even number.
Event *B*: The result is a prime number.

b. Event *A*: The result is 2 or 4.
Event *B*: The result is an odd number.

2 EXPLORATION: Finding the Probability that Two Events Occur

Work with a partner. A six-sided die is rolled. For each pair of events, find
(a) $P(A)$, (b) $P(B)$, (c) $P(A \text{ and } B)$, and (d) $P(A \text{ or } B)$.

a. Event *A*: The result is an even number.
Event *B*: The result is a prime number.

b. Event *A*: The result is a 2 or 4.
Event *B*: The result is an odd number.

5.4 Probability of Disjoint and Overlapping Events (continued)

---

3 EXPLORATION: Discovering Probability Formulas

Go to *BigIdeasMath.com* for an interactive tool to investigate this exploration.

Work with a partner.

   a. In general, if event A and event B are disjoint, then what is the probability that event A or event B will occur? Use a Venn diagram to justify your conclusion.

   b. In general, if event A and event B are overlapping, then what is the probability that event A or event B will occur? Use a Venn diagram to justify your conclusion.

   c. Conduct an experiment using a six-sided die. Roll the die 50 times and record the results. Then use the results to find the probabilities described in Exploration 2. How closely do your experimental probabilities compare to the theoretical probabilities you found in Exploration 2?

Communicate Your Answer

   4. How can you find probabilities of disjoint and overlapping events?

   5. Give examples of disjoint events and overlapping events that do not involve dice.

5.4 Notetaking with Vocabulary
For use after Lesson 5.4

In your own words, write the meaning of each vocabulary term.

compound event

overlapping events

disjoint or mutually exclusive events

Core Concepts

Probability of Compound Events

If A and B are any two events, then the probability of A or B is

$$P(A \text{ or } B) = P(A) + P(B) - P(A \text{ and } B).$$

If A and B are disjoint events, then the probability of A or B is

$$P(A \text{ or } B) = P(A) + P(B).$$

Notes:

5.4 **Notetaking with Vocabulary** (continued)

Extra Practice

1. Events A and B are disjoint. $P(A) = \frac{2}{3}$ and $P(B) = \frac{1}{6}$. Find $P(A \text{ or } B)$.

2. $P(A) = 0.8$, $P(B) = 0.05$, and $P(A \text{ or } B) = 0.6$. Find $P(A \text{ and } B)$.

In Exercises 3–6, a vehicle is randomly chosen from a parking lot. The parking lot contains three red minivans, two blue minivans, three blue convertibles, one black pickup truck, three black motorcycles, one red motorcycle and two blue scooters. Find the probability of selecting the type of vehicle.

3. A red vehicle or a minivan

4. A scooter or a black vehicle

5. A black vehicle or a motorcycle

6. A four-wheeled vehicle or a blue vehicle

5.4   **Notetaking with Vocabulary** (continued)

7. During a basketball game, the coach needs to select a player to make the free throw after a technical foul on the other team. There is a 68% chance that the coach will select you and a 26% chance that the coach will select your friend. What is the probability that you or your friend is selected to make the free throw?

8. Two six-sided dice are rolled. Find the probability of rolling the same number twice.

9. Out of 120 student parents, 90 of them can chaperone the Homecoming dance or the Prom. There are 40 parents who can chaperone the Homecoming dance and 65 parents who can chaperone the Prom. What is the probability that a randomly selected parent can chaperone both the Homecoming dance and the Prom?

10. A football team scores a touchdown first 75% of the time when they start with the ball. The team does not score first 51% of the time when their opponent starts with the ball. The team who gets the ball first is determined by a coin toss. What is the probability that the team scores a touchdown first?

Name _____ Date _____

5.5 Permutations and Combinations
For use with Exploration 5.5

Essential Question How can a tree diagram help you visualize the number of ways in which two or more events can occur?

1 **EXPLORATION: Reading a Tree Diagram**

Work with a partner. Two coins are flipped and the spinner is spun. The tree diagram shows the possible outcomes.

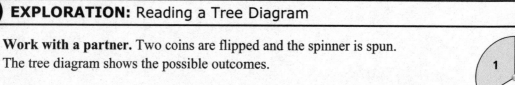

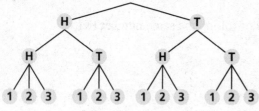

Coin is flipped.

Coin is flipped.

Spinner is spun.

a. How many outcomes are possible?

b. List the possible outcomes.

2 **EXPLORATION: Reading a Tree Diagram**

Work with a partner. Consider the tree diagram below.

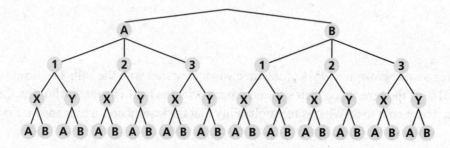

a. How many events are shown?

b. What outcomes are possible for each event?

c. How many outcomes are possible?

d. List the possible outcomes.

5.5 **Permutations and Combinations** (continued)

3 EXPLORATION: Writing a Conjecture

Work with a partner.

a. Consider the following general problem: Event 1 can occur in *m* ways and event 2 can occur in *n* ways. Write a conjecture about the number of ways the two events can occur. Explain your reasoning.

b. Use the conjecture you wrote in part (a) to write a conjecture about the number of ways *more than* two events can occur. Explain your reasoning.

c. Use the results of Explorations 1(a) and 2(c) to verify your conjectures.

Communicate Your Answer

4. How can a tree diagram help you visualize the number of ways in which two or more events can occur?

5. In Exploration 1, the spinner is spun a second time. How many outcomes are possible?

Name _____ Date _____

5.5 Notetaking with Vocabulary
For use after Lesson 5.5

In your own words, write the meaning of each vocabulary term.

permutation

n factorial

combination

Core Concepts

Permutations

Formulas

The number of permutations
of *n* objects is given by

$$_nP_n = n!.$$

Examples

The number of permutations of 4
objects is

$$_4P_4 = 4! = 4 \cdot 3 \cdot 2 \cdot 1 = 24.$$

The number of permutations
of *n* objects taken *r* at a time,
where $r \leq n$, is given by

$$_nP_r = \frac{n!}{(n-r)!}.$$

The number of permutations of 4
objects taken 2 at a time is

$$_4P_2 = \frac{4!}{(4-2)!} = \frac{4 \cdot 3 \cdot \cancel{2!}}{\cancel{2!}} = 12.$$

Notes:

178 **Integrated Mathematics II**
Student Journal

Name_____ Date_____

Combinations

Formula   The number of combinations of n objects taken r at a time, where $r \leq n$, is given by

$$_nC_r = \frac{n!}{(n-r)! \bullet r!}.$$

Example   The number of combinations of 4 objects taken 2 at a time is

$$_4C_2 = \frac{4!}{(4-2)! \bullet 2!} = \frac{4 \bullet 3 \bullet \cancel{2!}}{\cancel{2!} \bullet (2 \bullet 1)} = 6.$$

Notes:

5.5 **Notetaking with Vocabulary** (continued)

Extra Practice

In Exercises 1 and 2, find the number of ways you can arrange (a) all of the numbers and (b) 3 of the numbers in the given amount.

1. $2,564,783

2. $4,128,675,309

3. Your rock band has nine songs recorded but you only want to put five of them on your demo CD to hand out to local radio stations. How many possible ways could the five songs be ordered on your demo CD?

4. A witness at the scene of a hit-and-run accident saw that the car that caused the accident had a license plate with only the letters I, R, L, T, O, and A. Find the probability that the license plate starts with a T and ends with an R.

5. How many possible combinations of three colors can be chosen from the seven colors of the rainbow?

Name_____ Date_____

Essential Question How can you determine the frequency of each outcome of an event?

 EXPLORATION: Analyzing Histograms

Go to *BigIdeasMath.com* for an interactive tool to investigate this exploration.

Work with a partner. The histograms show the results when *n* coins are flipped.

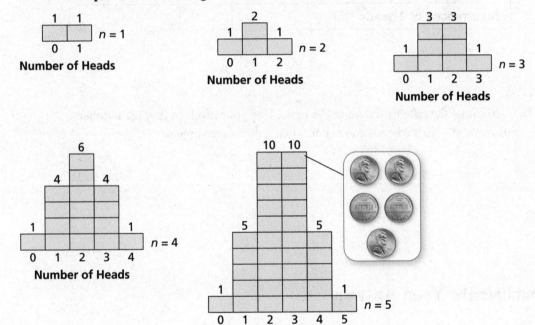

a. In how many ways can 3 heads occur when 5 coins are flipped?

b. Draw a histogram that shows the numbers of heads that can occur when 6 coins are flipped.

c. In how many ways can 3 heads occur when 6 coins are flipped?

5.6 **Binomial Distributions** (continued)

2 **EXPLORATION:** Determining the Number of Occurrences

Work with a partner.

a. Complete the table showing the numbers of ways in which 2 heads can occur when n coins are flipped.

n	3	4	5	6	7
Occurrences of 2 heads					

b. Determine the pattern shown in the table. Use your result to find the number of ways in which 2 heads can occur when 8 coins are flipped.

Communicate Your Answer

3. How can you determine the frequency of each outcome of an event?

4. How can you use a histogram to find the probability of an event?

5.6 Notetaking with Vocabulary
For use after Lesson 5.6

In your own words, write the meaning of each vocabulary term.

random variable

probability distribution

binomial distribution

binomial experiment

Core Concepts

Probability Distributions

A **probability distribution** is a function that gives the probability of each possible value of a random variable. The sum of all the probabilities in a probability distribution must equal 1.

Probability Distribution for Rolling a Six-Sided Die						
x	1	2	3	4	5	6
P(x)	$\frac{1}{6}$	$\frac{1}{6}$	$\frac{1}{6}$	$\frac{1}{6}$	$\frac{1}{6}$	$\frac{1}{6}$

Notes:

5.6 Notetaking with Vocabulary (continued)

Binomial Experiments

A **binomial experiment** meets the following conditions.

- There are n independent trials.

- Each trial has only two possible outcomes: success and failure.

- The probability of success is the same for each trial. This probability is denoted by p. The probability of failure is $1 - p$.

For a binomial experiment, the probability of exactly k successes in n trials is

$$P(k \text{ successes}) = {}_nC_k\, p^k (1 - p)^{n-k}.$$

Notes:

Extra Practice

1. Make a table and draw a histogram showing the probability distribution for the random variable P if $P = $ the product when two six-sided dice are rolled.

Name_____ Date_____

2. Use the probability distribution to determine (a) the number that is most likely to be spun on a spinner, and (b) the probability of spinning a perfect square.

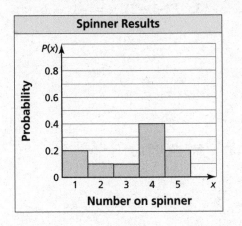

3. Calculate the probability of flipping a coin twenty times and getting nineteen heads.

4. According to a survey, 78% of women in a city watch professional football. You ask four randomly chosen women from the city whether they watch professional football.

   a. Draw a histogram of the binomial distribution for your survey.

   b. What is the most likely outcome of your survey?

   c. What is the probability that at most one woman watches professional football?

Name _____ Date _____

Chapter 6 **Maintaining Mathematical Proficiency**

Write an equation of the line passing through point _P_ that is perpendicular to the given line.

1. $P(5, 2)$, $y = 2x + 6$ 2. $P(4, 2)$, $y = 6x - 3$ 3. $P(-1, -2)$, $y = -3x + 6$

4. $P(-8, 3)$, $y = 3x - 1$ 5. $P(6, 7)$, $y = x - 5$ 6. $P(3, 7)$, $y = \frac{1}{4}x + 4$

Write the sentence as an inequality.

7. A number g is at least 4 and no more than 12.

8. A number r is more than 2 and less than 7.

9. A number q is less than or equal to 6 or greater than 1.

10. A number p is fewer than 17 or no less than 5.

11. A number k is greater than or equal to −4 and less than 1.

Name_____ Date_____

Essential Question How can you prove a mathematical statement?

A **proof** is a logical argument that uses deductive reasoning to show that a statement is true.

1 EXPLORATION: Writing Reasons in a Proof

Work with a partner. Four steps of a proof are shown. Write the reasons for each statement.

Given $AD = AB + AC$

Prove $CD = AB$

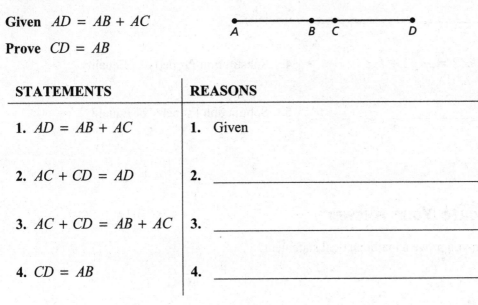

STATEMENTS	REASONS
1. $AD = AB + AC$	1. Given
2. $AC + CD = AD$	2. _____
3. $AC + CD = AB + AC$	3. _____
4. $CD = AB$	4. _____

2 EXPLORATION: Writing Steps in a Proof

Work with a partner. Five steps of a proof are shown. Complete the statements that correspond to each reason.

Given $m\angle ABD = m\angle CBE$

Prove $m\angle 1 = m\angle 3$

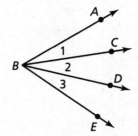

6.1 **Proving Geometric Relationships** (continued)

2 **EXPLORATION:** Writing Steps in a Proof (continued)

STATEMENTS	REASONS
1. $m\angle ABD = m\angle 1 + m\angle 2$	1. Angle Addition Postulate
2. $m\angle CBE =$ _____	2. Angle Addition Postulate
3. _____	3. Given
4. $m\angle 1 + m\angle 2 = m\angle 2 + m\angle 3$	4. Substitution Property of Equality
5. _____	5. Subtraction Property of Equality

Communicate Your Answer

3. How can you prove a mathematical statement?

4. In Exploration 2, can you prove that $m\angle 1 = m\angle 2$? Explain your reasoning.

Name_____ Date_____

6.1 Notetaking with Vocabulary
For use after Lesson 6.1

In your own words, write the meaning of each vocabulary term.

proof

two-column proof

paragraph proof

flowchart proof, or flow proof

coordinate proof

Notes:

6.1 Notetaking with Vocabulary (continued)

Extra Practice

1. Complete the proof.

   Given ∠AEB is a complement of ∠BEC.
   Prove m∠AED = 90°

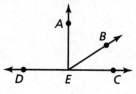

STATEMENTS	REASONS
1. ∠AEB is a complement of ∠BEC.	1. Given
2. _____	2. Definition of complementary angles
3. m∠AEC = m∠AEB + m∠BEC	3. _____
4. m∠AEC = 90°	4. _____
5. m∠AED + m∠AEC = 180°	5. Definition of supplementary angles
6. _____	6. Substitution Property of Equality
7. m∠AED = 90°	7. _____

2. Write a two-column proof.

   Given M is the midpoint of $\overline{RT}$.
   Prove MT = RS + SM

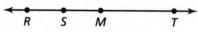

STATEMENTS	REASONS

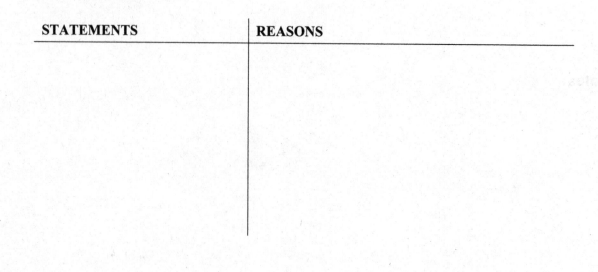

6.1 Notetaking with Vocabulary (continued)

3. Complete the flowchart proof. Then write a two-column proof.

Given $\angle ACB$ and $\angle ACD$ are supplementary.
$\angle EGF$ and $\angle ACD$ are supplementary.

Prove $\angle ACB \cong \angle EGF$

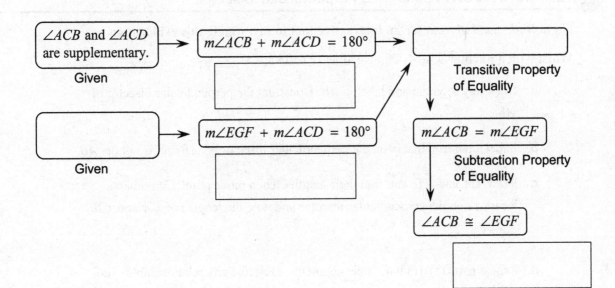

$\angle ACB$ and $\angle ACD$ are supplementary.	→	$m\angle ACB + m\angle ACD = 180°$	→	
Given				Transitive Property of Equality

	→	$m\angle EGF + m\angle ACD = 180°$		$m\angle ACB = m\angle EGF$
Given				Subtraction Property of Equality

$\angle ACB \cong \angle EGF$

Two-Column Proof

STATEMENTS	REASONS

6.2 Perpendicular and Angle Bisectors
For use with Exploration 6.2

Essential Question   What conjectures can you make about a point on the perpendicular bisector of a segment and a point on the bisector of an angle?

1 EXPLORATION: Points on a Perpendicular Bisector

Go to *BigIdeasMath.com* for an interactive tool to investigate this exploration.

Work with a partner. Use dynamic geometry software.

    a. Draw any segment and label it $\overline{AB}$. Construct the perpendicular bisector of $\overline{AB}$.

    b. Label a point C that is on the perpendicular bisector of $\overline{AB}$ but is not on $\overline{AB}$.

    c. Draw $\overline{CA}$ and $\overline{CB}$ and find their lengths. Then move point C to other locations on the perpendicular bisector and note the lengths of $\overline{CA}$ and $\overline{CB}$.

    d. Repeat parts (a)–(c) with other segments. Describe any relationship(s) you notice.

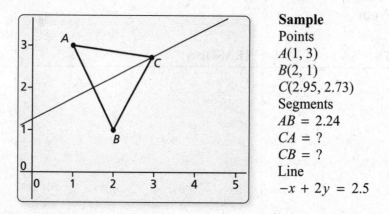

Sample
Points
$A(1, 3)$
$B(2, 1)$
$C(2.95, 2.73)$
Segments
$AB = 2.24$
$CA = ?$
$CB = ?$
Line
$-x + 2y = 2.5$

2 EXPLORATION: Points on an Angle Bisector

Go to *BigIdeasMath.com* for an interactive tool to investigate this exploration.

Work with a partner. Use dynamic geometry software.

    a. Draw two rays $\overrightarrow{AB}$ and $\overrightarrow{AC}$ to form $\angle BAC$. Construct the bisector of $\angle BAC$.

    b. Label a point D on the bisector of $\angle BAC$.

Name_____ Date_____

2 **EXPLORATION: Points on an Angle Bisector** (continued)

c. Construct and find the lengths of the perpendicular segments from D to the sides of $\angle BAC$. Move point D along the angle bisector and note how the lengths change.

d. Repeat parts (a)–(c) with other angles. Describe any relationship(s) you notice.

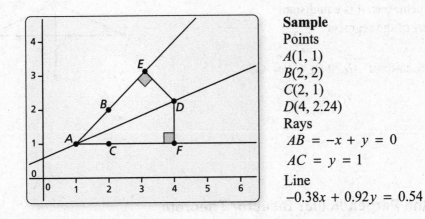

Sample
Points
$A(1, 1)$
$B(2, 2)$
$C(2, 1)$
$D(4, 2.24)$
Rays
$AB = -x + y = 0$
$AC = y = 1$
Line
$-0.38x + 0.92y = 0.54$

Communicate Your Answer

3. What conjectures can you make about a point on the perpendicular bisector of a segment and a point on the bisector of an angle?

4. In Exploration 2, what is the distance from point D to $\overrightarrow{AB}$ when the distance from D to $\overrightarrow{AC}$ is 5 units? Justify your answer.

6.2 Notetaking with Vocabulary
For use after Lesson 6.2

In your own words, write the meaning of each vocabulary term.

equidistant

Theorems

Perpendicular Bisector Theorem

In a plane, if a point lies on the perpendicular
bisector of a segment, then it is equidistant
from the endpoints of the segment.

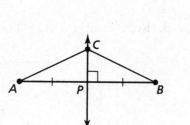

If $\overleftrightarrow{CP}$ is the $\perp$ bisector of $\overline{AB}$, then $CA = CB$.

Notes:

Converse of the Perpendicular Bisector Theorem

In a plane, if a point is equidistant from the
endpoints of a segment, then it lies on the
perpendicular bisector of the segment.

If $DA = DB$, then point D lies on the $\perp$ bisector of $\overline{AB}$.

Notes:

6.2   **Notetaking with Vocabulary** (continued)

Angle Bisector Theorem

If a point lies on the bisector of an angle, then it is
equidistant from the two sides of the angle.

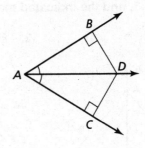

If $\overrightarrow{AD}$ bisects $\angle BAC$ and $\overline{DB} \perp \overrightarrow{AB}$ and $\overline{DC} \perp \overrightarrow{AC}$,
then $DB = DC$.

Notes:

Converse of the Angle Bisector Theorem

If a point is in the interior of an angle and is equidistant
from the two sides of the angle, then it lies on the
bisector of the angle.

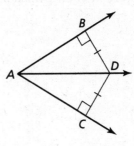

If $\overline{DB} \perp \overrightarrow{AB}$ and $\overline{DC} \perp \overrightarrow{AC}$ and $DB = DC$,

then $\overrightarrow{AD}$ bisects $\angle BAC$.

Notes:

6.2 **Notetaking with Vocabulary** (continued)

Extra Practice

In Exercises 1–3, find the indicated measure. Explain your reasoning.

1. *AB*

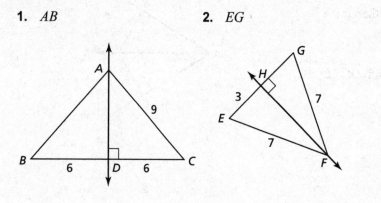

2. *EG*

3. *SU*

4. Find the equation of the perpendicular bisector of *AB*.

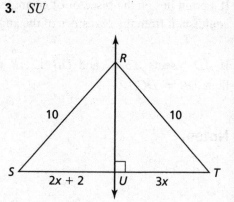

In Exercises 5–7, find the indicated measure. Explain your reasoning.

5. *m∠CAB*

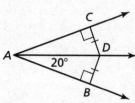

6. *DC*

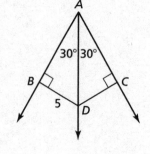

7. *BD*

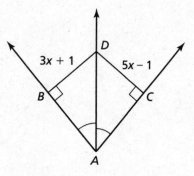

6.3 Bisectors of Triangles
For use with Exploration 6.3

Essential Question What conjectures can you make about the perpendicular bisectors and the angle bisectors of a triangle?

1 EXPLORATION: Properties of the Perpendicular Bisectors of a Triangle

Go to *BigIdeasMath.com* for an interactive tool to investigate this exploration.

Work with a partner. Use dynamic geometry software. Draw any $\triangle ABC$.

a. Construct the perpendicular bisectors of all three sides of $\triangle ABC$. Then drag the vertices to change $\triangle ABC$. What do you notice about the perpendicular bisectors?

b. Label a point D at the intersection of the perpendicular bisectors.

c. Draw the circle with center D through vertex A of $\triangle ABC$. Then drag the vertices to change $\triangle ABC$. What do you notice?

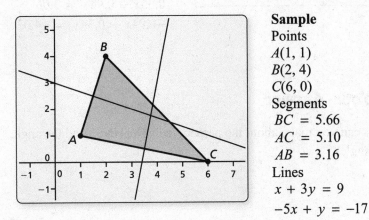

Sample
Points
$A(1, 1)$
$B(2, 4)$
$C(6, 0)$
Segments
$BC = 5.66$
$AC = 5.10$
$AB = 3.16$
Lines
$x + 3y = 9$
$-5x + y = -17$

2 EXPLORATION: Properties of the Angle Bisectors of a Triangle

Go to *BigIdeasMath.com* for an interactive tool to investigate this exploration.

Work with a partner. Use dynamic geometry software. Draw any $\triangle ABC$.

a. Construct the angle bisectors of all three angles of $\triangle ABC$. Then drag the vertices to change $\triangle ABC$. What do you notice about the angle bisectors?

Name_____ Date _____

2 **EXPLORATION:** Properties of the Angle Bisectors of a Triangle (continued)

b. Label a point D at the intersection of the angle bisectors.

c. Find the distance between D and $\overline{AB}$. Draw the circle with center D and this distance as a radius. Then drag the vertices to change $\triangle ABC$. What do you notice?

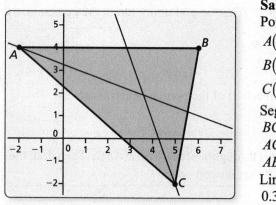

Sample
Points
$A(-2, 4)$
$B(6, 4)$
$C(5, -2)$
Segments
$BC = 6.08$
$AC = 9.22$
$AB = 8$
Lines
$0.35x + 0.94y = 3.06$
$-0.94x - 0.34y = -4.02$

Communicate Your Answer

3. What conjectures can you make about the perpendicular bisectors and the angle bisectors of a triangle?

6.3 Notetaking with Vocabulary
For use after Lesson 6.3

In your own words, write the meaning of each vocabulary term.

concurrent

point of concurrency

circumcenter

incenter

Theorems

Circumcenter Theorem

The circumcenter of a triangle is equidistant from the vertices of the triangle.

If $\overline{PD}$, $\overline{PE}$, and $\overline{PF}$ are perpendicular bisectors, then $PA = PB = PC$.

Notes:

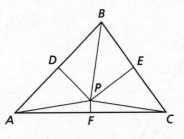

6.3 **Notetaking with Vocabulary** (continued)

Incenter Theorem

The incenter of a triangle is equidistant
from the sides of the triangle.

If $\overline{AP}$, $\overline{BP}$, and $\overline{CP}$ are angle bisectors of $\triangle ABC$,
then $PD = PE = PF$.

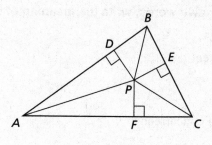

Notes:

Extra Practice

**In Exercises 1–3, N is the incenter of $\triangle ABC$. Use the given information to find the
indicated measure.**

1. $ND = 2x - 5$
$NE = -2x + 7$
Find NF.

2. $NG = x - 1$
$NH = 2x - 6$
Find NJ.

3. $NK = x + 10$
$NL = -2x + 1$
Find NM.

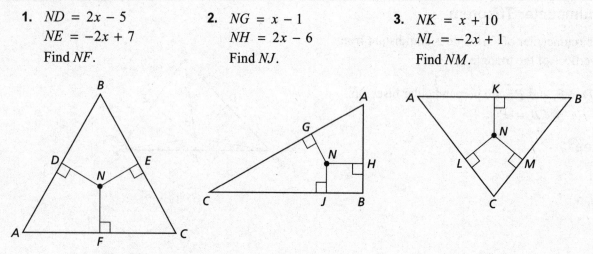

Name_____ Date_____

In Exercises 4–7, find the indicated measure.

4. *PA*

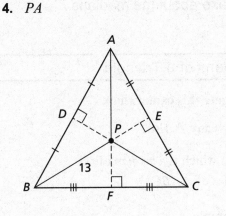

5. *PS*

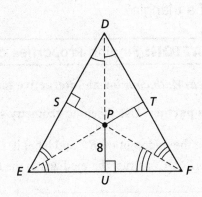

6. *GE*

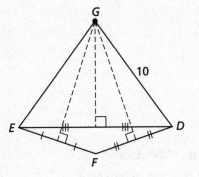

7. *NF*

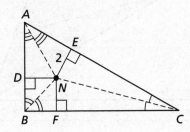

In Exercises 8–10, find the coordinates of the circumcenter of the triangle with the given vertices.

8. $A(-2, -2), B(-2, 4), C(6, 4)$ **9.** $D(3, 5), E(3, 1), F(9, 5)$ **10.** $J(4, -7), K(4, -3), L(-6, -3)$

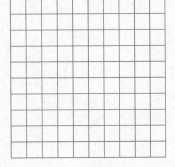
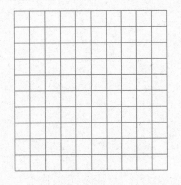

6.4 Medians and Altitudes of Triangles
For use with Exploration 6.4

Essential Question What conjectures can you make about the medians and altitudes of a triangle?

1 EXPLORATION: Finding Properties of the Medians of a Triangle

Go to *BigIdeasMath.com* for an interactive tool to investigate this exploration.

Work with a partner. Use dynamic geometry software. Draw any $\triangle ABC$.

a. Plot the midpoint of $\overline{BC}$ and label it D. Draw $\overline{AD}$, which is a *median* of $\triangle ABC$. Construct the medians to the other two sides of $\triangle ABC$.

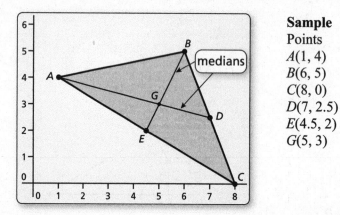

Sample
Points
$A(1, 4)$
$B(6, 5)$
$C(8, 0)$
$D(7, 2.5)$
$E(4.5, 2)$
$G(5, 3)$

b. What do you notice about the medians? Drag the vertices to change $\triangle ABC$. Use your observations to write a conjecture about the medians of a triangle.

c. In the figure above, point G divides each median into a shorter segment and a longer segment. Find the ratio of the length of each longer segment to the length of the whole median. Is this ratio always the same? Justify your answer.

Name_____ Date _____

---

2 **EXPLORATION:** Finding Properties of the Altitudes of a Triangle

Go to *BigIdeasMath.com* for an interactive tool to investigate this exploration.

Work with a partner. Use dynamic geometry software. Draw any △*ABC*.

    a. Construct the perpendicular segment from vertex *A* to $\overline{BC}$. Label the endpoint *D*. $\overline{AD}$ is an *altitude* of △*ABC*.

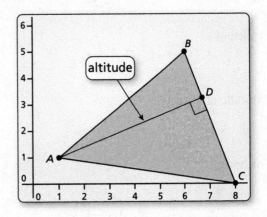

    b. Construct the altitudes to the other two sides of △*ABC*. What do you notice?

    c. Write a conjecture about the altitudes of a triangle. Test your conjecture by dragging the vertices to change △*ABC*.

Communicate Your Answer

    3. What conjectures can you make about the medians and altitudes of a triangle?

    4. The length of median $\overline{RU}$ in △*RST* is 3 inches. The point of concurrency of the three medians of △*RST* divides $\overline{RU}$ into two segments. What are the lengths of these two segments?

6.4 Notetaking with Vocabulary
For use after Lesson 6.4

In your own words, write the meaning of each vocabulary term.

median of a triangle

centroid

altitude of a triangle

orthocenter

Theorems

Centroid Theorem

The centroid of a triangle is two-thirds of the distance from each
vertex to the midpoint of the opposite side.

The medians of $\triangle ABC$ meet at point P, and

$AP = \dfrac{2}{3}AE$, $BP = \dfrac{2}{3}BF$, and $CP = \dfrac{2}{3}CD$.

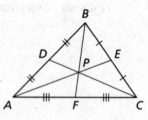

Notes:

6.4   Notetaking with Vocabulary (continued)

Core Concepts

Orthocenter

The lines containing the altitudes of a triangle are concurrent. This point of concurrency is the **orthocenter** of the triangle.

The lines containing $\overline{AF}$, $\overline{BD}$, and $\overline{CE}$ meet at the orthocenter G of $\triangle ABC$.

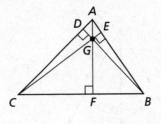

Notes:

Extra Practice

In Exercises 1–3, point P is the centroid of △LMN. Find PN and QP.

1. $QN = 33$ 2. $QN = 45$ 3. $QN = 39$

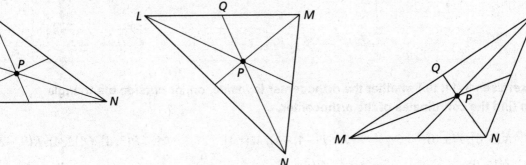

6.4 **Notetaking with Vocabulary** (continued)

In Exercises 4 and 5, point *D* is the centroid of △*ABC*. Find *CD* and *CE*.

4. $DE = 7$

5. $DE = 12$

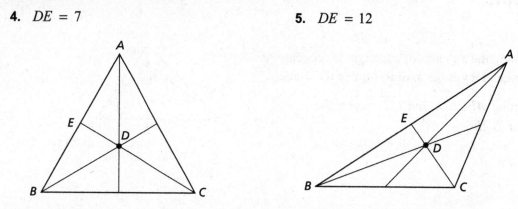

In Exercises 6–8, find the coordinates of the centroid of the triangle with the given vertices.

6. $A(-2, -1), B(1, 8),$
$C(4, -1)$

7. $D(-5, 4), E(-3, -2),$
$F(-1, 4)$

8. $J(8, 7), K(20, 5), L(8, 3)$

In Exercises 9–11, tell whether the orthocenter is *inside, on,* or *outside* the triangle. Then find the coordinates of the orthocenter.

9. $X(3, 6), Y(3, 0),$
$Z(11, 0)$

10. $L(-4, -4), M(1, 1),$
$N(6, -4)$

11. $P(3, 4), Q(11, 4), R(9, -2)$

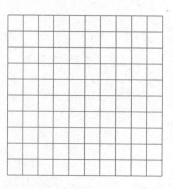
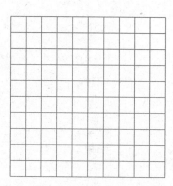

Name_____ Date_____

Essential Question How are the midsegments of a triangle related to the sides of the triangle?

---

1 EXPLORATION: Midsegments of a Triangle

Go to *BigIdeasMath.com* for an interactive tool to investigate this exploration.

Work with a partner. Use dynamic geometry software. Draw any $\triangle ABC$.

a. Plot midpoint D of $\overline{AB}$ and midpoint E of $\overline{BC}$. Draw $\overline{DE}$, which is a *midsegment* of $\triangle ABC$.

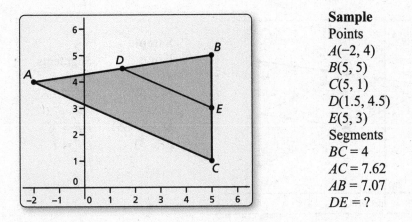

Sample
Points
$A(-2, 4)$
$B(5, 5)$
$C(5, 1)$
$D(1.5, 4.5)$
$E(5, 3)$
Segments
$BC = 4$
$AC = 7.62$
$AB = 7.07$
$DE = ?$

b. Compare the slope and length of $\overline{DE}$ with the slope and length of $\overline{AC}$.

c. Write a conjecture about the relationships between the midsegments and sides of a triangle. Test your conjecture by drawing the other midsegments of $\triangle ABC$, dragging vertices to change $\triangle ABC$, and noting whether the relationships hold.

Name _____ Date _____

2 **EXPLORATION:** Midsegments of a Triangle

Go to *BigIdeasMath.com* for an interactive tool to investigate this exploration.

Work with a partner. Use dynamic geometry software. Draw any $\triangle ABC$.

   a. Draw all three midsegments of $\triangle ABC$.

   b. Use the drawing to write a conjecture about the triangle formed by the midsegments of the original triangle.

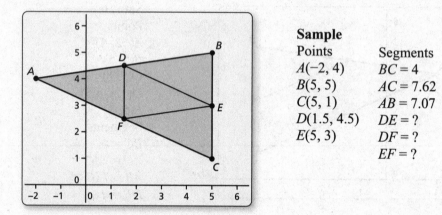

Sample

Points	Segments
$A(-2, 4)$	$BC = 4$
$B(5, 5)$	$AC = 7.62$
$C(5, 1)$	$AB = 7.07$
$D(1.5, 4.5)$	$DE = ?$
$E(5, 3)$	$DF = ?$
	$EF = ?$

Communicate Your Answer

3. How are the midsegments of a triangle related to the sides of the triangle?

4. In $\triangle RST$, $\overline{UV}$ is the midsegment connecting the midpoints of $\overline{RS}$ and $\overline{ST}$. Given $UV = 12$, find RT.

Name_____ Date_____

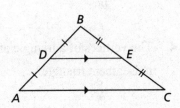

6.5 Notetaking with Vocabulary
For use after Lesson 6.5

In your own words, write the meaning of each vocabulary term.

midsegment of a triangle

Theorems

Triangle Midsegment Theorem

The segment connecting the midpoints of two sides of a
triangle is parallel to the third side and is half as long as that side.

$\overline{DE}$ is a midsegment of $\triangle ABC$, $\overline{DE} \parallel \overline{AC}$, and $DE = \dfrac{1}{2}AC$.

Notes:

6.5 Notetaking with Vocabulary (continued)

Extra Practice

In Exercises 1–3, **DE** is a midsegment of △ABC. Find the value of **x**.

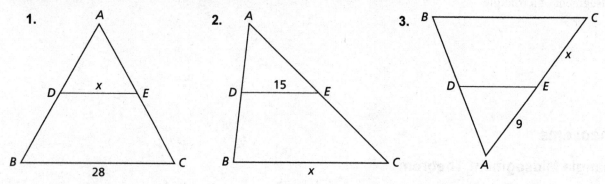

1.

2.

3.

4. The vertices of a triangle are $A(-5, 6)$, $B(3, 8)$, and $C(1, -4)$. What are the vertices of the midsegment triangle?

5. What is the perimeter of △DEF?

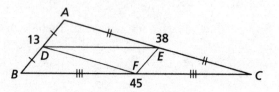

6. In the diagram, $\overline{DE}$ is a midsegment of △ABC, and $\overline{FG}$ is a midsegment of △ADE. Find FG.

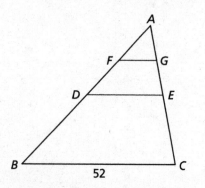

6.5 **Notetaking with Vocabulary** (continued)

7. The area of △*ABC* is 48 cm². $\overline{DE}$ is a midsegment of △*ABC*. What is the area of △*ADE*?

8. The diagram below shows a triangular wood shed. You want to install a shelf halfway up the 8-foot wall that will be built between the two walls.

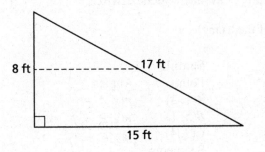

8 ft ----------- 17 ft

15 ft

a. How long will the shelf be?

b. How many feet should you measure from the ground along the slanting wall to find where to attach the opposite end of the shelf so that it will be level?

6.6 Indirect Proof and Inequalities in One Triangle
For use with Exploration 6.6

Essential Question How are the sides related to the angles of a triangle? How are any two sides of a triangle related to the third side?

---

1 EXPLORATION: Comparing Angle Measures and Side Lengths

Go to *BigIdeasMath.com* for an interactive tool to investigate this exploration.

Work with a partner. Use dynamic geometry software. Draw any scalene $\triangle ABC$.

a. Find the side lengths and angle measures of the triangle.

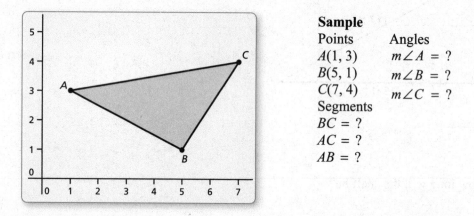

Sample
Points   Angles
$A(1, 3)$ $m\angle A = ?$
$B(5, 1)$ $m\angle B = ?$
$C(7, 4)$ $m\angle C = ?$
Segments
$BC = ?$
$AC = ?$
$AB = ?$

b. Order the side lengths. Order the angle measures. What do you observe?

c. Drag the vertices of $\triangle ABC$ to form new triangles. Record the side lengths and angle measures in the following table. Write a conjecture about your findings.

BC	AC	AB	$m\angle A$	$m\angle B$	$m\angle C$

Name_____ Date_____

2 **EXPLORATION:** A Relationship of the Side Lengths of a Triangle

Go to *BigIdeasMath.com* for an interactive tool to investigate this exploration.

Work with a partner. Use dynamic geometry software. Draw any $\triangle ABC$.

a. Find the side lengths of the triangle.

b. Compare each side length with the sum of the other two side lengths.

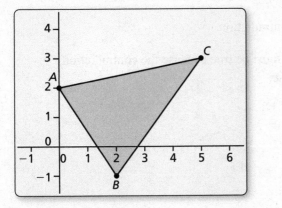

Sample
Points
$A(0, 2)$
$B(2, -1)$
$C(5, 3)$
Segments
$BC = ?$
$AC = ?$
$AB = ?$

c. Drag the vertices of $\triangle ABC$ to form new triangles and repeat parts (a) and (b). Organize your results in a table. Write a conjecture about your findings.

BC	AC	AB	Comparisons

Communicate Your Answer

3. How are the sides related to the angles of a triangle? How are any two sides of a triangle related to the third side?

4. Is it possible for a triangle to have side lengths of 3, 4, and 10? Explain.

6.6 Notetaking with Vocabulary
For use after Lesson 6.6

In your own words, write the meaning each vocabulary term.

indirect proof

Core Concepts

How to Write an Indirect Proof (Proof by Contradiction)

Step 1 Identify the statement you want to prove. Assume temporarily that this statement is false by assuming that its opposite is true.

Step 2 Reason logically until you reach a contradiction.

Step 3 Point out that the desired conclusion must be true because the contradiction proves the temporary assumption false.

Notes:

Theorems

Triangle Longer Side Theorem

If one side of a triangle is longer than another side, then the angle opposite the longer side is larger than the angle opposite the shorter side.

Notes:

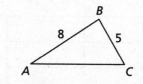

$AB > BC$, so $m\angle C > m\angle A$.

6.6 **Notetaking with Vocabulary** (continued)

Triangle Larger Angle Theorem

If one angle of a triangle is larger than another angle,
then the side opposite the larger angle is longer than
the side opposite the smaller angle.

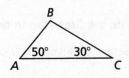

$$m\angle A > m\angle C, \text{ so } BC > AB.$$

Notes:

Triangle Inequality Theorem

The sum of the lengths of any two sides of a triangle is greater
than the length of the third side.

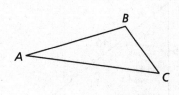

$$AB + BC > AC \qquad AC + BC > AB \qquad AB + AC > BC$$

Notes:

6.6 Notetaking with Vocabulary (continued)

Extra Practice

In Exercises 1–3, write the first step in an indirect proof of the statement.

1. Not all the students in a given class can be above average.

2. No number equals another number divided by zero.

3. The square root of 2 is not equal to the quotient of any two integers.

In Exercises 4 and 5, determine which two statements contradict each other. Explain your reasoning.

4. **A** $\triangle LMN$ is equilateral.

   B $LM \neq MN$

   C $\angle L = \angle M$

5. **A** $\triangle ABC$ is a right triangle.

   B $\angle A$ is acute.

   C $\angle C$ is obtuse.

In Exercises 6–8, list the angles of the given triangle from smallest to largest.

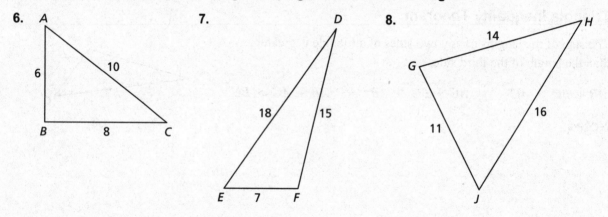

6.
7.
8.

In Exercises 9–12, is it possible to construct a triangle with the given side lengths? If not, explain why not.

9. 3, 12, 17
10. 5, 21, 16
11. 8, 5, 7
12. 10, 3, 11

13. A triangle has two sides with lengths 5 inches and 13 inches. Describe the possible lengths of the third side of the triangle.

Name_____ Date_____

6.7 Inequalities in Two Triangles
For use with Exploration 6.7

Essential Question If two sides of one triangle are congruent to two sides of another triangle, what can you say about the third sides of the triangles?

---

1 EXPLORATION: Comparing Measures in Triangles

Go to *BigIdeasMath.com* for an interactive tool to investigate this exploration.

Work with a partner. Use dynamic geometry software.

a. Draw $\triangle ABC$, as shown below.

b. Draw the circle with center $C(3, 3)$ through the point $A(1, 3)$.

c. Draw $\triangle DBC$ so that D is a point on the circle.

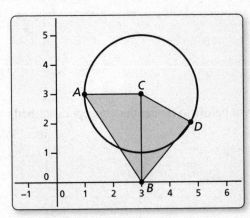

Sample
Points
$A(1, 3)$
$B(3, 0)$
$C(3, 3)$
$D(4.75, 2.03)$
Segments
$BC = 3$
$AC = 2$
$DC = 2$
$AB = 3.61$
$DB = 2.68$

d. Which two sides of $\triangle ABC$ are congruent to two sides of $\triangle DBC$? Justify your answer.

e. Compare the lengths of $\overline{AB}$ and $\overline{DB}$. Then compare the measures of $\angle ACB$ and $\angle DCB$. Are the results what you expected? Explain.

f. Drag point D to several locations on the circle. At each location, repeat part (e). Copy and record your results in the table below.

	D	AC	BC	AB	BD	$m\angle ACB$	$m\angle BCD$
1.	(4.75, 2.03)	2	3				
2.		2	3				
3.		2	3				
4.		2	3				
5.		2	3				

6.7 Inequalities in Two Triangles (continued)

---

1 EXPLORATION: Comparing Measures in Triangles (continued)

    g. Look for a pattern of the measures in your table. Then write a conjecture that summarizes your observations.

Communicate Your Answer

    2. If two sides of one triangle are congruent to two sides of another triangle, what can you say about the third sides of the triangles?

    3. Explain how you can use the hinge shown below to model the concept described in Question 2.

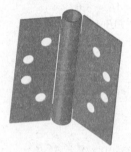

6.7 Notetaking with Vocabulary
For use after Lesson 6.7

In your own words, write the meaning of each vocabulary term.

indirect proof

inequality

Theorems

Hinge Theorem

If two sides of one triangle are congruent to two
sides of another triangle, and the included angle
of the first is larger than the included angle of the
second, then the third side of the first is longer than
the third side of the second.

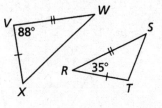

$$WX > ST$$

Notes:

Converse of the Hinge Theorem

If two sides of one triangle are congruent to
two sides of another triangle, and the third side
of the first is longer than the third side of the
second, then the included angle of the first is
larger than the included angle of the second.

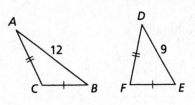

$$m\angle C > m\angle F$$

Notes:

6.7 **Notetaking with Vocabulary** (continued)

Extra Practice

In Exercises 1–9, complete the statement with **<**, **>**, or **=** . Explain your reasoning.

1. *BC* _____ *EF*

2. *BC* _____ *EF*

3. *BC* _____ *EF*

4. *m∠A* _____ *m∠D*

5. *m∠A* _____ *m∠D*

6. *m∠A* _____ *m∠D*

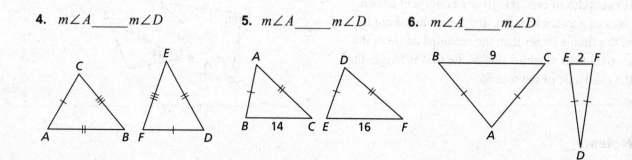

7. *AB* _____ *AC*

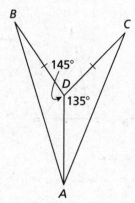

8. *AB* _____ *CD*

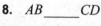
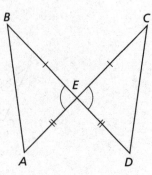

9. *m∠1* _____ *m∠2*

Name_____ Date_____

In Exercises 10 and 11, write a proof.

10. **Given** $\overline{XY} \cong \overline{YZ}$, $WX > WZ$

    Prove $m\angle WYX > m\angle WYZ$

    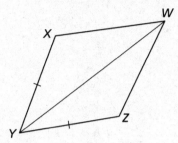

11. **Given** $\overline{AD} \cong \overline{BC}$, $m\angle DAC > m\angle ACB$

    Prove $DC > AB$

    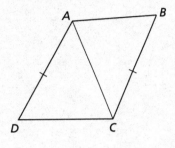

12. Loop a rubber band around the blade ends of a pair of scissors. Describe what happens to the rubber band as you open the scissors. How does that relate to the Hinge Theorem?

13. Starting from a point 10 miles north of Crow Valley, a crow flies northeast for 5 miles. Another crow, starting from a point 10 miles south of Crow Valley, flies due west for 5 miles. Which crow is farther from Crow Valley? Explain.

Chapter 7 Maintaining Mathematical Proficiency

Solve the equation by interpreting the expression in parentheses as a single quantity.

1. $5(10 - x) = 100$

2. $6(x + 8) - 12 = -48$

3. $3(2 - x) + 4(2 - x) = 56$

Determine which lines are parallel and which are perpendicular.

4. **5.** **6.**

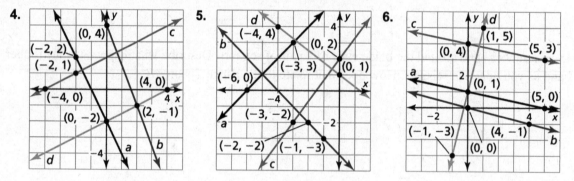

7. Explain why you can rewrite $4(x - 9) + 5(9 - x) = 11$ as $-(x - 9) = 11$? Then solve the equation.

Name_____ Date _____

7.1 Angles of Polygons
For use with Exploration 7.1

Essential Question What is the sum of the measures of the interior angles of a polygon?

1 EXPLORATION: The Sum of the Angle Measures of a Polygon

Go to *BigIdeasMath.com* for an interactive tool to investigate this exploration.

Work with a partner. Use dynamic geometry software.

a. Draw a quadrilateral and a pentagon. Find the sum of the measures of the interior angles of each polygon.

Sample

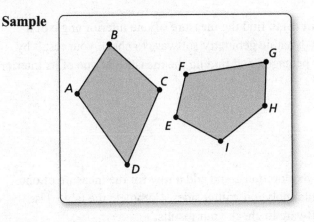

b. Draw other polygons and find the sums of the measures of their interior angles. Record your results in the table below.

Number of sides, n	3	4	5	6	7	8	9
Sum of angle measures, S							

c. Plot the data from your table in a coordinate plane.

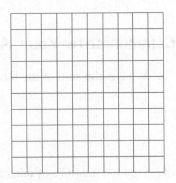

d. Write a function that fits the data. Explain what the function represents.

7.1 **Angles of Polygons** (continued)

2 **EXPLORATION:** Measure of One Angle in a Regular Polygon

Go to *BigIdeasMath.com* for an interactive tool to investigate this exploration.

Work with a partner.

 a. Use the function you found in Exploration 1 to write a new function that gives the measure of one interior angle in a regular polygon with n sides.

 b. Use the function in part (a) to find the measure of one interior angle of a regular pentagon. Use dynamic geometry software to check your result by constructing a regular pentagon and finding the measure of one of its interior angles.

 c. Copy your table from Exploration 1 and add a row for the measure of one interior angle in a regular polygon with n sides. Complete the table. Use dynamic geometry software to check your results.

Number of sides, n	3	4	5	6	7	8	9
Sum of angle measures, S							
Measure of one interior angle							

Communicate Your Answer

 3. What is the sum of the measures of the interior angles of a polygon?

 4. Find the measure of one interior angle in a regular dodecagon (a polygon with 12 sides).

7.1 Notetaking with Vocabulary
For use after Lesson 7.1

In your own words, write the meaning of each vocabulary term.

diagonal

equilateral polygon

equiangular polygon

regular polygon

Theorems

Polygon Interior Angles Theorem

The sum of the measures of the interior angles
of a convex n-gon is $(n - 2) \cdot 180°$.

$$m\angle 1 + m\angle 2 + \cdots + m\angle n = (n - 2) \cdot 180°$$

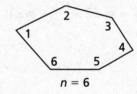

$n = 6$

Notes:

7.1 Notetaking with Vocabulary (continued)

Corollary to the Polygon Interior Angles Theorem

The sum of the measures of the interior angles of a quadrilateral is 360°.

Notes:

Polygon Exterior Angles Theorem

The sum of the measures of the exterior angles of a convex polygon, one angle at each vertex, is 360°.

$$m\angle 1 + m\angle 2 + \cdots + m\angle n = 360°$$

Notes:

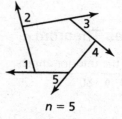

$n = 5$

7.1 Notetaking with Vocabulary (continued)

Extra Practice

In Exercises 1–3, find the sum of the measures of the interior angles of the indicated convex polygon.

1. octagon

2. 15-gon

3. 24-gon

In Exercises 4–6, the sum of the measures of the interior angles of a convex polygon is given. Classify the polygon by the number of sides.

4. 900°

5. 1620°

6. 2880°

In Exercises 7–10, find the value of x.

7.

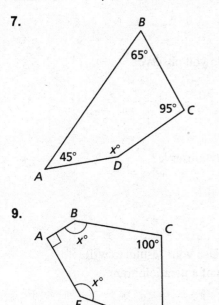

8.

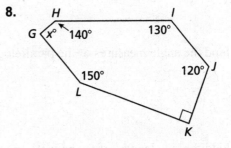

9.

10.

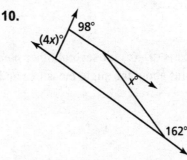

Name _____ Date _____

7.2 Properties of Parallelograms
For use with Exploration 7.2

Essential Question What are the properties of parallelograms?

1 **EXPLORATION:** Discovering Properties of Parallelograms

Go to *BigIdeasMath.com* for an interactive tool to investigate this exploration.

Work with a partner. Use dynamic geometry software.

a. Construct any parallelogram and label it *ABCD*. Explain your process.

Sample

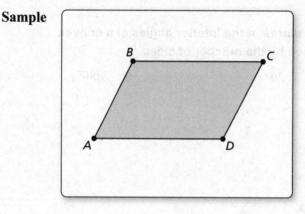

b. Find the angle measures of the parallelogram. What do you observe?

c. Find the side lengths of the parallelogram. What do you observe?

d. Repeat parts (a)–(c) for several other parallelograms. Use your results to write conjectures about the angle measures and side lengths of a parallelogram.

Name_____ Date_____

2 EXPLORATION: Discovering a Property of Parallelograms

Go to *BigIdeasMath.com* for an interactive tool to investigate this exploration.

Work with a partner. Use dynamic geometry software.

    a. Construct any parallelogram and label it *ABCD*.

    b. Draw the two diagonals of the parallelogram. Label the point of intersection *E*.

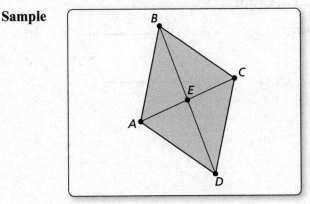

Sample

    c. Find the segment lengths *AE*, *BE*, *CE*, and *DE*. What do you observe?

    d. Repeat parts (a)–(c) for several other parallelograms. Use your results to write a conjecture about the diagonals of a parallelogram.

Communicate Your Answer

    3. What are the properties of parallelograms?

7.2 Notetaking with Vocabulary
For use after Lesson 7.2

In your own words, write the meaning of each vocabulary term.

parallelogram

Theorems

Parallelogram Opposite Sides Theorem

If a quadrilateral is a parallelogram, then
its opposite sides are congruent.

If $PQRS$ is a parallelogram, then $\overline{PQ} \cong \overline{RS}$
and $\overline{QR} \cong \overline{SP}$.

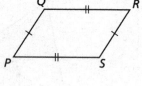

Notes:

Parallelogram Opposite Angles Theorem

If a quadrilateral is a parallelogram, then
its opposite angles are congruent.

If $PQRS$ is a parallelogram, then $\angle P \cong \angle R$
and $\angle Q \cong \angle S$.

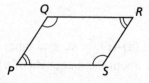

Notes:

7.2 **Notetaking with Vocabulary** (continued)

Parallelogram Consecutive Angles Theorem

If a quadrilateral is a parallelogram, then its consecutive angles are supplementary.

If *PQRS* is a parallelogram, then $x° + y° = 180°$.

Notes:

Parallelogram Diagonals Theorem

If a quadrilateral is a parallelogram, then its diagonals bisect each other.

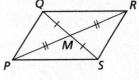

If *PQRS* is a parallelogram, then $\overline{QM} \cong \overline{SM}$ and $\overline{PM} \cong \overline{RM}$.

Notes:

Name_____ Date _____

Extra Practice

In Exercises 1–3, find the value of each variable in the parallelogram.

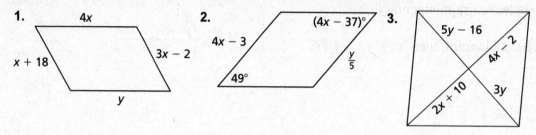

1.
4x
x + 18   3x − 2
y

2.
4x − 3   (4x − 37)°
49° $\frac{y}{5}$

3.
5y − 16
4x − 2
2x + 10   3y

In Exercises 4–11, find the indicated measure in □*MNOP*. Explain your reasoning.

4. *PO*

5. *OQ*

6. *NO*

7. *PQ*

8. *m∠PMN*

9. *m∠NOP*

10. *m∠OPM*

11. *m∠NMO*

M   24   N
14   20.7   68°
26
Q
59°
P   O

7.3 Proving That a Quadrilateral Is a Parallelogram
For use with Exploration 7.3

Essential Question How can you prove that a quadrilateral is a parallelogram?

---

1 EXPLORATION: Proving That a Quadrilateral Is a Parallelogram

Go to *BigIdeasMath.com* for an interactive tool to investigate this exploration.

Work with a partner. Use dynamic geometry software.

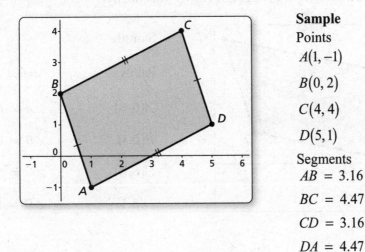

Sample
Points
$A(1, -1)$
$B(0, 2)$
$C(4, 4)$
$D(5, 1)$
Segments
$AB = 3.16$
$BC = 4.47$
$CD = 3.16$
$DA = 4.47$

a. Construct any quadrilateral *ABCD* whose opposite sides are congruent.

b. Is the quadrilateral a parallelogram? Justify your answer.

c. Repeat parts (a) and (b) for several other quadrilaterals. Then write a conjecture based on your results.

d. Write the converse of your conjecture. Is the converse true? Explain.

7.3 **Proving That a Quadrilateral Is a Parallelogram** (continued)

2 **EXPLORATION:** Proving That a Quadrilateral Is a Parallelogram

Go to *BigIdeasMath.com* for an interactive tool to investigate this exploration.

Work with a partner. Use dynamic geometry software.

    a. Construct any quadrilateral *ABCD* whose opposite angles are congruent.

    b. Is the quadrilateral a parallelogram? Justify your answer.

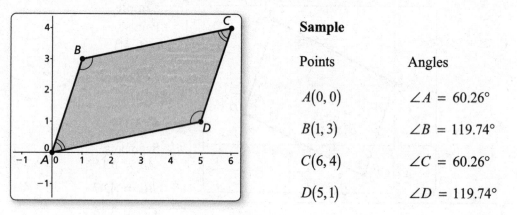

Sample

Points	Angles
$A(0, 0)$	$\angle A = 60.26°$
$B(1, 3)$	$\angle B = 119.74°$
$C(6, 4)$	$\angle C = 60.26°$
$D(5, 1)$	$\angle D = 119.74°$

    c. Repeat parts (a) and (b) for several other quadrilaterals. Then write a conjecture based on your results.

    d. Write the converse of your conjecture. Is the converse true? Explain.

Communicate Your Answer

    3. How can you prove that a quadrilateral is a parallelogram?

    4. Is the quadrilateral at the right a parallelogram? Explain your reasoning.

Name_____ Date_____

7.3 Notetaking with Vocabulary
For use after Lesson 7.3

In your own words, write the meaning of each vocabulary term.

diagonal

parallelogram

Theorems

Parallelogram Opposite Sides Converse

If both pairs of opposite sides of a quadrilateral are congruent, then the quadrilateral is a parallelogram.

If $\overline{AB} \cong \overline{CD}$ and $\overline{BC} \cong \overline{DA}$, then $ABCD$ is a parallelogram.

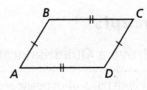

Notes:

Parallelogram Opposite Angles Converse

If both pairs of opposite angles of a quadrilateral are congruent, then the quadrilateral is a parallelogram.

If $\angle A \cong \angle C$ and $\angle B \cong \angle D$, then $ABCD$ is a parallelogram.

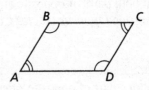

Notes:

Opposite Sides Parallel and Congruent Theorem

If one pair of opposite sides of a quadrilateral are congruent and parallel, then the quadrilateral is a parallelogram.

If $\overline{BC} \parallel \overline{AD}$ and $\overline{BC} \cong \overline{AD}$, then $ABCD$ is a parallelogram.

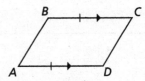

Notes:

7.3 **Notetaking with Vocabulary** (continued)

Parallelogram Diagonals Converse

If the diagonals of a quadrilateral bisect each other,
then the quadrilateral is a parallelogram.

If $\overline{BD}$ and $\overline{AC}$ bisect each other, then *ABCD* is a parallelogram.

Notes:

Core Concepts

Ways to Prove a Quadrilateral Is a Parallelogram

1. Show that both pairs of opposite sides are parallel. *(Definition)*	
2. Show that both pairs of opposite sides are congruent. *(Parallelogram Opposite Sides Converse)*	
3. Show that both pairs of opposite angles are congruent. *(Parallelogram Opposite Angles Converse)*	
4. Show that one pair of opposite sides are congruent and parallel. *(Opposite Sides Parallel and Congruent Theorem)*	
5. Show that the diagonals bisect each other. *(Parallelogram Diagonals Converse)*	

Name_____ Date_____

Extra Practice

In Exercises 1–3, state which theorem you can use to show that the quadrilateral is a parallelogram.

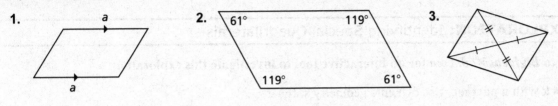

1.

2.

3.

In Exercises 4–7, find the values of x and y that make the quadrilateral a parallelogram.

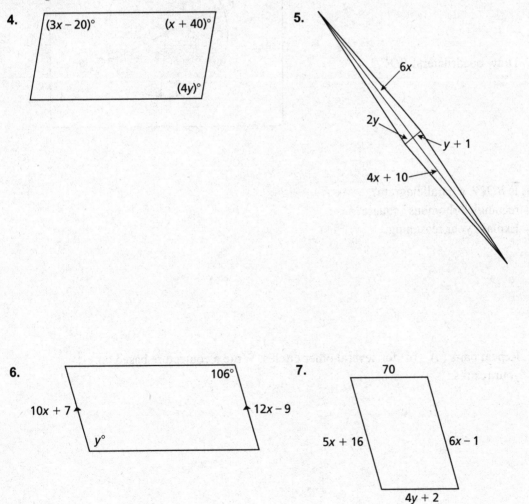

4. $(3x - 20)°$ $(x + 40)°$ $(4y)°$

5. $6x$ $2y$ $y + 1$ $4x + 10$

6. $106°$ $10x + 7$ $12x - 9$ $y°$

7. 70 $5x + 16$ $6x - 1$ $4y + 2$

7.4 Properties of Special Parallelograms
For use with Exploration 7.4

Essential Question What are the properties of the diagonals of rectangles, rhombuses, and squares?

1 EXPLORATION: Identifying Special Quadrilaterals

Go to *BigIdeasMath.com* for an interactive tool to investigate this exploration.

Work with a partner. Use dynamic geometry software.

a. Draw a circle with center *A*.

Sample

b. Draw two diameters of the circle. Label the endpoints *B, C, D,* and *E*.

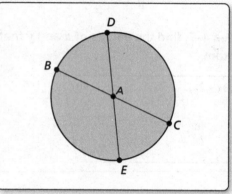

c. Draw quadrilateral *BDCE*.

d. Is *BDCE* a parallelogram? rectangle? rhombus? square? Explain your reasoning.

e. Repeat parts (a) – (d) for several other circles. Write a conjecture based on your results.

Name_____ Date_____

2   **EXPLORATION:** Identifying Special Quadrilaterals

Go to *BigIdeasMath.com* for an interactive tool to investigate this exploration.

Work with a partner. Use dynamic geometry software.

a. Construct two segments that are perpendicular bisectors of each other. Label the endpoints *A, B, D,* and *E.* Label the intersection *C.*

Sample

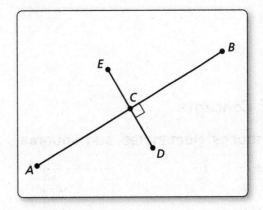

b. Draw quadrilateral *AEBD*.

c. Is *AEBD* a parallelogram? rectangle? rhombus? square? Explain your reasoning.

d. Repeat parts (a) – (c) for several other segments. Write a conjecture based on your results.

Communicate Your Answer

3. What are the properties of the diagonals of rectangles, rhombuses, and squares?

4. Is *RSTU* a parallelogram? rectangle? rhombus? square? Explain your reasoning.

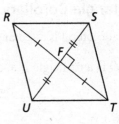

5. What type of quadrilateral has congruent diagonals that bisect each other?

Name _____ Date _____

7.4 Notetaking with Vocabulary
For use after Lesson 7.4

In your own words, write the meaning of each vocabulary term.

rhombus

rectangle

square

Core Concepts

Rhombuses, Rectangles, and Squares

A **rhombus** is a parallelogram with four congruent sides.

A **rectangle** is a parallelogram with four right angles.

A **square** is a parallelogram with four congruent sides and four right angles.

Notes:

Rhombus Corollary

A quadrilateral is a rhombus if and only if it has four congruent sides.

$ABCD$ is a rhombus if and only if $\overline{AB} \cong \overline{BC} \cong \overline{CD} \cong \overline{AD}$.

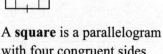

Rectangle Corollary

A quadrilateral is a rectangle if and only if it has four right angles.

$ABCD$ is a rectangle if and only if $\angle A$, $\angle B$, $\angle C$, and $\angle D$ are right angles.

7.4   Notetaking with Vocabulary (continued)

Square Corollary

A quadrilateral is a square if and only if it is a rhombus and a rectangle.

$ABCD$ is a square if and only if $\overline{AB} \cong \overline{BC} \cong \overline{CD} \cong \overline{AD}$ and $\angle A$, $\angle B$, $\angle C$, and $\angle D$ are right angles.

Notes:

Rhombus Diagonals Theorem

A parallelogram is a rhombus if and only if its diagonals are perpendicular.

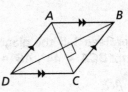

$\square ABCD$ is a rhombus if and only if $\overline{AC} \perp \overline{BD}$.

Notes:

Rhombus Opposite Angles Theorem

A parallelogram is a rhombus if and only if each diagonal bisects a pair of opposite angles.

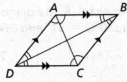

$\square ABCD$ is a rhombus if and only if $\overline{AC}$ bisects $\angle BCD$ and $\angle BAD$, and $\overline{BD}$ bisects $\angle ABC$ and $\angle ADC$.

Notes:

Rectangle Diagonals Theorem

A parallelogram is a rectangle if and only if its diagonals are congruent.

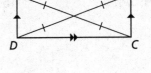

$\square ABCD$ is a rectangle if and only if $\overline{AC} \cong \overline{BD}$.

Notes:

Name _____ Date _____

Extra Practice

1. For any rhombus *MNOP*, decide whether the statement $\overline{MO} \cong \overline{NP}$ is *always* or *sometimes* true. Draw a diagram and explain your reasoning.

2. For any rectangle *PQRS*, decide whether the statement $\angle PQS \cong \angle RSQ$ is *always* or *sometimes* true. Draw a diagram and explain your reasoning.

In Exercises 3–5, the diagonals of rhombus *ABCD* intersect at *E*. Given that $m\angle BCA = 44°$, *AB* = 9, **and** *AE* = 7, **find the indicated measure.**

3. *BC*   4. *AC*   5. $m\angle ADC$

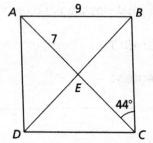

In Exercises 6–8, the diagonals of rectangle *EFGH* intersect at *I*. Given that $m\angle HFG = 31°$ **and** *EG* = 17, **find the indicated measure.**

6. $m\angle FHG$ 7. *HF*   8. $m\angle EFH$

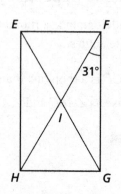

In Exercises 9–11, the diagonals of square *LMNP* intersect at *K*. Given that $MK = \dfrac{1}{2}$, **find the indicated measure.**

9. *PK*   10. $m\angle PKN$ 11. $m\angle MNK$

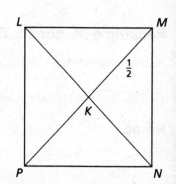

7.5 Properties of Trapezoids and Kites
For use with Exploration 7.5

Essential Question What are some properties of trapezoids and kites?

---

1 **EXPLORATION:** Making a Conjecture about Trapezoids

Go to *BigIdeasMath.com* **for an interactive tool to investigate this exploration.**

Work with a partner. Use dynamic geometry software.

a. Construct a trapezoid whose base angles are congruent. Explain your process.

Sample

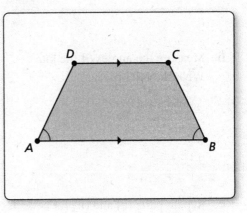

b. Is the trapezoid isosceles? Justify your answer.

c. Repeat parts (a) and (b) for several other trapezoids. Write a conjecture based on your results.

7.5 **Properties of Trapezoids and Kites** (continued)

---

2 **EXPLORATION:** Discovering a Property of Kites

Go to *BigIdeasMath.com* for an interactive tool to investigate this exploration.

Work with a partner. Use dynamic geometry software.

   a. Construct a kite. Explain your process.

Sample

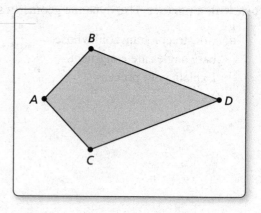

   b. Measure the angles of the kite. What do you observe?

   c. Repeat parts (a) and (b) for several other kites. Write a conjecture based on your results.

Communicate Your Answer

   3. What are some properties of trapezoids and kites?

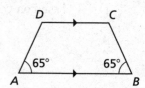

   4. Is the trapezoid at the right isosceles? Explain.

   5. A quadrilateral has angle measures of 70°, 70°, 110°, and 110°. Is the quadrilateral a kite? Explain.

Name_____ Date _____

In your own words, write the meaning of each vocabulary term.

trapezoid

bases

base angles

legs

isosceles trapezoid

midsegment of a trapezoid

kite

Theorems

Isosceles Trapezoid Base Angles Theorem

If a trapezoid is isosceles, then each pair of base angles is congruent.

If trapezoid $ABCD$ is isosceles, then $\angle A \cong \angle D$ and $\angle B \cong \angle C$.

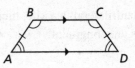

Isosceles Trapezoid Base Angles Converse

If a trapezoid has a pair of congruent base angles, then it is an isosceles trapezoid.

If $\angle A \cong \angle D$ (or if $\angle B \cong \angle C$), then trapezoid $ABCD$ is isosceles.

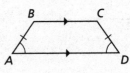

7.5 Notetaking with Vocabulary (continued)

Isosceles Trapezoid Diagonals Theorem

A trapezoid is isosceles if and only if its diagonals are congruent.

Trapezoid $ABCD$ is isosceles if and only if $\overline{AC} \cong \overline{BD}$.

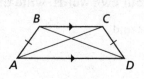

Trapezoid Midsegment Theorem

The midsegment of a trapezoid is parallel to each base, and its length is one-half the sum of the lengths of the bases.

If $\overline{MN}$ is the midsegment of trapezoid $ABCD$, then $\overline{MN} \parallel \overline{AB}$, $\overline{MN} \parallel \overline{DC}$, and $MN = \frac{1}{2}(AB + CD)$.

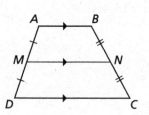

Kite Diagonals Theorem

If a quadrilateral is a kite, then its diagonals are perpendicular.

If quadrilateral $ABCD$ is a kite, then $\overline{AC} \perp \overline{BD}$.

Kite Opposite Angles Theorem

If a quadrilateral is a kite, then exactly one pair of opposite angles are congruent.

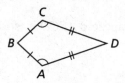

If quadrilateral $ABCD$ is a kite and $\overline{BC} \cong \overline{BA}$, then $\angle A \cong \angle C$ and $\angle B \not\cong \angle D$.

Notes:

7.5 **Notetaking with Vocabulary** (continued)

Extra Practice

1. Show that the quadrilateral with vertices at
   $Q(0, 3)$, $R(0, 6)$, $S(-6, 0)$, and $T(-3, 0)$ is
   a trapezoid. Decide whether the trapezoid
   is isosceles. Then find the length of the
   midsegment of the trapezoid.

In Exercises 2 and 3, find $m\angle K$ **and** $m\angle L$.

2.

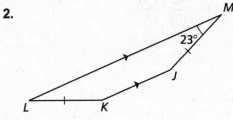

3.

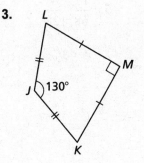

In Exercises 4 and 5, find CD.

4.

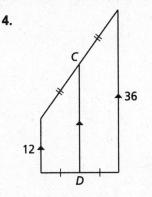

5.

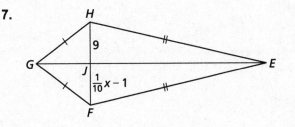

In Exercises 6 and 7, find the value of x.

6.

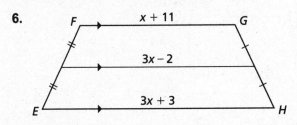

7.

Chapter 8 Maintaining Mathematical Proficiency

Tell whether the ratios form a proportion.

1. $\dfrac{3}{4}, \dfrac{16}{12}$

2. $\dfrac{35}{63}, \dfrac{45}{81}$

3. $\dfrac{12}{96}, \dfrac{16}{100}$

4. $\dfrac{15}{24}, \dfrac{75}{100}$

5. $\dfrac{17}{68}, \dfrac{32}{128}$

6. $\dfrac{65}{105}, \dfrac{156}{252}$

Tell whether the two figures are similar. Explain your reasoning.

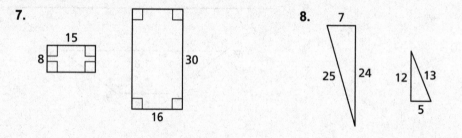

7.

8.

Name_____ Date_____

8.1 Dilations
For use with Exploration 8.1

Essential Question What does it mean to dilate a figure?

---

1 **EXPLORATION: Dilating a Triangle in a Coordinate Plane**

Go to *BigIdeasMath.com* **for an interactive tool to investigate this exploration.**

Work with a partner. Use dynamic geometry software to draw any triangle and label it $\triangle ABC$.

a. *Dilate* $\triangle ABC$ using a *scale factor* of 2 and a *center of dilation* at the origin to form $\triangle A'B'C'$. Compare the coordinates, side lengths, and angle measures of $\triangle ABC$ and $\triangle A'B'C'$.

Sample

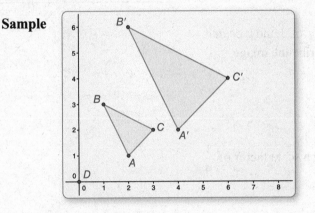

b. Repeat part (a) using a *scale factor* of $\frac{1}{2}$.

c. What do the results of parts (a) and (b) suggest about the coordinates, side lengths, and angle measures of the image of $\triangle ABC$ after a dilation with a scale factor of k?

8.1 **Dilations** (continued)

---

2 **EXPLORATION: Dilating Lines in a Coordinate Plane**

Go to *BigIdeasMath.com* for an interactive tool to investigate this exploration.

Work with a partner. Use dynamic geometry software to draw $\overleftrightarrow{AB}$ that passes through the origin and $\overleftrightarrow{AC}$ that does not pass through the origin.

a. *Dilate* $\overleftrightarrow{AB}$ *using a scale factor* of 3 *and a center of dilation* at the origin. Describe the image.

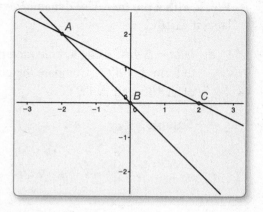

b. *Dilate* $\overleftrightarrow{AC}$ *using a scale factor* of 3 *and a center of dilation* at the origin. Describe the image.

c. Repeat parts (a) and (b) using a scale factor of $\dfrac{1}{4}$.

d. What do you notice about dilations of lines passing through the center of dilation and dilations of lines not passing through the center of dilation?

Communicate Your Answer

3. What does it mean to dilate a figure?

4. Repeat Exploration 1 using a center of dilation at a point other than the origin.

Name_____ Date _____

8.1 Notetaking with Vocabulary
For use after Lesson 8.1

In your own words, write the meaning of each vocabulary term.

dilation

center of dilation

scale factor

enlargement

reduction

Core Concepts

Dilations

A **dilation** is a transformation in which a figure is enlarged or reduced
with respect to a fixed point C called the **center of dilation** and a **scale
factor** k, which is the ratio of the lengths of the corresponding sides of
the image and the preimage.

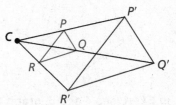

A dilation with center of dilation C and scale factor k maps every point P
in a figure to a point P' so that the following are true.

- If P is the center point C, then $P = P'$.

- If P is not the center point C, then the image point P' lies on $\overrightarrow{CP}$.
  The scale factor k is a positive number such that $k = \dfrac{CP'}{CP}$.

- Angle measures are preserved.

Notes:

Name _____ Date _____

Coordinate Rule for Dilations

If $P(x, y)$ is the preimage of a point, then its image after a dilation centered
at the origin $(0, 0)$ with scale factor k is the point $P'(kx, ky)$.

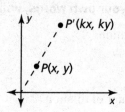

Notes:

Extra Practice

**In Exercises 1–3, find the scale factor of the dilation. Then tell whether the dilation
is a *reduction* or an *enlargement*.**

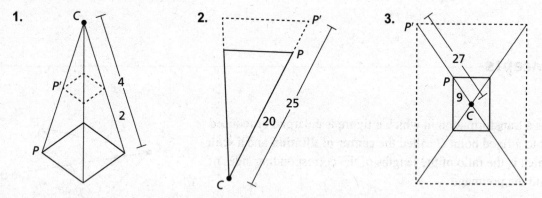

1.

2.

3.

**In Exercises 4 and 5, graph the polygon and its image after a dilation with scale
factor k.**

4. $A(-3, 1)$, $B(-4, -1)$, $C(-2, -1)$; $k = 2$

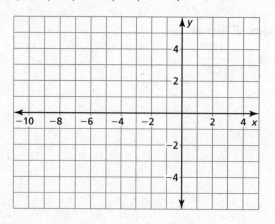

8.1   **Notetaking with Vocabulary** (continued)

5. $P(-10, 0), Q(-5, 0), R(0, 5), S(-5, 5); k = \frac{1}{5}$

In Exercises 6 and 7, find the coordinates of the image of the polygon after a dilation with scale factor *k*.

6. $A(-3, 1), B(-4, -1), C(-2, -1); k = -6$

7. $P(-8, 4), Q(20, -8), R(16, 4), S(0, 12); k = -0.25$

8. You design a poster on an 8.5-inch by 11-inch paper for a contest at your school. The poster of the winner will be printed on a 34-inch by 44-inch canvas to be displayed. What is the scale factor of this dilation?

9. A biology book shows the image of an insect that is 10 times its actual size. The image of the insect is 8 centimeters long. What is the actual length of the insect?

Name_____ Date _____

8.2 Similarity and Transformations
For use with Exploration 8.2

Essential Question When a figure is translated, reflected, rotated, or dilated in the plane, is the image always similar to the original figure?

---

1 EXPLORATION: Dilations and Similarity

Go to *BigIdeasMath.com* for an interactive tool to investigate this exploration.

Work with a partner.

a. Use dynamic geometry software to draw any triangle and label it △*ABC*.

b. Dilate the triangle using a scale factor of 3. Is the image similar to the original triangle? Justify your answer.

Sample

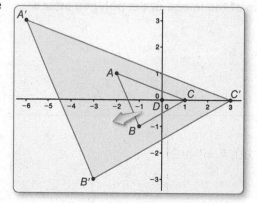

Name_____ Date _____

2   EXPLORATION: Rigid Motions and Similarity

Go to *BigIdeasMath.com* for an interactive tool to investigate this exploration.

Work with a partner.

   a. Use dynamic geometry software to draw any triangle.

   b. Copy the triangle and translate it 3 units left and 4 units up. Is the image similar to the original triangle? Justify your answer.

   c. Reflect the triangle in the *y*-axis. Is the image similar to the original triangle? Justify your answer.

   d. Rotate the original triangle 90° counterclockwise about the origin. Is the image similar to the original triangle? Justify your answer.

Communicate Your Answer

   3. When a figure is translated, reflected, rotated, or dilated in the plane, is the image always similar to the original figure? Explain your reasoning.

   4. A figure undergoes a composition of transformations, which includes translations, reflections, rotations, and dilations. Is the image similar to the original figure? Explain your reasoning.

8.2 Notetaking with Vocabulary
For use after Lesson 8.2

In your own words, write the meaning of each vocabulary term.

similarity transformation

similar figures

Notes:

Name _____ Date _____

Extra Practice

In Exercises 1–3, graph the polygon with the given vertices and its image after the similarity transformation.

1. $A(3, 6)$, $B(2, 5)$, $C(4, 3)$, $D(5, 5)$

    Translation: $(x, y) \rightarrow (x - 5, y - 3)$

    Dilation: $(x, y) \rightarrow (3x, 3y)$

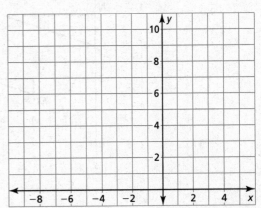

2. $R(12, 8)$, $S(8, 0)$, $T(0, 4)$

    Dilation: $(x, y) \rightarrow \left(\frac{1}{4}x, \frac{1}{4}y\right)$

    Reflection: in the y-axis

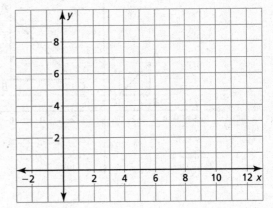

3. $X(9, 6)$, $Y(3, 3)$, $Z(3, 6)$

    Rotation: 90° about the origin

    Dilation: $(x, y) \rightarrow \left(\frac{2}{3}x, \frac{2}{3}y\right)$

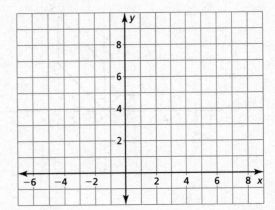

8.2 **Notetaking with Vocabulary** (continued)

In Exercises 4–6, describe the similarity transformation that maps the preimage to the image.

4.

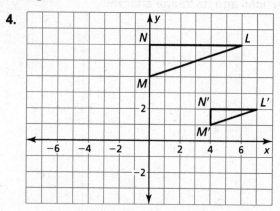

5.

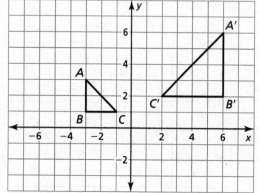

6.

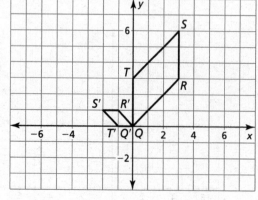

8.3 Similar Polygons
For use with Exploration 8.3

Essential Question How are similar polygons related?

> **1 EXPLORATION: Comparing Triangles after a Dilation**

Go to *BigIdeasMath.com* for an interactive tool to investigate this exploration.

Work with a partner. Use dynamic geometry software to draw any $\triangle ABC$. Dilate $\triangle ABC$ to form a similar $\triangle A'B'C'$ using any scale factor k and any center of dilation.

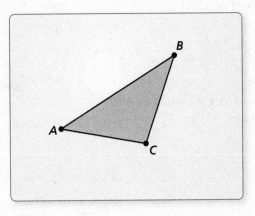

a. Compare the corresponding angles of $\triangle A'B'C'$ and $\triangle ABC$.

b. Find the ratios of the lengths of the sides of $\triangle A'B'C'$ to the lengths of the corresponding sides of $\triangle ABC$. What do you observe?

c. Repeat parts (a) and (b) for several other triangles, scale factors, and centers of dilation. Do you obtain similar results?

Name _____ Date _____

---

2 **EXPLORATION: Comparing Triangles after a Dilation**

Go to *BigIdeasMath.com* **for an interactive tool to investigate this exploration.**

Work with a partner. Use dynamic geometry software to draw any $\triangle ABC$. Dilate $\triangle ABC$ to form a similar $\triangle A'B'C'$ using any scale factor k and any center of dilation.

    a. Compare the perimeters of $\triangle A'B'C'$ and $\triangle ABC$. What do you observe?

    b. Compare the areas of $\triangle A'B'C'$ and $\triangle ABC$. What do you observe?

    c. Repeat parts (a) and (b) for several other triangles, scale factors, and centers of dilation. Do you obtain similar results?

Communicate Your Answer

    3. How are similar polygons related?

    4. A $\triangle RST$ is dilated by a scale factor of 3 to form $\triangle R'S'T'$. The area of $\triangle RST$ is 1 square inch. What is the area of $\triangle R'S'T'$?

8.3 Notetaking with Vocabulary
For use after Lesson 8.3

In your own words, write the meaning of each vocabulary term.

similar figures

similarity transformation

corresponding parts

Core Concepts

Corresponding Parts of Similar Polygons

In the diagram below, $\triangle ABC$ is similar to $\triangle DEF$. You can write "$\triangle ABC$ is similar to $\triangle DEF$" as $\triangle ABC \sim \triangle DEF$. A similarity transformation preserves angle measure. So, corresponding angles are congruent. A similarity transformation also enlarges or reduces side lengths by a scale factor k. So, corresponding side lengths are proportional.

Corresponding angles

$\angle A \cong \angle D, \angle B \cong \angle E, \angle C \cong \angle F$

Ratios of corresponding side lengths

$$\frac{DE}{AB} = \frac{EF}{BC} = \frac{FD}{CA} = k$$

Notes:

Name _____ Date _____

Corresponding Lengths in Similar Polygons

If two polygons are similar, then the ratio of any two corresponding lengths in the
polygons is equal to the scale factor of the similar polygons.

Notes:

Theorems

Perimeters of Similar Polygons

If two polygons are similar, then the ratio of
their perimeters is equal to the ratios of their
corresponding side lengths.

If $KLMN \sim PQRS$, then

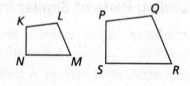

$$\frac{PQ + QR + RS + SP}{KL + LM + MN + NK} = \frac{PQ}{KL} = \frac{QR}{LM} = \frac{RS}{MN} = \frac{SP}{NK}.$$

Notes:

Areas of Similar Polygons

If two polygons are similar, then the ratio of their areas is
equal to the squares of the ratios of their corresponding side
lengths.

If $KLMN \sim PQRS$, then

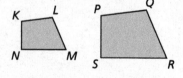

$$\frac{\text{Area of } PQRS}{\text{Area of } KLMN} = \left(\frac{PQ}{KL}\right)^2 = \left(\frac{QR}{LM}\right)^2 = \left(\frac{RS}{MN}\right)^2 = \left(\frac{SP}{NK}\right)^2.$$

Notes:

Name_____ Date_____

Extra Practice

In Exercises 1 and 2, the polygons are similar. Find the value of x.

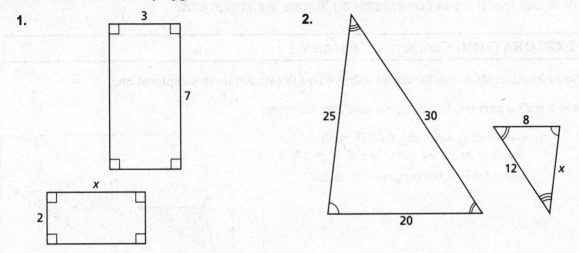

1.

2.

In Exercises 3–8, *ABCDE ~ KLMNP*.

3. Find the scale factor from *ABCDE* to *KLMNP*.

4. Find the scale factor from *KLMNP* to *ABCDE*.

5. Find the values of *x*, *y*, and *z*.

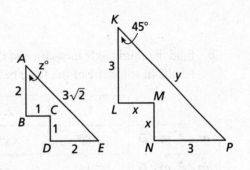

6. Find the perimeter of each polygon.

7. Find the ratio of the perimeters of *ABCDE* to *KLMNP*.

8. Find the ratio of the areas of *ABCDE* to *KLMNP*.

8.4 Proving Triangle Similarity by AA
For use with Exploration 8.4

Essential Question What can you conclude about two triangles when you know that two pairs of corresponding angles are congruent?

---

1 **EXPLORATION:** Comparing Triangles

Go to BigIdeasMath.com for an interactive tool to investigate this exploration.

Work with a partner. Use dynamic geometry software.

a. Construct $\triangle ABC$ and $\triangle DEF$ so that
$m\angle A = m\angle D = 106°$, $m\angle B = m\angle E = 31°$,
and $\triangle DEF$ is not congruent to $\triangle ABC$.

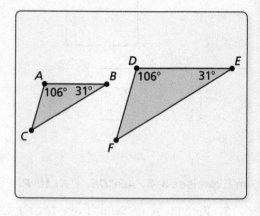

b. Find the third angle measure and the side lengths of each triangle. Record your results in column 1 of the table below.

	1.	2.	3.	4.	5.	6.
$m\angle A, m\angle D$	106°	88°	40°			
$m\angle B, m\angle E$	31°	42°	65°			
$m\angle C$						
$m\angle F$						
AB						
DE						
BC						
EF						
AC						
DF						

8.4 **Proving Triangle Similarity by AA** (continued)

1 **EXPLORATION: Comparing Triangles** (continued)

    c. Are the two triangles similar? Explain.

    d. Repeat parts (a)–(c) to complete columns 2 and 3 of the table for the given angle measures.

    e. Complete each remaining column of the table using your own choice of two pairs of equal corresponding angle measures. Can you construct two triangles in this way that are *not* similar?

    f. Make a conjecture about any two triangles with two pairs of congruent corresponding angles.

Communicate Your Answer

2. What can you conclude about two triangles when you know that two pairs of corresponding angles are congruent?

3. Find *RS* in the figure at the right.

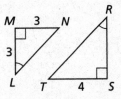

8.4 Notetaking with Vocabulary
For use after Lesson 8.4

In your own words, write the meaning of each vocabulary term.

similar figures

similarity transformation

Theorems

Angle-Angle (AA) Similarity Theorem

If two angles of one triangle are congruent to two angles of
another triangle, then the two triangles are similar.

If $\angle A \cong \angle D$ and $\angle B \cong \angle E$, then $\triangle ABC \sim \triangle DEF$.

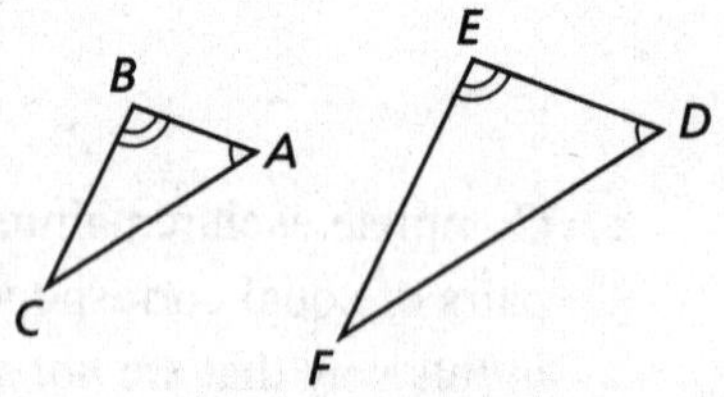

Notes:

8.4 **Notetaking with Vocabulary** (continued)

Extra Practice

In Exercises 1 and 2, determine whether the triangles are similar. If they are, write a similarity statement. Explain your reasoning.

1.

2.

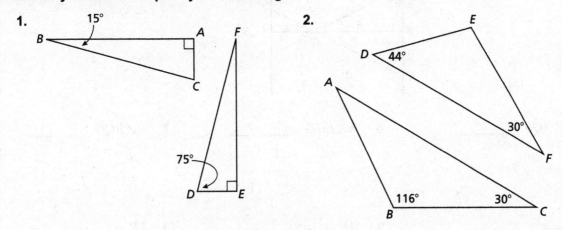

In Exercises 3 and 4, show that the two triangles are similar.

3.

4.

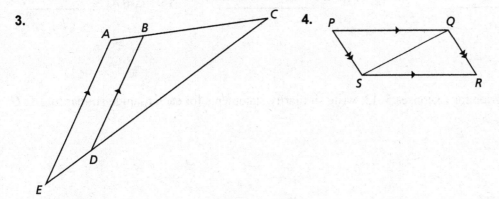

8.4   **Notetaking with Vocabulary** (continued)

In Exercises 5–13, use the diagram to complete the statement.

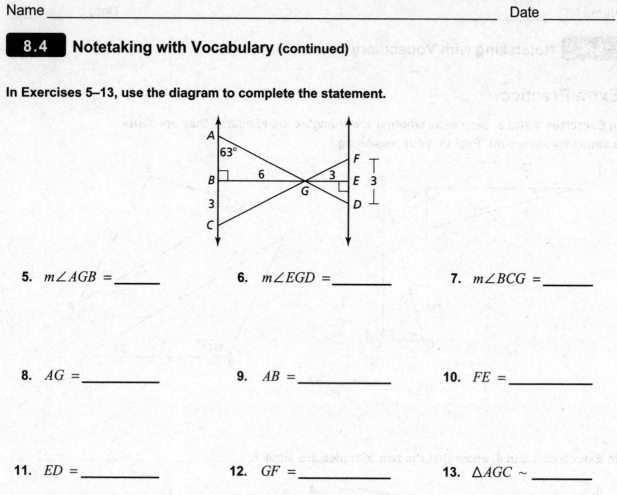

5. $m\angle AGB = $ _____

6. $m\angle EGD = $ _____

7. $m\angle BCG = $ _____

8. $AG = $ _____

9. $AB = $ _____

10. $FE = $ _____

11. $ED = $ _____

12. $GF = $ _____

13. $\triangle AGC \sim$ _____

14. Using the diagram for Exercises 5–13, write similarity statements for each triangle similar to $\triangle EFG$.

15. Determine if it is possible for $\triangle HJK$ and $\triangle PQR$ to be similar. Explain your reasoning.

$$m\angle H = 100°, m\angle K = 46°, m\angle P = 44°, \text{ and } m\angle Q = 46°$$

8.5 Proving Triangle Similarity by SSS and SAS
For use with Exploration 8.5

Essential Question   What are two ways to use corresponding sides of two triangles to determine that the triangles are similar?

---

1   EXPLORATION: Deciding Whether Triangles Are Similar

Go to *BigIdeasMath.com* for an interactive tool to investigate this exploration.

Work with a partner. Use dynamic geometry software.

a. Construct $\triangle ABC$ and $\triangle DEF$ with the side lengths given in column 1 of the table below.

	1.	2.	3.	4.	5.	6.	7.
AB	5	5	6	15	9	24	
BC	8	8	8	20	12	18	
AC	10	10	10	10	8	16	
DE	10	15	9	12	12	8	
EF	16	24	12	16	15	6	
DF	20	30	15	8	10	8	
m∠A							
m∠B							
m∠C							
m∠D							
m∠E							
m∠F							

b. Complete column 1 in the table above.

c. Are the triangles similar? Explain your reasoning.

d. Repeat parts (a)–(c) for columns 2–6 in the table.

e. How are the corresponding side lengths related in each pair of triangles that are similar? Is this true for each pair of triangles that are not similar?

8.5 Proving Triangle Similarity by SSS and SAS (continued)

---

1 EXPLORATION: Deciding Whether Triangles Are Similar (continued)

    f. Make a conjecture about the similarity of two triangles based on their corresponding side lengths.

    g. Use your conjecture to write another set of side lengths of two similar triangles. Use the side lengths to complete column 7 of the table.

---

2 EXPLORATION: Deciding Whether Triangles Are Similar

Go to *BigIdeasMath.com* **for an interactive tool to investigate this exploration.**

Work with a partner. Use dynamic geometry software. Construct any $\triangle ABC$.

    a. Find AB, AC, and $m\angle A$. Choose any positive rational number k and construct $\triangle DEF$ so that $DE = k \bullet AB$, $DF = k \bullet AC$, and $m\angle D = m\angle A$.

    b. Is $\triangle DEF$ similar to $\triangle ABC$? Explain your reasoning.

    c. Repeat parts (a) and (b) several times by changing $\triangle ABC$ and k. Describe your results.

Communicate Your Answer

    3. What are two ways to use corresponding sides of two triangles to determine that the triangles are similar?

8.5 Notetaking with Vocabulary
For use after Lesson 8.5

In your own words, write the meaning of each vocabulary term.

similar figures

corresponding parts

parallel lines

Theorems

Side-Side-Side (SSS) Similarity Theorem

If the corresponding side lengths of two
triangles are proportional, then the
triangles are similar.

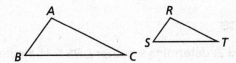

If $\dfrac{AB}{RS} = \dfrac{BC}{ST} = \dfrac{CA}{TR}$, then $\triangle ABC \sim \triangle RST$.

Notes:

8.5 **Notetaking with Vocabulary** (continued)

Side-Angle-Side (SAS) Similarity Theorem

If an angle of one triangle is congruent to an angle
of a second triangle and the lengths of the sides
including these angles are proportional, then the
triangles are similar.

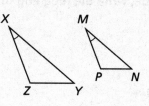

If $\angle X \cong \angle M$ and $\dfrac{ZX}{PM} = \dfrac{XY}{MN}$, then
$\triangle XYZ \sim \triangle MNP$.

Notes:

Extra Practice

In Exercises 1 and 2, determine whether $\triangle RST$ is similar to $\triangle ABC$.

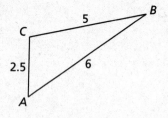

1.

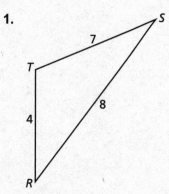

2.

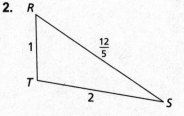

8.5 **Notetaking with Vocabulary** (continued)

3. Find the value of x that makes $\triangle RST \sim \triangle HGK$.

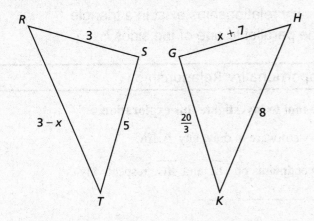

4. Verify that $\triangle RST \sim \triangle XYZ$. Find the scale factor of $\triangle RST$ to $\triangle XYZ$.

$$\triangle RST : RS = 12, ST = 15, TR = 24$$
$$\triangle XYZ : XY = 28, YZ = 35, ZX = 56$$

In Exercises 5 and 6, use $\triangle ABC$.

5. The shortest side of a triangle similar to $\triangle ABC$ is 15 units long. Find the other side lengths of the triangle.

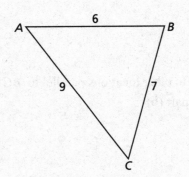

6. The longest side of a triangle similar to $\triangle ABC$ is 6 units long. Find the other side lengths of the triangle.

8.6 Proportionality Theorems
For use with Exploration 8.6

Essential Question What proportionality relationships exist in a triangle intersected by an angle bisector or by a line parallel to one of the sides?

---

1 **EXPLORATION:** Discovering a Proportionality Relationship

Go to *BigIdeasMath.com* for an interactive tool to investigate this exploration.

Work with a partner. Use dynamic geometry software to draw any $\triangle ABC$.

    a. Construct $\overline{DE}$ parallel to $\overline{BC}$ with endpoints on $\overline{AB}$ and $\overline{AC}$, respectively.

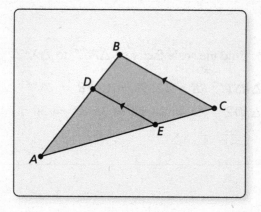

    b. Compare the ratios of AD to BD and AE to CE.

    c. Move $\overline{DE}$ to other locations parallel to $\overline{BC}$ with endpoints on $\overline{AB}$ and $\overline{AC}$, and repeat part (b).

    d. Change $\triangle ABC$ and repeat parts (a)–(c) several times. Write a conjecture that summarizes your results.

8.6 **Proportionality Theorems** (continued)

2 EXPLORATION: Discovering a Proportionality Relationship

Go to *BigIdeasMath.com* for an interactive tool to investigate this exploration.

Work with a partner. Use dynamic geometry software to draw any $\triangle ABC$.

    a. Bisect $\angle B$ and plot point D at the intersection of the angle bisector and $\overline{AC}$.

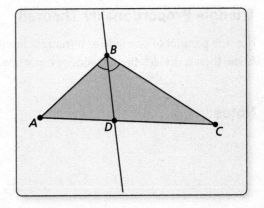

    b. Compare the ratios of AD to DC and BA to BC.

    c. Change $\triangle ABC$ and repeat parts (a) and (b) several times. Write a conjecture that summarizes your results.

Communicate Your Answer

    3. What proportionality relationships exist in a triangle intersected by an angle bisector or by a line parallel to one of the sides?

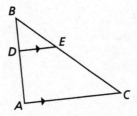

    4. Use the figure at the right to write a proportion.

8.6   Notetaking with Vocabulary
For use after Lesson 8.6

In your own words, write the meaning of each vocabulary term.

directed line segment

Theorems

Triangle Proportionality Theorem

If a line parallel to one side of a triangle intersects the other two
sides, then it divides the two sides proportionally.

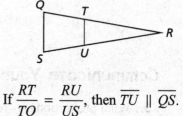

Notes:

If $\overline{TU} \parallel \overline{QS}$, then $\dfrac{RT}{TQ} = \dfrac{RU}{US}$.

Converse of the Triangle Proportionality Theorem

If a line divides two sides of a triangle proportionally, then it is
parallel to the third side.

Notes:

If $\dfrac{RT}{TQ} = \dfrac{RU}{US}$, then $\overline{TU} \parallel \overline{QS}$.

Name_____ Date_____

Three Parallel Lines Theorem

If three parallel lines intersect two transversals, then they divide
the transversals proportionally.

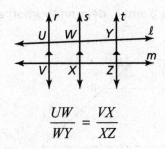

Notes:

$$\frac{UW}{WY} = \frac{VX}{XZ}$$

Triangle Angle Bisector Theorem

If a ray bisects an angle of a triangle, then it divides the opposite
side into segments whose lengths are proportional to the lengths
of the other two sides.

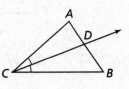

Notes:

$$\frac{AD}{DB} = \frac{CA}{CB}$$

Extra Practice

In Exercises 1 and 2, find the length of $\overline{AB}$.

1.

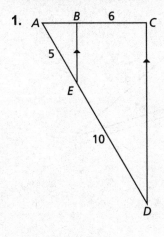

2.

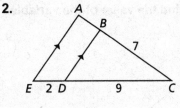

8.6 Notetaking with Vocabulary (continued)

In Exercises 3 and 4, determine whether $\overline{AB} \parallel \overline{XY}$.

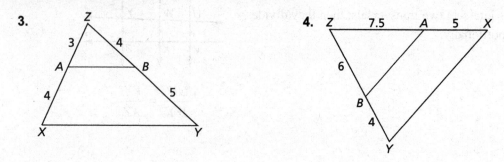

3.

4.

In Exercises 5–7, use the diagram to complete the proportion.

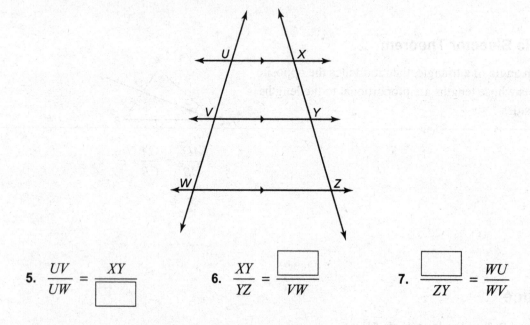

5. $\dfrac{UV}{UW} = \dfrac{XY}{\boxed{}}$

6. $\dfrac{XY}{YZ} = \dfrac{\boxed{}}{VW}$

7. $\dfrac{\boxed{}}{ZY} = \dfrac{WU}{WV}$

In Exercises 8 and 9, find the value of the variable.

8.

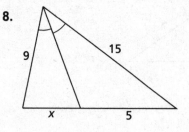

9.

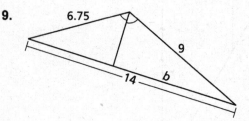

Name_____ Date_____

Chapter 9

Maintaining Mathematical Proficiency

Simplify the expression.

1. $\sqrt{500}$

2. $\sqrt{189}$

3. $\sqrt{252}$

4. $\dfrac{4}{\sqrt{3}}$

5. $\dfrac{11}{\sqrt{5}}$

6. $\dfrac{8}{\sqrt{2}}$

Solve the proportion.

7. $\dfrac{x}{21} = \dfrac{2}{7}$

8. $\dfrac{x}{5} = \dfrac{9}{4}$

9. $\dfrac{3}{x} = \dfrac{14}{42}$

10. $\dfrac{20}{27} = \dfrac{6}{x}$

11. $\dfrac{x-4}{5} = \dfrac{10}{9}$

12. $\dfrac{15}{5x+25} = \dfrac{3}{9}$

13. The Pythagorean Theorem states that $a^2 + b^2 = c^2$, where a and b are legs of a right triangle and c is the hypotenuse. Are you able to simplify the Pythagorean Theorem further to say that $a + b = c$? Explain.

9.1 The Pythagorean Theorem
For use with Exploration 9.1

Essential Question How can you prove the Pythagorean Theorem?

1 EXPLORATION: Proving the Pythagorean Theorem without Words

Go to *BigIdeasMath.com* for an interactive tool to investigate this exploration.

Work with a partner.

a. Draw and cut out a right triangle with legs *a* and *b*, and hypotenuse *c*.

b. Make three copies of your right triangle. Arrange all four triangles to form a large square as shown.

c. Find the area of the large square in terms of *a*, *b*, and *c* by summing the areas of the triangles and the small square.

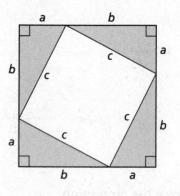

d. Copy the large square. Divide it into two smaller squares and two equally-sized rectangles, as shown.

e. Find the area of the large square in terms of *a* and *b* by summing the areas of the rectangles and the smaller squares.

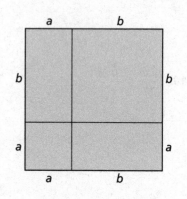

f. Compare your answers to parts (c) and (e). Explain how this proves the Pythagorean Theorem.

9.1   **The Pythagorean Theorem** (continued)

2   **EXPLORATION:** Proving the Pythagorean Theorem

Work with a partner.

     a. Consider the triangle shown.

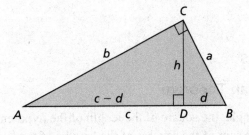

     b. Explain why $\triangle ABC$, $\triangle ACD$, and $\triangle CBD$ are similar.

     c. Write a two-column proof using the similar triangles in part (b) to prove that $a^2 + b^2 = c^2$.

Communicate Your Answer

     3. How can you prove the Pythagorean Theorem?

     4. Use the Internet or some other resource to find a way to prove the Pythagorean Theorem that is different from Explorations 1 and 2.

9.1 Notetaking with Vocabulary
For use after Lesson 9.1

In your own words, write the meaning of each vocabulary term.

Pythagorean triple

Theorems

Pythagorean Theorem

In a right triangle, the square of the length of the hypotenuse is equal to the sum of the squares of the lengths of the legs.

Notes:

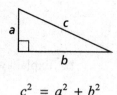

$$c^2 = a^2 + b^2$$

Core Concepts

Common Pythagorean Triples and Some of Their Multiples

3, 4, 5	**5, 12, 13**	**8, 15, 17**	**7, 24, 25**
6, 8, 10	10, 24, 26	16, 30, 34	14, 48, 50
9, 12, 15	15, 36, 39	24, 45, 51	21, 72, 75
$3x, 4x, 5x$	$5x, 12x, 13x$	$8x, 15x, 17x$	$7x, 24x, 25x$

The most common Pythagorean triples are in bold. The other triples are the result of multiplying each integer in a bold-faced triple by the same factor.

Notes:

9.1 **Notetaking with Vocabulary** (continued)

Theorems

Converse of the Pythagorean Theorem

If the square of the length of the longest side of a triangle
is equal to the sum of the squares of the lengths of the other
two sides, then the triangle is a right triangle.

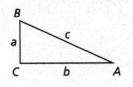

If $c^2 = a^2 + b^2$, then $\triangle ABC$ is a right triangle.

Notes:

Pythagorean Inequalities Theorem

For any $\triangle ABC$, where c is the length of the longest side, the following statements
are true.

If $c^2 < a^2 + b^2$, then $\triangle ABC$ is acute.   If $c^2 > a^2 + b^2$, then $\triangle ABC$ is obtuse.

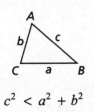

$$c^2 < a^2 + b^2$$

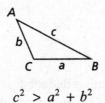

$$c^2 > a^2 + b^2$$

Notes:

9.1 **Notetaking with Vocabulary** (continued)

Extra Practice

In Exercises 1–6, find the value of x. Then tell whether the side lengths form a
Pythagorean triple.

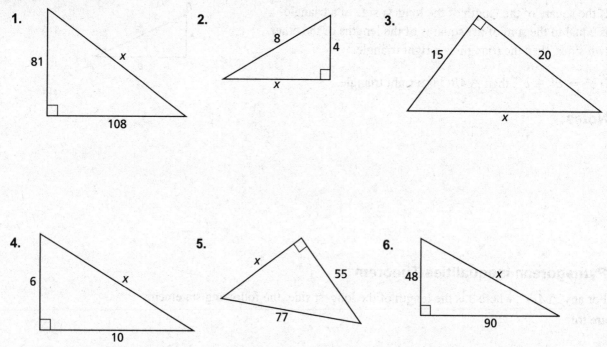

1.
81
x
108

2.
8
4
x

3.
15
20
x

4.
6
x
10

5.
x
55
77

6.
48
x
90

7. From school, you biked 1.2 miles due south and then 0.5 mile due east to your house.
    If you had biked home on the street that runs directly diagonal from your school to your
    house, how many fewer miles would you have biked?

In Exercises 8 and 9, verify that the segment lengths form a triangle. Is the triangle
acute, *right*, or *obtuse*?

8. 90, 216, and 234

9. 1, 1, and $\sqrt{3}$

9.2 **Special Right Triangles**
For use with Exploration 9.2

Essential Question What is the relationship among the side lengths of 45°-45°-90° triangles? 30°-60°-90° triangles?

---

1 **EXPLORATION:** Side Ratios of an Isosceles Right Triangle

Go to *BigIdeasMath.com* for an interactive tool to investigate this exploration.

Work with a partner.

    a. Use dynamic geometry software to construct an isosceles right triangle with a leg length of 4 units.

    b. Find the acute angle measures. Explain why this triangle is called a 45°-45°-90° triangle.

    c. Find the exact ratios of the side lengths (using square roots).

$$\frac{AB}{AC} = \underline{\hspace{2cm}}$$

$$\frac{AB}{BC} = \underline{\hspace{2cm}}$$

$$\frac{AC}{BC} = \underline{\hspace{2cm}}$$

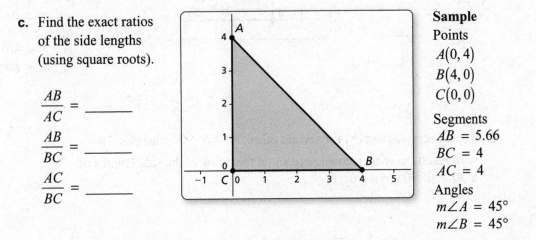

Sample
Points
$A(0, 4)$
$B(4, 0)$
$C(0, 0)$

Segments
$AB = 5.66$
$BC = 4$
$AC = 4$

Angles
$m\angle A = 45°$
$m\angle B = 45°$

    d. Repeat parts (a) and (c) for several other isosceles right triangles. Use your results to write a conjecture about the ratios of the side lengths of an isosceles right triangle.

Name_____ Date _____

2 EXPLORATION: Side Ratios of a 30°-60°-90° Triangle

Go to *BigIdeasMath.com* for an interactive tool to investigate this exploration.

Work with a partner.

a. Use dynamic geometry software to construct a right triangle with acute angle measures of 30° and 60° (a 30°-60°-90° triangle), where the shorter leg length is 3 units.

b. Find the exact ratios of the side lengths (using square roots).

$$\frac{AB}{AC} = \underline{\hspace{1.5cm}}$$

$$\frac{AB}{BC} = \underline{\hspace{1.5cm}}$$

$$\frac{AC}{BC} = \underline{\hspace{1.5cm}}$$

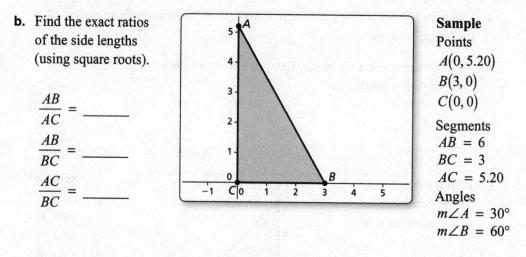

Sample
Points
$A(0, 5.20)$
$B(3, 0)$
$C(0, 0)$

Segments
$AB = 6$
$BC = 3$
$AC = 5.20$

Angles
$m\angle A = 30°$
$m\angle B = 60°$

c. Repeat parts (a) and (b) for several other 30°-60°-90° triangles. Use your results to write a conjecture about the ratios of the side lengths of a 30°-60°-90° triangle.

Communicate Your Answer

3. What is the relationship among the side lengths of 45°-45°-90° triangles? 30°-60°-90° triangles?

9.2 Notetaking with Vocabulary
For use after Lesson 9.2

In your own words, write the meaning of each vocabulary term.

isosceles triangle

Theorems

45°-45°-90° Triangle Theorem

In a 45°-45°-90° triangle, the hypotenuse is $\sqrt{2}$ times as long as each leg.

Notes:

hypotenuse = leg • $\sqrt{2}$

30°-60°-90° Triangle Theorem

In a 30°-60°-90° triangle, the hypotenuse is twice as long as the shorter leg, and the longer leg is $\sqrt{3}$ times as long as the shorter leg.

Notes:

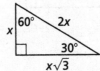

hypotenuse = shorter leg • 2

longer leg = shorter leg • $\sqrt{3}$

9.2   Notetaking with Vocabulary (continued)

Extra Practice

In Exercises 1–4, find the value of *x*. Write your answer in simplest form.

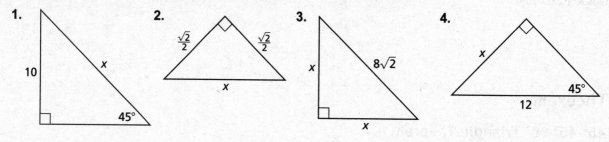

1.

10

x

45°

2.

$\frac{\sqrt{2}}{2}$ $\frac{\sqrt{2}}{2}$

x

3.

x

$8\sqrt{2}$

x

4.

x

45°

12

In Exercises 5–7, find the values of *x* and *y*. Write your answers in simplest form.

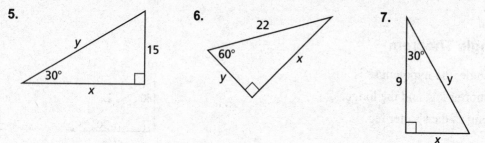

5.

y

15

30°

x

6.

22

60°

x

y

7.

30°

9

y

x

Name_____ Date_____

In Exercises 8 and 9, sketch the figure that is described. Find the indicated length.
Round decimal answers to the nearest tenth.

8. The length of a diagonal in a square is 32 inches. Find the perimeter of the square.

9. An isosceles triangle with 30° base angles has an altitude of $\sqrt{3}$ meters. Find the length of the base of the isosceles triangle.

10. Find the area of $\triangle DEF$. Round decimal answers to the nearest tenth.

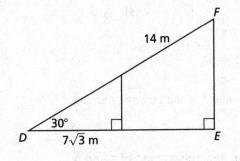

9.3 Similar Right Triangles
For use with Exploration 9.3

Essential Question How are altitudes and geometric means of right triangles related?

> **1** **EXPLORATION:** Writing a Conjecture

Go to *BigIdeasMath.com* for an interactive tool to investigate this exploration.

Work with a partner.

a. Use dynamic geometry software to construct right $\triangle ABC$, as shown. Draw $\overline{CD}$ so that it is an altitude from the right angle to the hypotenuse of $\triangle ABC$.

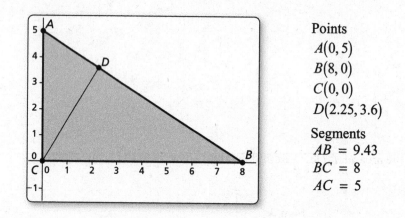

Points
$A(0, 5)$
$B(8, 0)$
$C(0, 0)$
$D(2.25, 3.6)$

Segments
$AB = 9.43$
$BC = 8$
$AC = 5$

b. The **geometric mean** of two positive numbers a and b is the positive number x that satisfies

$$\frac{a}{x} = \frac{x}{b}.$$

x is the geometric mean of a and b.

Write a proportion involving the side lengths of $\triangle CBD$ and $\triangle ACD$ so that CD is the geometric mean of two of the other side lengths. Use similar triangles to justify your steps.

9.3 **Similar Right Triangles** (continued)

1 **EXPLORATION:** Writing a Conjecture (continued)

    c. Use the proportion you wrote in part (b) to find *CD*.

    d. Generalize the proportion you wrote in part (b). Then write a conjecture about how the geometric mean is related to the altitude from the right angle to the hypotenuse of a right triangle.

2 **EXPLORATION:** Comparing Geometric and Arithmetic Means

Go to *BigIdeasMath.com* for an interactive tool to investigate this exploration.

Work with a partner. Use a spreadsheet to find the arithmetic mean and the geometric mean of several pairs of positive numbers. Compare the two means. What do you notice?

	A	B	C	D
	a	b	Arithmetic Mean	Geometric Mean
1				
2	3	4	3.5	3.464
3	4	5		
4	6	7		
5	0.5	0.5		
6	0.4	0.8		
7	2	5		
8	1	4		
9	9	16		
10	10	100		
11				

Communicate Your Answer

    3. How are altitudes and geometric means of right triangles related?

9.3 Notetaking with Vocabulary
For use after Lesson 9.3

In your own words, write the meaning of each vocabulary term.

geometric mean

Theorems

Right Triangle Similarity Theorem

If the altitude is drawn to the hypotenuse of a right triangle, then the two triangles formed are similar to the original triangle and to each other.

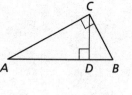

$\triangle CBD \sim \triangle ABC$, $\triangle ACD \sim \triangle ABC$, and $\triangle CBD \sim \triangle ACD$.

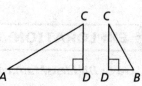

Notes:

Core Concepts

Geometric Mean

The **geometric mean** of two positive numbers a and b is the positive number x that satisfies $\dfrac{a}{x} = \dfrac{x}{b}$. So, $x^2 = ab$ and $x = \sqrt{ab}$.

Notes:

9.3   **Notetaking with Vocabulary** (continued)

Theorems

Geometric Mean (Altitude) Theorem

In a right triangle, the altitude from the right angle to the hypotenuse divides the hypotenuse into two segments.

The length of the altitude is the geometric mean of the lengths of the two segments of the hypotenuse.

$$CD^2 = AD \cdot BD$$

Notes:

Geometric Mean (Leg) Theorem

In a right triangle, the altitude from the right angle to the hypotenuse divides the hypotenuse into two segments.

The length of each leg of the right triangle is the geometric mean of the lengths of the hypotenuse and the segment of the hypotenuse that is adjacent to the leg.

$$CB^2 = DB \cdot AB$$
$$AC^2 = AD \cdot AB$$

Notes:

Name _____ Date _____

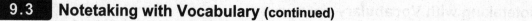

9.3 Notetaking with Vocabulary (continued)

Extra Practice

In Exercises 1 and 2, identify the similar triangles.

1.

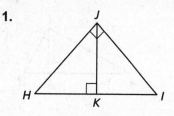

2.

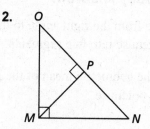

In Exercises 3 and 4, find the geometric mean of the two numbers.

3. 2 and 6

4. 5 and 45

In Exercises 5–8, find the value of the variable.

5.

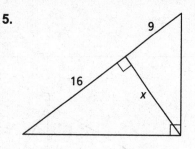

6.

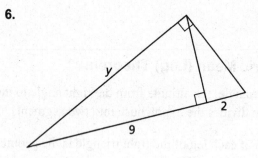

7.

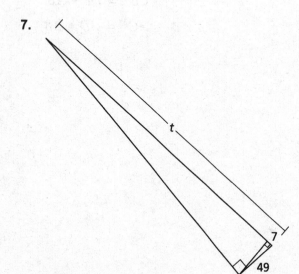

8.

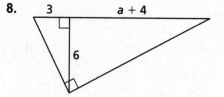

9.4 The Tangent Ratio
For use with Exploration 9.4

Essential Question How is a right triangle used to find the tangent of an acute angle? Is there a unique right triangle that must be used?

Let $\triangle ABC$ be a right triangle with acute $\angle A$.
The *tangent* of $\angle A$ (written as $\tan A$) is defined as follows.

$$\tan A = \frac{\text{length of leg opposite } \angle A}{\text{length of leg adjacent to } \angle A} = \frac{BC}{AC}$$

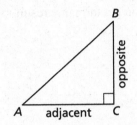

---

1 EXPLORATION: Calculating a Tangent Ratio

Go to *BigIdeasMath.com* for an interactive tool to investigate this exploration.

Work with a partner. Use dynamic geometry software.

a. Construct $\triangle ABC$, as shown. Construct segments perpendicular to $\overline{AC}$ to form right triangles that share vertex A and are similar to $\triangle ABC$ with vertices, as shown.

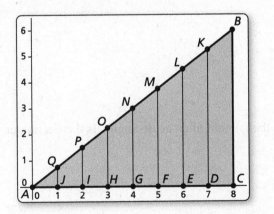

Sample
Points
$A(0, 0)$
$B(8, 6)$
$C(8, 0)$
Angle
$m\angle BAC = 36.87°$

b. Calculate each given ratio to complete the table for the decimal value of $\tan A$ for each right triangle. What can you conclude?

Ratio	$\dfrac{BC}{AC}$	$\dfrac{KD}{AD}$	$\dfrac{LE}{AE}$	$\dfrac{MF}{AF}$	$\dfrac{NG}{AG}$	$\dfrac{OH}{AH}$	$\dfrac{PI}{AI}$	$\dfrac{QJ}{AJ}$
tan A								

9.4 **The Tangent Ratio** (continued)

---

2 **EXPLORATION:** Using a Calculator

Work with a partner. Use a calculator that has a tangent key to calculate the tangent of $36.87°$. Do you get the same result as in Exploration 1? Explain.

Communicate Your Answer

3. Repeat Exploration 1 for $\triangle ABC$ with vertices $A(0, 0)$, $B(8, 5)$, and $C(8, 0)$.

Construct the seven perpendicular segments so that not all of them intersect $\overline{AC}$ at integer values of x. Discuss your results.

4. How is a right triangle used to find the tangent of an acute angle? Is there a unique right triangle that must be used?

Name_____ Date_____

Notetaking with Vocabulary
For use after Lesson 9.4

In your own words, write the meaning of each vocabulary term.

trigonometric ratio

tangent

angle of elevation

Core Concepts

Tangent Ratio

Let $\triangle ABC$ be a right triangle with acute $\angle A$.

The tangent of $\angle A$ (written as $\tan A$) is defined as follows.

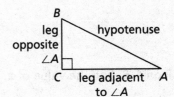

$$\tan A = \frac{\text{length of leg opposite } \angle A}{\text{length of leg adjacent to } \angle A} = \frac{BC}{AC}$$

Notes:

9.4 Notetaking with Vocabulary (continued)

Extra Practice

In Exercises 1–3, find the tangents of the acute angles in the right triangle. Write each answer as a fraction and as a decimal rounded to four decimal places.

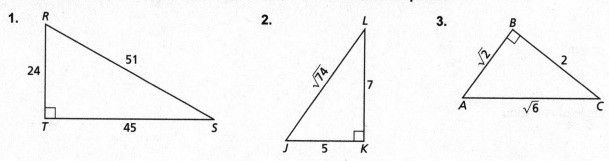

1.

2.

3.

In Exercises 4–6, find the value of *x*. Round your answer to the nearest tenth.

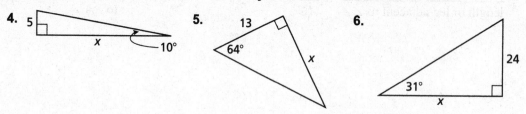

4.

5.

6.

7. In $\triangle CDE$, $\angle E = 90°$ and $\tan C = \dfrac{4}{3}$. Find $\tan D$? Write your answer as a fraction.

9.4 **Notetaking with Vocabulary** (continued)

8. An environmentalist wants to measure the width of a river to monitor its erosion. From point A, she walks downstream 100 feet and measures the angle from this point to point C to be 40°.

   a. How wide is the river? Round to the nearest tenth.

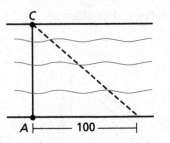

   b. One year later, the environmentalist returns to measure the same river. From point A, she again walks downstream 100 feet and measures the angle from this point to point C to be now 51°. By how many feet has the width of the river increased?

9. A boy flies a kite at an angle of elevation of 18°. The kite reaches its maximum height 300 feet away from the boy. What is the maximum height of the kite? Round to the nearest tenth.

10. Find the perimeter of the figure.

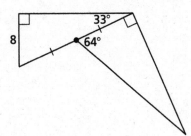

9.5 The Sine and Cosine Ratios

For use with Exploration 9.5

Essential Question   How is a right triangle used to find the sine and cosine of an acute angle? Is there a unique right triangle that must be used?

Let $\triangle ABC$ be a right triangle with acute $\angle A$. The *sine* of $\angle A$ and *cosine* of $\angle A$ (written as $\sin A$ and $\cos A$, respectively) are defined as follows.

$$\sin A = \frac{\text{length of leg opposite } \angle A}{\text{length of hypotenuse}} = \frac{BC}{AB}$$

$$\cos A = \frac{\text{length of leg adjacent to } \angle A}{\text{length of hypotenuse}} = \frac{AC}{AB}$$

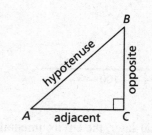

---

1   EXPLORATION: Calculating Sine and Cosine Ratios

Go to *BigIdeasMath.com* for an interactive tool to investigate this exploration.

Work with a partner. Use dynamic geometry software.

a. Construct $\triangle ABC$, as shown. Construct segments perpendicular to $\overline{AC}$ to form right triangles that share vertex A and are similar to $\triangle ABC$ with vertices, as shown.

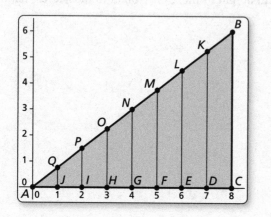

Sample
Points
$A(0, 0)$
$B(8, 6)$
$C(8, 0)$
Angle
$m\angle BAC = 36.87°$

9.5 **The Sine and Cosine Ratios** (continued)

---

1 **EXPLORATION: Calculating Sine and Cosine Ratios** (continued)

b. Calculate each given ratio to complete the table for the decimal values of sin A and cos A for each right triangle. What can you conclude?

Sine ratio	$\dfrac{BC}{AB}$	$\dfrac{KD}{AK}$	$\dfrac{LE}{AL}$	$\dfrac{MF}{AM}$	$\dfrac{NG}{AN}$	$\dfrac{OH}{AO}$	$\dfrac{PI}{AP}$	$\dfrac{QJ}{AQ}$
sin A								
Cosine ratio	$\dfrac{AC}{AB}$	$\dfrac{AD}{AK}$	$\dfrac{AE}{AL}$	$\dfrac{AF}{AM}$	$\dfrac{AG}{AN}$	$\dfrac{AH}{AO}$	$\dfrac{AI}{AP}$	$\dfrac{AJ}{AQ}$
cos A								

Communicate Your Answer

2. How is a right triangle used to find the sine and cosine of an acute angle? Is there a unique right triangle that must be used?

3. In Exploration 1, what is the relationship between $\angle A$ and $\angle B$ in terms of their measures? Find sin B and cos B. How are these two values related to sin A and cos A? Explain why these relationships exist.

9.5 Notetaking with Vocabulary
For use after Lesson 9.5

In your own words, write the meaning of each vocabulary term.

sine

cosine

angle of depression

Core Concepts

Sine and Cosine Ratios

Let $\triangle ABC$ be a right triangle with acute $\angle A$.
The sine of $\angle A$ and cosine of $\angle A$ (written as
$\sin A$ and $\cos A$) are defined as follows.

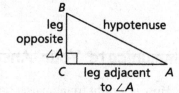

$$\sin A = \frac{\text{length of leg opposite } \angle A}{\text{length of hypotenuse}} = \frac{BC}{AB}$$

$$\cos A = \frac{\text{length of leg adjacent to } \angle A}{\text{length of hypotenuse}} = \frac{AC}{AB}$$

Notes:

Name_____ Date_____

Sine and Cosine of Complementary Angles

The sine of an acute angle is equal to the cosine of its complement. The cosine of an acute angle is equal to the sine of its complement.

Let A and B be complementary angles. Then the following statements are true.

$$\sin A = \cos(90° - A) = \cos B \qquad \sin B = \cos(90° - B) = \cos A$$
$$\cos A = \sin(90° - A) = \sin B \qquad \cos B = \sin(90° - B) = \sin A$$

Notes:

Extra Practice

In Exercises 1–3, find sin *F*, sin *G*, cos *F*, and cos *G*. Write each answer as a fraction and as a decimal rounded to four places.

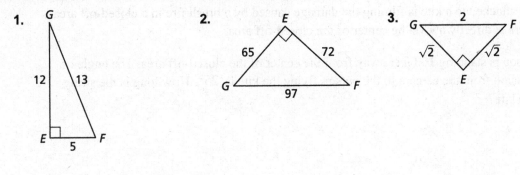

1.

2.

3.

In Exercises 4–6, write the expression in terms of cosine.

4. sin 9°

5. sin 30°

6. sin 77°

9.5 Notetaking with Vocabulary (continued)

In Exercises 7–9, write the expression in terms of sine.

7. $\cos 15°$

8. $\cos 83°$

9. $\cos 45°$

In Exercises 10–13, find the value of each variable using sine and cosine. Round your answers to the nearest tenth.

10.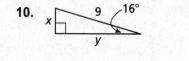

11.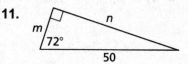

12.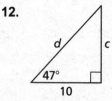

13.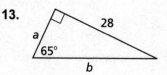

14. A camera attached to a kite is filming the damage caused by a brush fire in a closed-off area. The camera is directly above the center of the closed-off area.

    a. A person is standing 100 feet away from the center of the closed-off area. The angle of depression from the camera to the person flying the kite is 25°. How long is the string on the kite?

    b. If the string on the kite is 200 feet long, how far away must the person flying the kite stand from the center of the closed-off area, assuming the same angle of depression of 25°, to film the damage?

9.6 Solving Right Triangles

For use with Exploration 9.6

Essential Question When you know the lengths of the sides of a right triangle, how can you find the measures of the two acute angles?

---

1   EXPLORATION: Solving Special Right Triangles

Go to *BigIdeasMath.com* for an interactive tool to investigate this exploration.

Work with a partner. Use the figures to find the values of the sine and cosine of ∠A and ∠B. Use these values to find the measures of ∠A and ∠B. Use dynamic geometry software to verify your answers.

a.

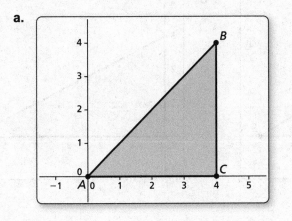

b.

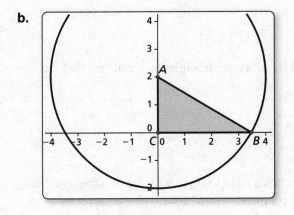

9.6   **Solving Right Triangles** (continued)

---

2   **EXPLORATION:** Solving Right Triangles

Go to *BigIdeasMath.com* for an interactive tool to investigate this exploration.

Work with a partner. You can use a calculator to find the measure of an angle when you know the value of the sine, cosine, or tangent of the angle. Use the inverse sine, inverse cosine, or inverse tangent feature of your calculator to approximate the measures of $\angle A$ and $\angle B$ to the nearest tenth of a degree. Then use dynamic geometry software to verify your answers.

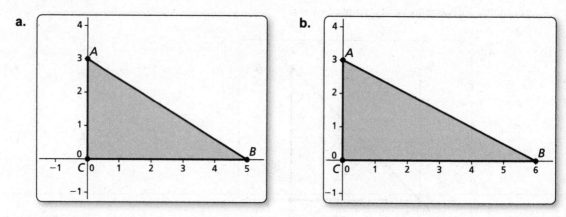

a.

b.

Communicate Your Answer

3. When you know the lengths of the sides of a right triangle, how can you find the measures of the two acute angles?

4. A ladder leaning against a building forms a right triangle with the building and the ground. The legs of the right triangle (in meters) form a 5-12-13 Pythagorean triple. Find the measures of the two acute angles to the nearest tenth of a degree.

9.6 Notetaking with Vocabulary
For use after Lesson 9.6

In your own words, write the meaning of each vocabulary term.

inverse tangent

inverse sine

inverse cosine

solve a right triangle

Core Concepts

Inverse Trigonometric Ratios

Let $\angle A$ be an acute angle.

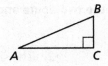

Inverse Tangent   If $\tan A = x$, then $\tan^{-1} x = m\angle A$. $\tan^{-1}\dfrac{BC}{AC} = m\angle A$

Inverse Sine   If $\sin A = y$, then $\sin^{-1} y = m\angle A$. $\sin^{-1}\dfrac{BC}{AB} = m\angle A$

Inverse Cosine   If $\cos A = z$, then $\cos^{-1} z = m\angle A$. $\cos^{-1}\dfrac{AC}{AB} = m\angle A$

Notes:

Name _____ Date _____

Solving a Right Triangle

To **solve a right triangle** means to find all unknown side lengths and angle measures.
You can solve a right triangle when you know either of the following.

- two side lengths

- one side length and the measure of one acute angle

Notes:

Extra Practice

In Exercises 1 and 2, determine which of the two acute angles has the given trigonometric ratio.

1. The cosine of the angle is $\frac{24}{25}$.

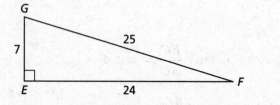

2. The sine of the angle is about 0.38.

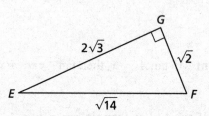

In Exercises 3–6, let ∠H be an acute angle. Use a calculator to approximate the measure of ∠H to the nearest tenth of a degree.

3. $\sin H = 0.2$ **4.** $\tan H = 1$ **5.** $\cos H = 0.33$ **6.** $\sin H = 0.89$

9.6   Notetaking with Vocabulary (continued)

In Exercises 7–10, solve the right triangle. Round decimal answers to the nearest tenth.

7.

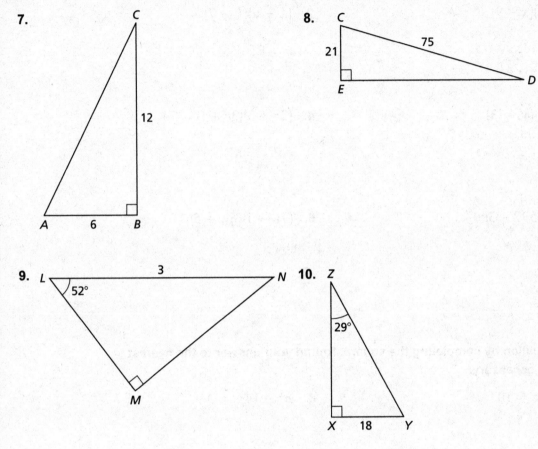

8.

75

21

9.   L   3   N

52°

M

10.   Z

29°

X   18   Y

11.   A boat is pulled in by a winch on a dock 12 feet above the deck of the boat. When the winch is fully extended to 25 feet, what is the angle of elevation from the boat to the winch?

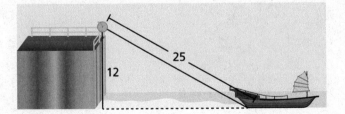

25

12

Chapter 10 Maintaining Mathematical Proficiency

Find the product.

1. $(x - 4)(x - 9)$

2. $(k + 6)(k - 7)$

3. $(y + 5)(y - 13)$

4. $(2r + 3)(3r + 1)$

5. $(4m - 5)(2 - 3m)$

6. $(7w - 1)(6w + 5)$

Solve the equation by completing the square. Round your answer to the nearest hundredth, if necessary.

7. $x^2 + 6x = 10$

8. $p^2 - 14p = 5$

9. $z^2 + 16z + 7 = 0$

10. $z^2 + 5z - 2 = 0$

11. $x^2 + 2x - 5 = 0$

12. $c^2 - c - 1 = 0$

10.1 Lines and Segments That Intersect Circles
For use with Exploration 10.1

Essential Question What are the definitions of the lines and segments that intersect a circle?

---

1 EXPLORATION: Lines and Line Segments That Intersect Circles

Work with a partner. The drawing at the right shows five lines or segments that intersect a circle. Use the relationships shown to write a definition for each type of line or segment. Then use the Internet or some other resource to verify your definitions.

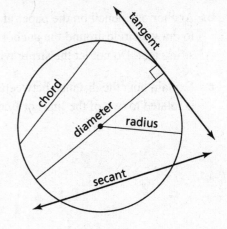

Chord:

Secant:

Tangent:

Radius:

Diameter:

10.1 **Lines and Segments That Intersect Circles** (continued)

2 **EXPLORATION:** Using String to Draw a Circle

Work with a partner. Use two pencils, a piece of string, and a piece of paper.

    a. Tie the two ends of the piece of string loosely around the two pencils.

    b. Anchor one pencil on the paper at the center of the circle. Use the other pencil to draw a circle around the anchor point while using slight pressure to keep the string taut. Do not let the string wind around either pencil.

    c. Explain how the distance between the two pencil points as you draw the circle is related to two of the lines or line segments you defined in Exploration 1.

Communicate Your Answer

    3. What are the definitions of the lines and segments that intersect a circle?

    4. Of the five types of lines and segments in Exploration 1, which one is a subset of another? Explain.

    5. Explain how to draw a circle with a diameter of 8 inches.

Name_____ Date_____

10.1 Notetaking with Vocabulary
For use after Lesson 10.1

In your own words, write the meaning of each vocabulary term.

circle

center

radius

chord

diameter

secant

tangent

point of tangency

tangent circles

concentric circles

common tangent

Notes:

10.1 Notetaking with Vocabulary (continued)

Core Concepts

Lines and Segments That Intersect Circles

A segment whose endpoints are the center and any point on a circle is a
radius.

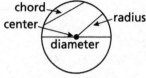

A **chord** is a segment whose endpoints are on a circle. A **diameter** is a chord
that contains the center of the circle.

A **secant** is a line that intersects a circle in two points.

A **tangent** is a line in the plane of a circle that intersects the circle in exactly
one point, the **point of tangency**. The *tangent ray* $\overrightarrow{AB}$ and the *tangent
segment* $\overline{AB}$ are also called tangents.

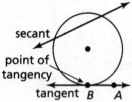
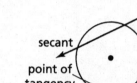

Notes:

Coplanar Circles and Common Tangents

In a plane, two circles can intersect in two points, one point, or no points. Coplanar
circles that intersect in one point are called **tangent circles**. Coplanar circles that have a
common center are called **concentric circles**.

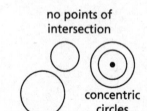

2 points of
intersection

1 point of intersection
(tangent circles)

no points of
intersection

concentric
circles

A line or segment that is tangent to two coplanar circles is called a **common tangent**. A
common internal tangent intersects the segment that joins the centers of the two circles.
A *common external tangent* does not intersect the segment that joins the centers of the
two circles.

Notes:

10.1 **Notetaking with Vocabulary** (continued)

Extra Practice

In Exercises 1–6, use the diagram.

1. Name two radii.

2. Name a chord.

3. Name a diameter.

4. Name a secant.

5. Name a tangent.

6. Name a point of tangency.

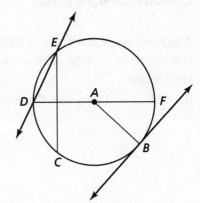

In Exercises 7 and 8, use the diagram.

7. Tell how many common tangents the circles have and draw them.

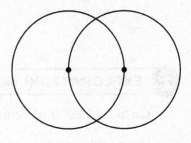

8. Tell whether each common tangent identified in Exercise 7 is internal or external.

In Exercises 9 and 10, point *D* is a point of tangency.

9. Find *BD*.

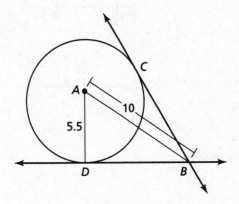

10. Point *C* is also a point of tangency. If $BC = 4x + 6$, find the value of *x* to the nearest tenth.

10.2 Finding Arc Measures
For use with Exploration 10.2

Essential Question   How are circular arcs measured?

A **central angle** of a circle is an angle whose vertex is the center of the circle. A *circular arc* is a portion of a circle, as shown below. The measure of a circular arc is the measure of its central angle.

If $m\angle AOB < 180°$, then the circular arc is called a **minor arc** and is denoted by $\overset{\frown}{AB}$.

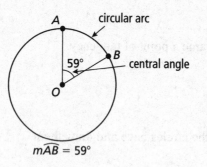

$m\overset{\frown}{AB} = 59°$

---

1   EXPLORATION: Measuring Circular Arcs

Go to *BigIdeasMath.com* for an interactive tool to investigate this exploration.

Work with a partner. Use dynamic geometry software to find the measure of $\overset{\frown}{BC}$. Verify your answers using trigonometry.

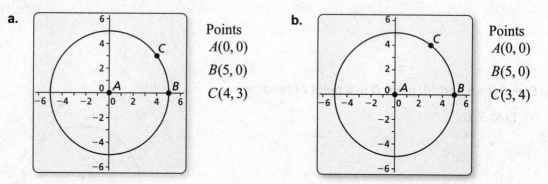

a.
Points
$A(0, 0)$
$B(5, 0)$
$C(4, 3)$

b.
Points
$A(0, 0)$
$B(5, 0)$
$C(3, 4)$

10.2 **Finding Arc Measures** (continued)

---

1 **EXPLORATION:** Measuring Circular Arcs (continued)

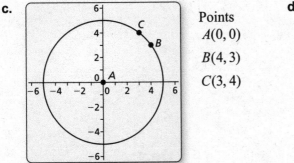

c.

Points
$A(0, 0)$
$B(4, 3)$
$C(3, 4)$

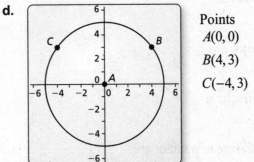

d.

Points
$A(0, 0)$
$B(4, 3)$
$C(-4, 3)$

Communicate Your Answer

2. How are circular arcs measured?

3. Use dynamic geometry software to draw a circular arc with the given measure.

   a. 30°   **b.** 45°

   c. 60°   **d.** 90°

10.2 Notetaking with Vocabulary
For use after Lesson 10.2

In your own words, write the meaning of each vocabulary term.

central angle

minor arc

major arc

semicircle

measure of a minor arc

measure of a major arc

adjacent arcs

congruent circles

congruent arcs

similar arcs

Core Concepts

Measuring Arcs

The **measure of a minor arc** is the measure of its central angle. The
expression $m\overarc{AB}$ is read as "the measure of arc AB."

The measure of the entire circle is 360°. The **measure of a major arc**
is the difference of 360° and the measure of the related minor arc. The
measure of a semicircle is 180°.

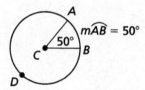

$m\overarc{AB} = 50°$

$m\overarc{ADB} = 360° - 50° = 310°$

Notes:

10.2 Notetaking with Vocabulary (continued)

Postulates

Arc Addition Postulate

The measure of an arc formed by two adjacent arcs is the sum of
the measures of the two arcs.

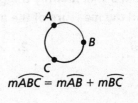

$$m\overarc{ABC} = m\overarc{AB} + m\overarc{BC}$$

Notes:

Theorems

Congruent Circles Theorem

Two circles are congruent circles if and only if they have the same radius.

Notes:

$\odot A \cong \odot B$ if and only if $\overline{AC} \cong \overline{BD}$.

Congruent Central Angles Theorem

In the same circle, or in congruent circles, two minor arcs are congruent
if and only if their corresponding central angles are congruent.

Notes:

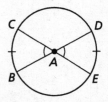

$\overarc{BC} \cong \overarc{DE}$ if and only if
$\angle BAC \cong \angle DAE$.

Similar Circles Theorem

All circles are similar.

Notes:

10.2 Notetaking with Vocabulary (continued)

Extra Practice

In Exercises 1–8, identify the given arc as a *major arc*, *minor arc*, or *semicircle*. Then find the measure of the arc.

1. $\overset{\frown}{AB}$

2. $\overset{\frown}{ABC}$

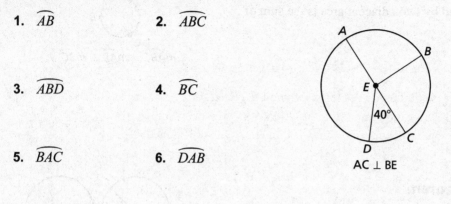

AC ⊥ BE

3. $\overset{\frown}{ABD}$

4. $\overset{\frown}{BC}$

5. $\overset{\frown}{BAC}$

6. $\overset{\frown}{DAB}$

7. $\overset{\frown}{AD}$

8. $\overset{\frown}{CD}$

9. In $\odot E$ above, tell whether $\overset{\frown}{ABC} \cong \overset{\frown}{ADC}$. Explain why or why not.

10. In $\odot K$, find the measure of $\overset{\frown}{DE}$.

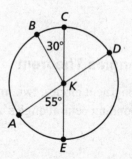

11. Find the value of x. Then find the measure of $\overset{\frown}{AB}$.

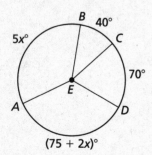

10.3 Using Chords
For use with Exploration 10.3

Essential Question What are two ways to determine when a chord is a diameter of a circle?

---

1 EXPLORATION: Drawing Diameters

Go to *BigIdeasMath.com* for an interactive tool to investigate this exploration.

Work with a partner. Use dynamic geometry software to construct a circle of radius 5 with center at the origin. Draw a diameter that has the given point as an endpoint. Explain how you know that the chord you drew is a diameter.

   a. $(4, 3)$ **b.** $(0, 5)$

   c. $(-3, 4)$ **d.** $(-5, 0)$

---

2 EXPLORATION: Writing a Conjecture about Chords

Go to *BigIdeasMath.com* for an interactive tool to investigate this exploration.

Work with a partner. Use dynamic geometry software to construct a chord $\overline{BC}$ of a circle A. Construct a chord on the perpendicular bisector of $\overline{BC}$. What do you notice? Change the original chord and the circle several times. Are your results always the same? Use your results to write a conjecture.

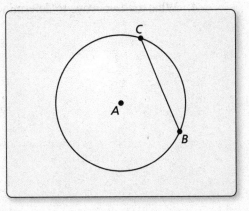

Name _____ Date _____

---

3 **EXPLORATION:** A Chord Perpendicular to a Diameter

Go to *BigIdeasMath.com* for an interactive tool to investigate this exploration.

Work with a partner. Use dynamic geometry software to construct a diameter $\overline{BC}$ of a circle A. Then construct a chord $\overline{DE}$ perpendicular to $\overline{BC}$ at point F. Find the lengths DF and EF. What do you notice? Change the chord perpendicular to $\overline{BC}$ and the circle several times. Do you always get the same results? Write a conjecture about a chord that is perpendicular to a diameter of a circle.

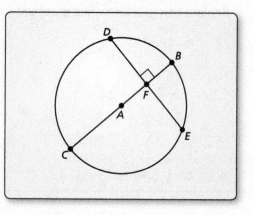

Communicate Your Answer

4. What are two ways to determine when a chord is a diameter of a circle?

10.3 Notetaking with Vocabulary
For use after Lesson 10.3

In your own words, write the meaning of each vocabulary term.

chord

arc

diameter

Theorems

Congruent Corresponding Chords Theorem

In the same circle, or in congruent circles, two minor arcs are congruent if and only if their corresponding chords are congruent.

Notes:

$\overset{\frown}{AB} \cong \overset{\frown}{CD}$ if and only if $\overline{AB} \cong \overline{CD}$.

10.3   Notetaking with Vocabulary (continued)

Perpendicular Chord Bisector Theorem

If a diameter of a circle is perpendicular to a chord, then
the diameter bisects the chord and its arc.

Notes:

If $\overline{EG}$ is a diameter and $\overline{EG} \perp \overline{DF}$,
then $\overline{HD} \cong \overline{HF}$ and $\overarc{GD} \cong \overarc{GF}$.

Perpendicular Chord Bisector Converse

If one chord of a circle is a perpendicular bisector of
another chord, then the first chord is a diameter.

Notes:

If $\overline{QS}$ is a perpendicular bisector of $\overline{TR}$,
then $\overline{QS}$ is a diameter of the circle.

Equidistant Chords Theorem

In the same circle, or in congruent circles, two chords
are congruent if and only if they are equidistant from the
center.

Notes:

$\overline{AB} \cong \overline{CD}$ if and only if $EF = EG$.

10.3 Notetaking with Vocabulary (continued)

Extra Practice

In Exercises 1–4, find the measure of the arc or chord in ⊙Q.

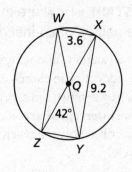

1. $m\widehat{WX}$

2. YZ

3. WZ

4. $m\widehat{XY}$

In Exercises 5 and 6, find the value of x.

5.

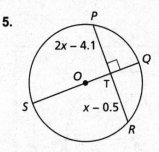

6.

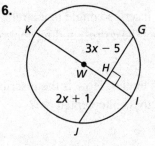

In Exercises 7 and 8, find the radius of the circle.

7.

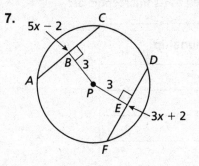

8.

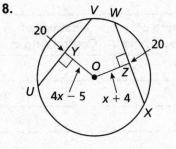

10.4 Inscribed Angles and Polygons
For use with Exploration 10.4

Essential Question How are inscribed angles related to their intercepted arcs? How are the angles of an inscribed quadrilateral related to each other?

An **inscribed angle** is an angle whose vertex is on a circle and whose sides contain chords of the circle. An arc that lies between two lines, rays, or segments is called an **intercepted arc**. Recall that a polygon is an inscribed polygon when all its vertices lie on a circle.

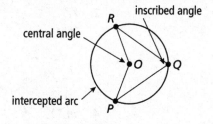

1 EXPLORATION: Inscribed Angles and Central Angles

Go to *BigIdeasMath.com* for an interactive tool to investigate this exploration.

Work with a partner. Use dynamic geometry software.

a. Construct an inscribed angle in a circle. Then construct the corresponding central angle.

Sample

b. Measure both angles. How is the inscribed angle related to its intercepted arc?

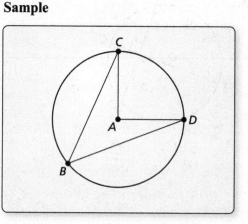

c. Repeat parts (a) and (b) several times. Record your results in the following table. Write a conjecture about how an inscribed angle is related to its intercepted arc.

Measure of Inscribed Angle	Measure of Central Angle	Relationship

10.4 **Inscribed Angles and Polygons** (continued)

---

2 **EXPLORATION:** A Quadrilateral with Inscribed Angles

Go to *BigIdeasMath.com* for an interactive tool to investigate this exploration.

Work with a partner. Use dynamic geometry software.

a. Construct a quadrilateral with each vertex on a circle.

Sample

b. Measure all four angles. What relationships do you notice?

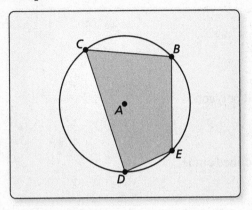

c. Repeat parts (a) and (b) several times. Record your results in the following table. Then write a conjecture that summarizes the data.

Angle Measure 1	Angle Measure 2	Angle Measure 3	Angle Measure 4

Communicate Your Answer

3. How are inscribed angles related to their intercepted arcs? How are the angles of an inscribed quadrilateral related to each other?

4. Quadrilateral *EFGH* is inscribed in $\odot C$, and $m\angle E = 80°$. What is $m\angle G$? Explain.

Name_____ Date _____

10.4 Notetaking with Vocabulary
For use after Lesson 10.4

In your own words, write the meaning of each vocabulary term.

inscribed angle

intercepted arc

subtend

inscribed polygon

circumscribed circle

Core Concepts

Inscribed Angle and Intercepted Arc

An **inscribed angle** is an angle whose vertex is on a circle and
whose sides contain chords of the circle. An arc that lies between
two lines, rays, or segments is called an **intercepted arc**. If the
endpoints of a chord or arc lie on the sides of an inscribed angle,
then the chord or arc is said to **subtend** the angle.

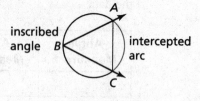

Notes:

$\angle B$ intercepts $\overparen{AC}$.
$\overline{AC}$ subtends $\angle B$.
$\overparen{AC}$ subtends $\angle B$.

Theorems

Measure of an Inscribed Angle Theorem

The measure of an inscribed angle is one-half the measure of its
intercepted arc.

Notes:

$$m\angle ADB = \frac{1}{2}m\overparen{AB}$$

328 **Integrated Mathematics II**
Student Journal

10.4 **Notetaking with Vocabulary** (continued)

Inscribed Angles of a Circle Theorem

If two inscribed angles of a circle intercept the same arc, then the
angles are congruent.

Notes:

$\angle ADB \cong \angle ACB$

Theorems

Inscribed Right Triangle Theorem

If a right triangle is inscribed in a circle, then the hypotenuse is a
diameter of the circle. Conversely, if one side of an inscribed
triangle is a diameter of the circle, then the triangle is a right
triangle and the angle opposite the diameter is the right angle.

Notes:

$m\angle ABC = 90°$ if and only if
$\overline{AC}$ is a diameter of the circle.

Inscribed Quadrilateral Theorem

A quadrilateral can be inscribed in a circle if and only if its
opposite angles are supplementary.

Notes:

D, E, F, and G lie on $\odot C$ if and only if
$m\angle D + m\angle F = m\angle E + m\angle G = 180°.$

10.4 Notetaking with Vocabulary (continued)

Extra Practice

In Exercises 1–5, use the diagram to find the indicated measure.

1. $m\angle A$

2. $m\angle C$

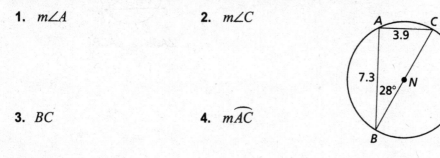

3. BC

4. $m\widehat{AC}$

5. $m\widehat{AB}$

6. Name two pairs of congruent angles.

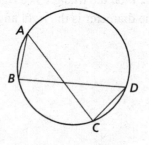

7. Find the value of each variable.

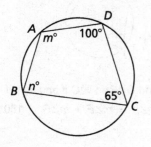

10.5 Angle Relationships in Circles
For use with Exploration 10.5

Essential Question When a chord intersects a tangent line or another chord, what relationships exist among the angles and arcs formed?

1 EXPLORATION: Angles Formed by a Chord and Tangent Line

Go to *BigIdeasMath.com* for an interactive tool to investigate this exploration.

Work with a partner. Use dynamic geometry software.   **Sample**

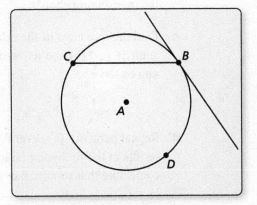

a. Construct a chord in a circle. At one of the endpoints of the chord, construct a tangent line to the circle.

b. Find the measures of the two angles formed by the chord and the tangent line.

c. Find the measures of the two circular arcs determined by the chord.

d. Repeat parts (a)–(c) several times. Record your results in the following table. Then write a conjecture that summarizes the data.

Angle Measure 1	Angle Measure 2	Circular Arc Measure 1	Circular Arc Measure 2

10.5 Angle Relationships in Circles (continued)

2 **EXPLORATION: Angles Formed by Intersecting Chords**

Go to *BigIdeasMath.com* for an interactive tool to investigate this exploration.

Work with a partner. Use dynamic geometry software.   **Sample**

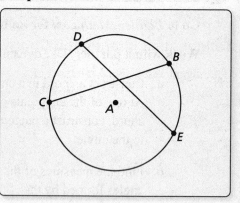

a. Construct two chords that intersect inside a circle.

b. Find the measure of one of the angles formed by the intersecting chords.

c. Find the measures of the arcs intercepted by the angle in part (b) and its vertical angle. What do you observe?

d. Repeat parts (a)–(c) several times. Record your results in the following table. Then write a conjecture that summarizes the data.

Angle Measure	Arc Measures	Observations

Communicate Your Answer

3. When a chord intersects a tangent line or another chord, what relationships exist among the angles and arcs formed?

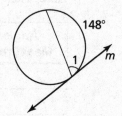

4. Line *m* is tangent to the circle in the figure at the right. Find the measure of ∠1.

5. Two chords intersect inside a circle to form a pair of vertical angles with measures of 55°. Find the sum of the measures of the arcs intercepted by the two angles.

10.5 Notetaking with Vocabulary
For use after Lesson 10.5

In your own words, write the meaning of each vocabulary term.

circumscribed angle

Theorems

Tangent and Intersected Chord Theorem

If a tangent and a chord intersect at a point on a circle, then the measure of each angle formed is one-half the measure of its intercepted arc.

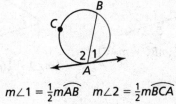

$$m\angle 1 = \tfrac{1}{2}m\widehat{AB} \quad m\angle 2 = \tfrac{1}{2}m\widehat{BCA}$$

Notes:

Core Concepts

Intersecting Lines and Circles

If two nonparallel lines intersect a circle, there are three places where the lines can intersect.

on the circle   inside the circle   outside the circle

Notes:

Theorems

Angles Inside the Circle Theorem

If two chords intersect *inside* a circle, then the measure of each angle is one-half the *sum* of the measures of the arcs intercepted by the angle and its vertical angle.

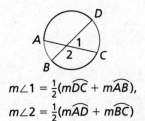

$$m\angle 1 = \tfrac{1}{2}(m\widehat{DC} + m\widehat{AB}),$$
$$m\angle 2 = \tfrac{1}{2}(m\widehat{AD} + m\widehat{BC})$$

Notes:

10.5 Notetaking with Vocabulary (continued)

Angles Outside the Circle Theorem

If a tangent and a secant, two tangents, or two secants
intersect *outside* a circle, then the measure of the angle formed
is one-half the *difference* of the measures of the intercepted
arcs.

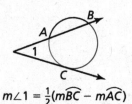

$$m\angle 1 = \tfrac{1}{2}(m\widehat{BC} - m\widehat{AC})$$

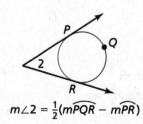

$$m\angle 2 = \tfrac{1}{2}(m\widehat{PQR} - m\widehat{PR})$$

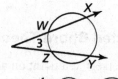

$$m\angle 3 = \tfrac{1}{2}(m\widehat{XY} - m\widehat{WZ})$$

Notes:

Core Concepts

Circumscribed Angle

A **circumscribed angle** is an angle whose sides are tangent to
a circle.

Notes:

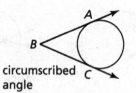

circumscribed
angle

Theorems

Circumscribed Angle Theorem

The measure of a circumscribed angle is equal to 180° minus
the measure of the central angle that intercepts the same arc.

Notes:

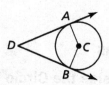

$$m\angle ADB = 180° - m\angle ACB$$

10.5 Notetaking with Vocabulary (continued)

Extra Practice

In Exercises 1–3, $\overrightarrow{CD}$ is tangent to the circle. Find the indicated measure.

1. $m\angle ABC$

2. $m\overarc{AB}$

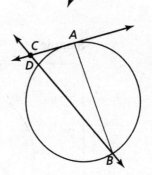

3. $m\overarc{AEB}$

In Exercises 4 and 5, $m\overarc{ADB} = 220°$ and $m\angle B = 21°$.
Find the indicated measure.

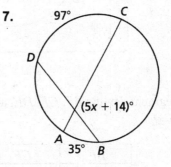

4. $m\overarc{AB}$

5. $m\angle ACB$

In Exercises 6–9, find the value of x.

6.

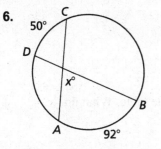

50°

7.

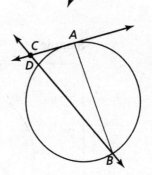

97°

$(5x + 14)°$

35°

8.

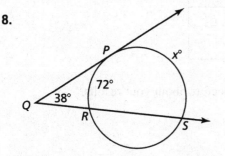

72°

38°

$x°$

9.

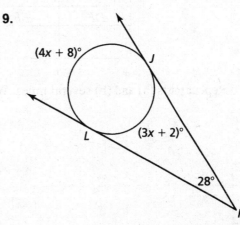

$(4x + 8)°$

$(3x + 2)°$

28°

Name _____ Date _____

Essential Question   What relationships exist among the segments
formed by two intersecting chords or among segments of two secants that
intersect outside a circle?

---

1 ▶ **EXPLORATION:** Segments Formed by Two Intersecting Chords

---

Go to *BigIdeasMath.com* for an interactive tool to investigate this exploration.

Work with a partner. Use dynamic geometry software.

  a. Construct two chords $\overline{BC}$ and $\overline{DE}$ that intersect in the interior of a circle at
    point F.

Sample

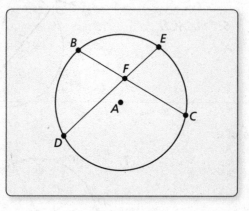

  b. Find the segment lengths BF, CF, DF, and EF and complete the table. What do
    you observe?

BF	CF	BF • CF

DF	EF	DF • EF

  c. Repeat parts (a) and (b) several times. Write a conjecture about your results.

10.6 **Segment Relationships in Circles** (continued)

2 **EXPLORATION:** Secants Intersecting Outside a Circle

Go to *BigIdeasMath.com* for an interactive tool to investigate this exploration.

Work with a partner. Use dynamic geometry software.

a. Construct two secants $\overrightarrow{BC}$ and $\overrightarrow{BD}$ that intersect at a point B outside a circle, as shown.

Sample

b. Find the segment lengths BE, BC, BF, and BD, and complete the table. What do you observe?

BE	BC	BE • BC

BF	BD	BF • BD

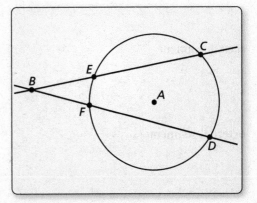

c. Repeat parts (a) and (b) several times. Write a conjecture about your results.

Communicate Your Answer

3. What relationships exist among the segments formed by two intersecting chords or among segments of two secants that intersect outside a circle?

4. Find the segment length AF in the figure at the right.

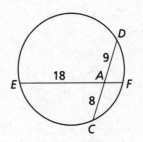

10.6 Notetaking with Vocabulary
For use after Lesson 10.6

In your own words, write the meaning of each vocabulary term.

segments of a chord

tangent segment

secant segment

external segment

Theorems

Segments of Chords Theorem

If two chords intersect in the interior of a circle, then the product of the lengths of the segments of one chord is equal to the product of the lengths of the segments of the other chord.

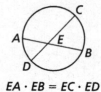

$$EA \cdot EB = EC \cdot ED$$

Notes:

10.6 **Notetaking with Vocabulary** (continued)

Core Concepts

Tangent Segment and Secant Segment

A **tangent segment** is a segment that is tangent to a circle at an endpoint. A **secant segment** is a segment that contains a chord of a circle and has exactly one endpoint outside the circle. The part of a secant segment that is outside the circle is called an **external segment**.

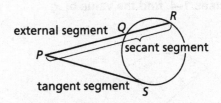

$\overline{PS}$ is a tangent segment.
$\overline{PR}$ is a secant segment.
$\overline{PQ}$ is the external segment of $\overline{PR}$.

Notes:

Theorems

Segments of Secants Theorem

If two secant segments share the same endpoint outside a circle, then the product of the lengths of one secant segment and its external segment equals the product of the lengths of the other secant segment and its external segment.

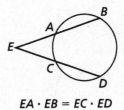

Notes:

$$EA \cdot EB = EC \cdot ED$$

Segments of Secants and Tangents Theorem

If a secant segment and a tangent segment share an endpoint outside a circle, then the product of the lengths of the secant segment and its external segment equals the square of the length of the tangent segment.

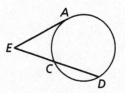

Notes:

$$EA^2 = EC \cdot ED$$

10.6 **Notetaking with Vocabulary** (continued)

Extra Practice

In Exercises 1–4, find the value of x.

1.

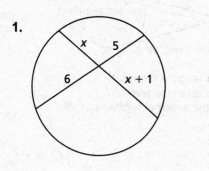

2.

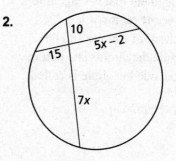

3.

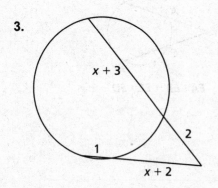

4.

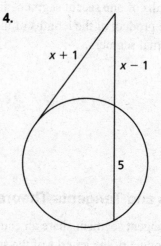

Name_____ Date _____

10.7 Circles in the Coordinate Plane
For use with Exploration 10.7

Essential Question What is the equation of a circle with center (h, k) and radius r in the coordinate plane?

1 EXPLORATION: The Equation of a Circle with Center at the Origin

Go to *BigIdeasMath.com* for an interactive tool to investigate this exploration.

Work with a partner. Use dynamic geometry software to construct and determine the equations of circles centered at $(0, 0)$ in the coordinate plane, as described below.

a. Complete the first two rows of the table for circles with the given radii. Complete the other rows for circles with radii of your choice.

Radius	Equation of circle
1	
2	

b. Write an equation of a circle with center $(0, 0)$ and radius r.

2 EXPLORATION: The Equation of a Circle with Center (h, k)

Go to *BigIdeasMath.com* for an interactive tool to investigate this exploration.

Work with a partner. Use dynamic geometry software to construct and determine the equations of circles of radius 2 in the coordinate plane, as described below.

a. Complete the first two rows of the table for circles with the given centers. Complete the other rows for circles with centers of your choice.

Center	Equation of circle
$(0, 0)$	
$(2, 0)$	

b. Write an equation of a circle with center (h, k) and radius 2.

c. Write an equation of a circle with center (h, k) and radius r.

10.7 Circles in the Coordinate Plane (continued)

---

3 **EXPLORATION:** Deriving the Standard Equation of a Circle

Work with a partner. Consider a circle with radius r and center (h, k).

Write the Distance Formula to represent the distance d between a point (x, y) on the circle and the center (h, k) of the circle. Then square each side of the Distance Formula equation.

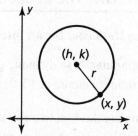

How does your result compare with the equation you wrote in part (c) of Exploration 2?

Communicate Your Answer

4. What is the equation of a circle with center (h, k) and radius r in the coordinate plane?

5. Write an equation of the circle with center $(4, -1)$ and radius 3.

Name_____ Date_____

10.7 Notetaking with Vocabulary
For use after Lesson 10.7

In your own words, write the meaning of each vocabulary term.

standard equation of a circle

Core Concepts

Standard Equation of a Circle

Let (x, y) represent any point on a circle with center (h, k) and radius r. By the Pythagorean Theorem (Theorem 9.1),

$$(x - h)^2 + (y - k)^2 = r^2.$$

This is the **standard equation of a circle** with center (h, k) and radius r.

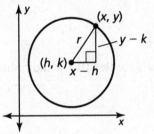

Notes:

10.7 Notetaking with Vocabulary (continued)

Extra Practice

In Exercises 1–4, write the standard equation of the circle.

1.

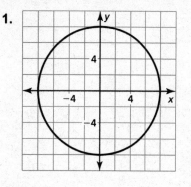

2.

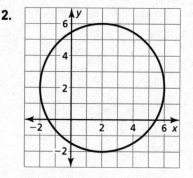

3. a circle with center $(0, 0)$ and radius $\dfrac{1}{3}$

4. a circle with center $(-3, -5)$ and radius 8

In Exercises 5 and 6, use the given information to write the standard equation of the circle.

5. The center is $(0, 0)$, and a point on the circle is $(4, -3)$.

6. The center is $(4, 5)$, and a point on the circle is $(0, 8)$.

Name_____ Date _____

In Exercises 7–10, find the center and radius of the circle. Then graph the circle.

7. $x^2 + y^2 = 225$

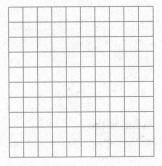

8. $(x - 3)^2 + (y + 2)^2 = 16$

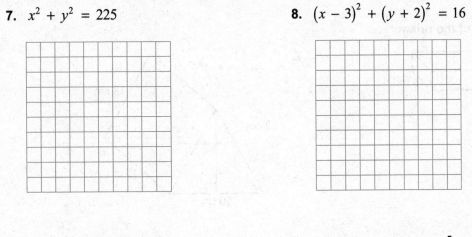

9. $x^2 + y^2 + 2x + 2y = 2$

10. $x^2 + y^2 - 3x + y = \dfrac{5}{2}$

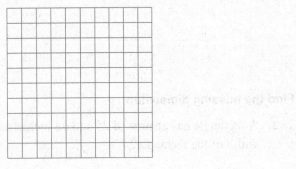

In Exercises 11 and 12, prove or disprove the statement.

11. The point $(-4, 4)$ lies on the circle centered at the origin with radius 6.

12. The point $(-1, 2)$ lies on the circle centered at $(-4, -1)$ with radius $3\sqrt{2}$.

13. Solve the system.

$$x^2 + y^2 = 16$$
$$y = -x - 4$$

Name _____ Date _____

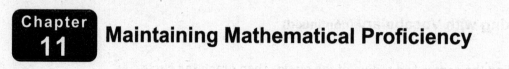
Find the surface area of the prism.

1.
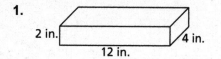

2.
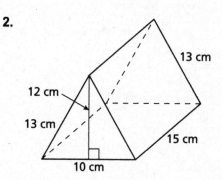

Find the missing dimension.

3. A rectangle has an area of 25 square inches and a length of 10 inches. What is the width of the rectangle?

4. A triangle has an area of 32 square centimeters and a base of 8 centimeters. What is the height of the triangle?

Name_____ Date _____

11.1 Circumference and Arc Length
For use with Exploration 11.1

Essential Question How can you find the length of a circular arc?

1 EXPLORATION: Finding the Length of a Circular Arc

Work with a partner. Find the length of each gray circular arc.

a. entire circle

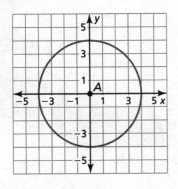

b. one-fourth of a circle

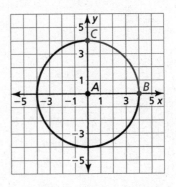

c. one-third of a circle

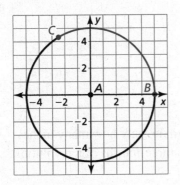

d. five-eighths of a circle

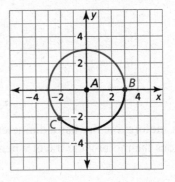

11.1 Circumference and Arc Length (continued)

2 EXPLORATION: Using Arc Length

Work with a partner. The rider is attempting to stop with the front tire of the motorcycle in the painted rectangular box for a skills test. The front tire makes exactly one-half additional revolution before stopping. The diameter of the tire is 25 inches. Is the front tire still in contact with the painted box? Explain.

├────── 3 ft ──────┤

Communicate Your Answer

3. How can you find the length of a circular arc?

4. A motorcycle tire has a diameter of 24 inches. Approximately how many inches does the motorcycle travel when its front tire makes three-fourths of a revolution?

11.1 Notetaking with Vocabulary
For use after Lesson 11.1

In your own words, write the meaning of each vocabulary term.

circumference

arc length

radian

Core Concepts

Circumference of a Circle

The circumference C of a circle is $C = \pi d$ or $C = 2\pi r$, where d is the diameter of the circle and r is the radius of the circle.

$$C = \pi d = 2\pi r$$

Notes:

11.1 Notetaking with Vocabulary (continued)

Arc Length

In a circle, the ratio of the length of a given arc to the circumference
is equal to the ratio of the measure of the arc to 360°.

$$\frac{\text{Arc length of } \widehat{AB}}{2\pi r} = \frac{m\widehat{AB}}{360°}, \text{ or}$$

$$\text{Arc length of } \widehat{AB} = \frac{m\widehat{AB}}{360°} \cdot 2\pi r$$

Notes:

Converting Between Degrees and Radians

Degrees to radians

Multiply degree measure by

$$\frac{2\pi \text{ radians}}{360°}, \text{ or } \frac{\pi \text{ radians}}{180°}.$$

Radians to degrees

Multiply radian measure by

$$\frac{360°}{2\pi \text{ radians}}, \text{ or } \frac{180°}{\pi \text{ radians}}.$$

Notes:

Name_____ Date_____

Extra Practice

In Exercises 1–5, find the indicated measure.

1. diameter of a circle with a circumference of 10 inches

2. circumference of a circle with a radius of 3 centimeters

3. radius of a circle with a circumference of 8 feet

4. circumference of a circle with a diameter of 2.4 meters

5. arc length of $\overset{\frown}{AC}$

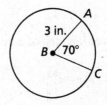

In Exercises 6 and 7, convert the angle measure.

6. Convert 60° to radians.

7. Convert $\dfrac{5\pi}{6}$ radians to degrees.

11.2 Areas of Circles and Sectors

For use with Exploration 11.2

Essential Question How can you find the area of a sector of a circle?

1 EXPLORATION: Finding the Area of a Sector of a Circle

Work with a partner. A **sector of a circle** is the region bounded by two radii of the circle and their intercepted arc. Find the area of each shaded circle or sector of a circle.

a. entire circle

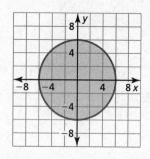

b. one-fourth of a circle

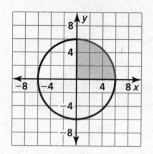

c. seven-eighths of a circle

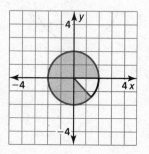

d. two-thirds of a circle

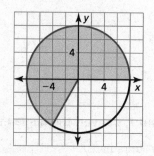

11.2 Areas of Circles and Sectors (continued)

---

2 **EXPLORATION:** Finding the Area of a Circular Sector

Work with a partner. A center pivot irrigation system consists of 400 meters of sprinkler equipment that rotates around a central pivot point at a rate of once every 3 days to irrigate a circular region with a diameter of 800 meters. Find the area of the sector that is irrigated by this system in one day.

 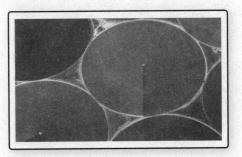

Communicate Your Answer

3. How can you find the area of a sector of a circle?

4. In Exploration 2, find the area of the sector that is irrigated in 2 hours.

11.2 Notetaking with Vocabulary
For use after Lesson 11.2

In your own words, write the meaning of each vocabulary term.

geometric probability

sector of a circle

Core Concepts

Area of a Circle

The area of a circle is

$$A = \pi r^2$$

where r is the radius of the circle.

Notes:

11.2 **Notetaking with Vocabulary** (continued)

Area of a Sector

The ratio of the area of a sector of a circle to the area of the whole circle $\left(\pi r^2\right)$ is equal to the ratio of the measure of the intercepted arc to 360°.

$$\frac{\text{Area of sector } APB}{\pi r^2} = \frac{m\overset{\frown}{AB}}{360°}, \text{ or}$$

$$\text{Area of sector } APB = \frac{m\overset{\frown}{AB}}{360°} \cdot \pi r^2$$

Notes:

Extra Practice

In Exercises 1–2, find the indicated measure.

  1. area of $\odot M$

  2. area of $\odot R$

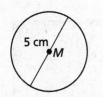

In Exercises 3–8, find the indicated measure.

  3. area of a circle with a diameter of 1.8 inches

  4. diameter of a circle with an area of 10 square feet

Name _____ Date _____

5. radius of a circle with an area of 65 square centimeters

6. area of a circle with a radius of 6.1 yards

7. areas of the sectors formed by ∠*PQR*

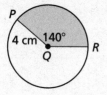

8. area of ⊙*Y*

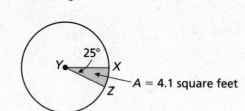

9. You throw a dart at the board shown. Your dart is equally likely to hit any point inside the square board.

   a. What is the probability your dart lands in the smallest triangle?

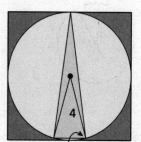

   b. What is the probability your dart does not land anywhere in the circle?

11.3 Areas of Polygons
For use with Exploration 11.3

Essential Question How can you find the area of a regular polygon?

The **center of a regular polygon** is the center of its circumscribed circle.

The distance from the center to any side of a regular polygon is called the **apothem of a regular polygon**.

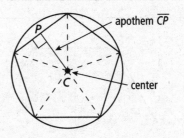

apothem $\overline{CP}$

center

---

1   EXPLORATION: Finding the Area of a Regular Polygon

Go to *BigIdeasMath.com* for an interactive tool to investigate this exploration.

Work with a partner. Use dynamic geometry software to construct each regular polygon with side lengths of 4, as shown. Find the apothem and use it to find the area of the polygon. Describe the steps that you used.

a.

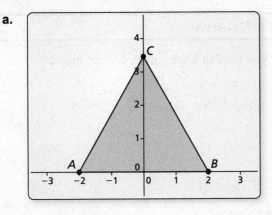

b.

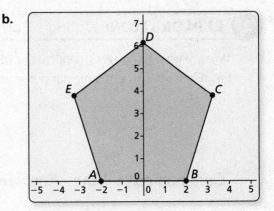

Name _____ Date _____

1 EXPLORATION: Finding the Area of a Regular Polygon (continued)

c.   d.

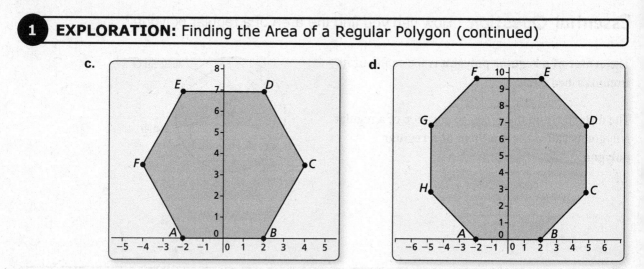

2 EXPLORATION: Writing a Formula for Area

Work with a partner. Generalize the steps you used in Exploration 1 to develop a formula for the area of a regular polygon.

Communicate Your Answer

3. How can you find the area of a regular polygon?

4. Regular pentagon *ABCDE* has side lengths of 6 meters and an apothem of approximately 4.13 meters. Find the area of *ABCDE*.

11.3 Notetaking with Vocabulary
For use after Lesson 11.3

In your own words, write the meaning of each vocabulary term.

center of a regular polygon

radius of a regular polygon

apothem of a regular polygon

central angle of a regular polygon

Core Concepts

Area of a Rhombus or Kite

The area of a rhombus or kite with diagonals d_1 and d_2 is $\frac{1}{2}d_1d_2$.

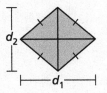 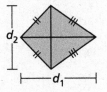

Notes:

11.3 Notetaking with Vocabulary (continued)

Area of a Regular Polygon

The area of a regular *n*-gon with side length *s* is one-half the product of the apothem *a* and the perimeter *P*.

$$A = \frac{1}{2}aP, \text{ or } A = \frac{1}{2}a \cdot ns$$

Notes:

Extra Practice

In Exercises 1 and 2, find the area of the kite or rhombus.

1.

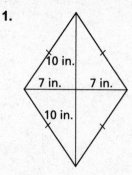

2.

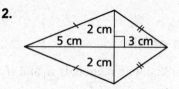

11.3 Notetaking with Vocabulary (continued)

3. Find the measure of a central angle of a regular polygon with 8 sides.

4. The central angles of a regular polygon are 40°. How many sides does the polygon have?

5. A regular pentagon has a radius of 4 inches and a side length of 3 inches.

   a. Find the apothem of the pentagon.

   b. Find the area of the pentagon.

6. A regular hexagon has an apothem of 10 units.

   a. Find the radius of the hexagon and the length of one side.

   b. Find the area of the hexagon.

11.4 Volumes of Prisms and Cylinders
For use with Exploration 11.4

Essential Question How can you find the volume of a prism or cylinder that is not a right prism or right cylinder?

Recall that the volume V of a right prism or a right cylinder is equal to the product of the area of a base B and the height h.

$$V = Bh$$

right prisms   right cylinder

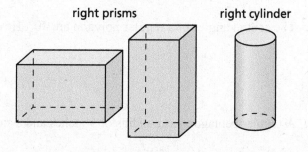

---

1 EXPLORATION: Finding Volume

Work with a partner. Consider a stack of square papers that is in the form of a right prism.

a. What is the volume of the prism?

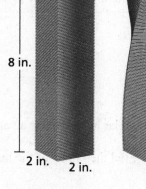

8 in.

2 in.   2 in.

b. When you twist the stack of papers, as shown at the right, do you change the volume? Explain your reasoning.

c. Write a carefully worded conjecture that describes the conclusion you reached in part (b).

d. Use your conjecture to find the volume of the twisted stack of papers.

11.4 **Volumes of Prisms and Cylinders** (continued)

---

2 **EXPLORATION:** Finding Volume

Work with a partner. Use the conjecture you wrote in Exploration 1 to find the volume of the cylinder.

a.

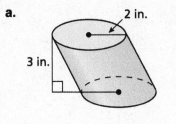

2 in.

3 in.

b.

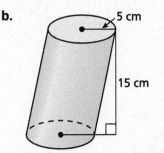

5 cm

15 cm

Communicate Your Answer

3. How can you find the volume of a prism or cylinder that is not a right prism or right cylinder?

4. In Exploration 1, would the conjecture you wrote change if the papers in each stack were not squares? Explain your reasoning.

11.4 Notetaking with Vocabulary
For use after Lesson 11.4

In your own words, write the meaning of each vocabulary term.

polyhedron

face

edge

vertex

volume

Cavalieri's Principle

similar solids

Notes:

11.4 **Notetaking with Vocabulary** (continued)

Core Concepts

Types of Solids

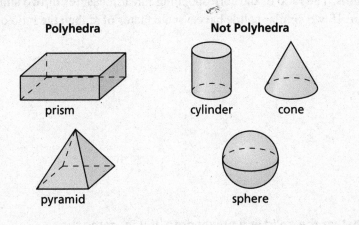

Polyhedra

prism

pyramid

Not Polyhedra

cylinder

cone

sphere

Notes:

Volume of a Prism

The volume V of a prism is

$$V = Bh$$

where B is the area of a base and h is the height.

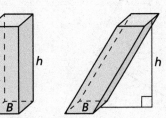

Notes:

Volume of a Cylinder

The volume V of a cylinder is

$$V = Bh = \pi r^2 h$$

where B is the area of a base, h is the height, and r is the radius of a base.

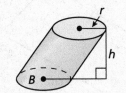

Notes:

Name_____ Date _____

Similar Solids

Two solids of the same type with equal ratios of corresponding linear measures, such as heights or radii, are called **similar solids**. The ratio of the corresponding linear measures of two similar solids is called the *scale factor*. If two similar solids have a scale factor of k, then the ratio of their volumes is equal to k^3.

Notes:

Extra Practice

In Exercises 1 and 2, tell whether the solid is a polyhedron. If it is, name the polyhedron.

1.

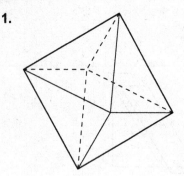

2.

In Exercises 3 and 4, find the volume of the prism.

3.

4. Area of base 10 in.²

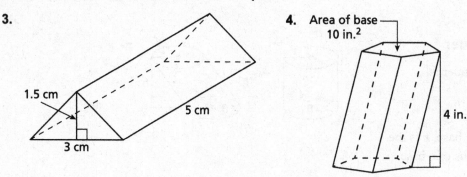

Name_____ Date_____

11.4 Notetaking with Vocabulary (continued)

In Exercises 5 and 6, find the volume of the cylinder.

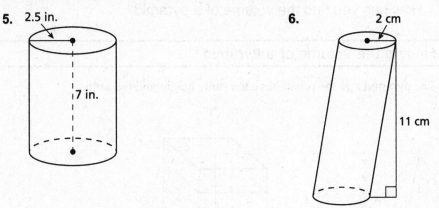

5. 2.5 in.

7 in.

6. 2 cm

11 cm

In Exercises 7 and 8, find the indicated measure.

7. height of a cylinder with a base radius of 8 inches and a volume of 2010 cubic inches

8. area of the base of a pentagonal prism with a volume of 50 cubic centimeters and a height of 7.5 centimeters

In Exercises 9 and 10, find the missing dimension of the prism or cylinder.

9. Volume = 661.5 cm^3

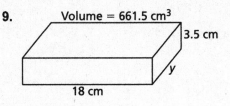

3.5 cm

y

18 cm

10. Volume = 75.36 in.^{3}

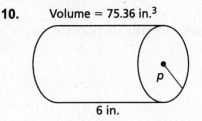

p

6 in.

11.5 Volumes of Pyramids
For use with Exploration 11.5

Essential Question How can you find the volume of a pyramid?

---

1 EXPLORATION: Finding the Volume of a Pyramid

Work with a partner. The pyramid and the prism have the same height and the same square base.

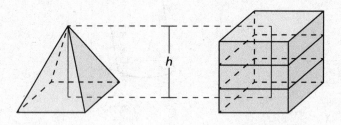

When the pyramid is filled with sand and poured into the prism, it takes three pyramids to fill the prism.

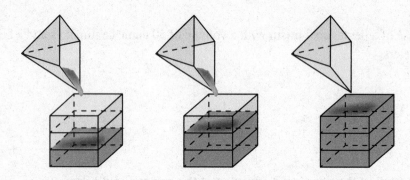

Use this information to write a formula for the volume V of a pyramid.

11.5 **Volumes of Pyramids** (continued)

2 **EXPLORATION:** Finding the Volume of a Pyramid

Work with a partner. Use the formula you wrote in Exploration 1 to find the volume of the hexagonal pyramid.

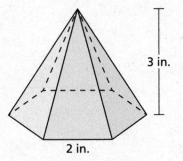

3 in.

2 in.

Communicate Your Answer

3. How can you find the volume of a pyramid?

4. In Section 11.5, you will study volumes of cones. How do you think you could use a method similar to the one presented in Exploration 1 to write a formula for the volume of a cone? Explain your reasoning.

Name _____ Date _____

In your own words, write the meaning of each vocabulary term.

pyramid

composite solid

Core Concepts

Volume of a Pyramid

The volume V of a pyramid is

$$V = \frac{1}{3}Bh$$

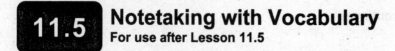

where B is the area of the base and h is the height.

Notes:

Name_____ Date _____

11.5 Notetaking with Vocabulary (continued)

Extra Practice

In Exercises 1–6, find the volume of the pyramid.

1.

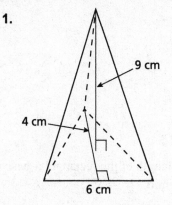

9 cm

4 cm

6 cm

2.

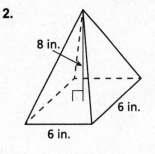

8 in.

6 in.

6 in.

3.

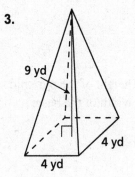

9 yd

4 yd

4 yd

4.

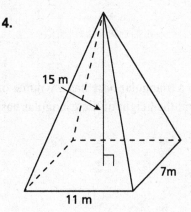

15 m

7m

11 m

5.

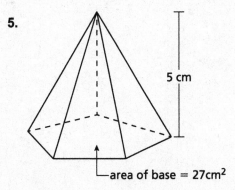

5 cm

area of base = 27cm²

6.

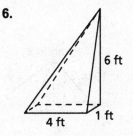

6 ft

1 ft

4 ft

11.5 Notetaking with Vocabulary (continued)

In Exercises 7–9, find the indicated measure.

7. A pyramid with a square base has a volume of 128 cubic inches and a height of 6 inches. Find the side length of the square base.

8. A pyramid with a rectangular base has a volume of 6 cubic feet. The length of the rectangular base is 3 feet and the width of the base is 1.5 feet. Find the height of the pyramid.

9. A pyramid with a triangular base has a volume of 18 cubic centimeters. The height of the pyramid is 9 centimeters and the height of the triangular base is 3 centimeters. Find the width of the base.

10. The pyramids are similar. Find the volume of pyramid B.

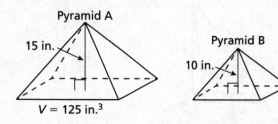

Pyramid A

15 in.

$V = 125$ in.^{3}

Pyramid B

10 in.

11.6 Surface Areas and Volumes of Cones
For use with Exploration 11.6

Essential Question How can you find the surface area and the volume of a cone?

---

1 EXPLORATION: Finding the Surface Area of a Cone

Work with a partner. Construct a circle with a radius of 3 inches. Mark the circumference of the circle into six equal parts, and label the length of each part. Then cut out one sector of the circle and make a cone.

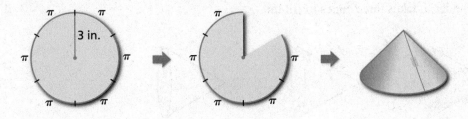

a. Explain why the base of the cone is a circle. What are the circumference and radius of the base?

b. What is the area of the original circle? What is the area with one sector missing?

c. Describe the surface area of the cone, including the base. Use your description to find the surface area.

11.6 **Surface Areas and Volumes of Cones** (continued)

---

2 **EXPLORATION:** Finding the Volume of a Cone

Work with a partner. The cone and the cylinder have the same height and the same circular base.

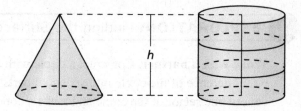

When the cone is filled with sand and poured into the cylinder, it takes three cones to fill the cylinder.

Use this information to write a formula for the volume V of a cone.

Communicate Your Answer

3. How can you find the surface area and the volume of a cone?

4. In Exploration 1, cut another sector from the circle and make a cone. Find the radius of the base and the surface area of the cone. Repeat this three times, recording your results in a table. Describe the pattern.

Radius of Base	Surface Area of Cone

Name_____ Date_____

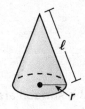

11.6 Notetaking with Vocabulary
For use after Lesson 11.6

In your own words, write the meaning of each vocabulary term.

lateral surface of a cone

Notes:

Core Concepts

Surface Area of a Right Cone

The surface area S of a right cone is

$$S = \pi r^2 + \pi r \ell$$

where r is the radius of the base and ℓ is the slant height.

Notes:

11.6 **Notetaking with Vocabulary** (continued)

Volume of a Cone

The volume V of a cone is

$$V = \frac{1}{3}Bh = \frac{1}{3}\pi r^2 h$$

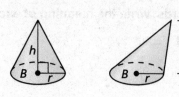

where B is the area of the base, h is the height, and r is the radius of the base.

Notes:

Extra Practice

In Exercises 1 and 2, find the surface area of the right cone.

1.

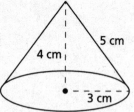

2. A right cone has a diameter of 1.8 inches and a height of 3 inches.

Name_____ Date_____

In Exercises 3 and 4, find the volume of the cone.

3.

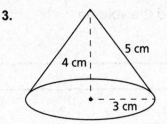

5 cm

4 cm

3 cm

4. A right cone has a radius of 5 feet and a slant height of 13 feet.

In Exercises 5–7, find the indicated measure.

5. A right cone has a surface area of 440 square inches and a radius of 7 inches. Find its slant height.

6. A right cone has a volume of 528 cubic meters and a diameter of 12 meters. Find its height.

7. Cone A and cone B are similar. The radius of cone A is 4 cm and the radius of cone B is 10 cm. The volume of cone A is 134 cm^3. Find the volume of cone B.

8. Find the volume of the composite solid.

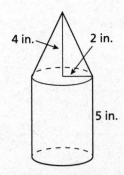

4 in. 2 in.

5 in.

11.7 Surface Areas and Volumes of Spheres
For use with Exploration 11.7

Essential Question   How can you find the surface area and the volume of a sphere?

---

1   EXPLORATION: Finding the Surface Area of a Sphere

Work with a partner. Remove the covering from a baseball or softball.

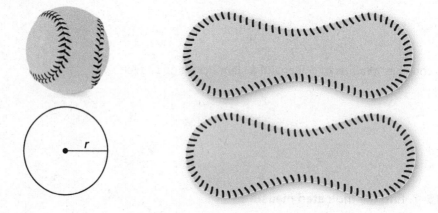

You will end up with two "figure 8" pieces of material, as shown above. From the amount of material it takes to cover the ball, what would you estimate the surface area S of the ball to be? Express your answer in terms of the radius r of the ball.

$S = $ _____   Surface area of a sphere

Use the Internet or some other resource to confirm that the formula you wrote for the surface area of a sphere is correct.

11.7 **Surface Areas and Volumes of Spheres** (continued)

---

2 **EXPLORATION:** Finding the Volume of a Sphere

Work with a partner. A cylinder is circumscribed about a sphere, as shown. Write a formula for the volume V of the cylinder in terms of the radius r.

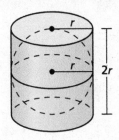

$V =$ _____   Volume of cylinder

When half of the sphere (a *hemisphere*) is filled with sand and poured into the cylinder, it takes three hemispheres to fill the cylinder. Use this information to write a formula for the volume V of a sphere in terms of the radius r

$V =$ _____   Volume of a sphere

Communicate Your Answer

3. How can you find the surface area and the volume of a sphere?

4. Use the results of Explorations 1 and 2 to find the surface area and the volume of a sphere with a radius of (a) 3 inches and (b) 2 centimeters.

11.7 Notetaking with Vocabulary
For use after Lesson 11.7

In your own words, write the meaning of each vocabulary term.

chord of a sphere

great circle

Core Concepts

Surface Area of a Sphere

The surface area S of a sphere is

$$S = 4\pi r^2$$

where r is the radius of the sphere.

$S = 4\pi r^2$

Notes:

11.7 Notetaking with Vocabulary (continued)

Volume of a Sphere

The volume V of a sphere is

$$V = \frac{4}{3}\pi r^3$$

where r is the radius of the sphere.

$V = \frac{4}{3}\pi r^3$

Notes:

Extra Practice

In Exercises 1–4, find the surface area of the solid.

1.

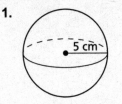

5 cm

2.

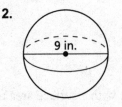

9 in.

3.

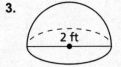

2 ft

4.

11.2 m

11.7   Notetaking with Vocabulary (continued)

In Exercises 5–8, find the volume of the sphere.

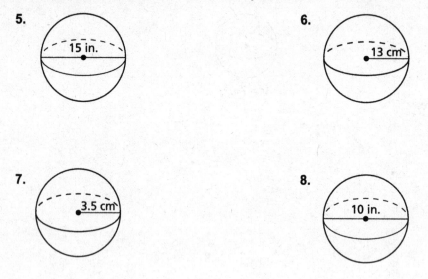

5.

15 in.

6.

13 cm

7.

3.5 cm

8.

10 in.

In Exercises 9–11, find the indicated measure.

9. Find the diameter of a sphere with a surface area of 144π square centimeters.

10. Find the volume of a sphere with a surface area of 256π square inches.

11. Find the volume of a sphere with a surface area of 400π square feet.